VITAL POINT STRIKES

THE ART & SCIENCE OF STRIKING VITAL TARGETS
FOR SELF-DEFENSE AND COMBAT SPORTS

OTHER TITLES BY THE AUTHOR

BOOKS
Ultimate Flexibility
Ultimate Fitness Through Martial Arts
Combat Strategy
The Art of Harmony
Teaching Martial Arts: The Way of The Master
Martial Arts Instructor's Desk Reference
1,001 Ways To Motivate Yourself & Others
Martial Arts After 40
Complete Taekwondo Poomsae
Taekwondo Kyorugi: Olympic Style Sparring
Muye Dobo Tongji: The Comprehensive Illustrated Manual of Martial Arts of Ancient Korea

DVDs
Ultimate Flexibility
Power Breathing
Ultimate Fitness
Self-defense Encyclopedia
Junsado: Combat Strategy
Junsado: Short Stick Combat (1 & 2)
Junsado: Long Stick
Junsado: Double Sticks
Wrist & Arresting Locks
Knife Defense (1 & 2)
Complete Kicking (1 & 2)
Complete Sparring (1 & 2)
Ultimate Kicking Drills
Aero Kicks
Top 100 Scoring Techniques
Taegeuk Poomsae
Palgwae Poomsae
and more

VITAL POINT STRIKES

THE ART & SCIENCE OF STRIKING VITAL TARGETS FOR SELF-DEFENSE AND COMBAT SPORTS

Sang H. Kim, Ph.D.

 Turtle Press   Santa Fe

VITAL POINT STRIKES
A Turtle Press Book / 2008
Copyright © 2008 Sang H. Kim. All Rights Reserved.
Printed in the United States of America. No part of this book may be reproduced without written permission except in the case of brief quotations embodied in articles or reviews.

For information, address Turtle Press, PO Box 34010, Santa Fe, NM 87594-0410

Photo models: Sang H. Kim, Alan Tafoya
Photographer: Cynthia A. Kim

ISBN 978-1-934903-05-6
LCCN 2008016681
Printed in the United States of America

10 9 8 7 6 5 4

Warning-Disclaimer

This book is designed to provide information on specific skills used in martial arts and self-defense. It is not the purpose of this book to reprint all the information that is otherwise available to the author, publisher, printer or distributors, but instead to complement, amplify and supplement other texts. You are urged to read all available material, learn as much as you wish about the subjects covered in this book and tailor the information to your individual needs. Anyone practicing the skills presented in this book should be physically capable to do so and have the permission of a licensed physician before participating in this activity or any physical activity.

Every effort has been made to make this book as complete and accurate as possible. However, there may be mistakes, both typographical and in content. Therefore, this text should be used only as a general guide and not the ultimate source of information on the subjects presented here in this book on any skill or subject. The purpose of this book is to provide information and entertain. The author, publisher, printer and distributors shall neither have liability nor responsibility to any person or entity with respect to loss or damages caused, or alleged to have been caused, directly or indirectly, by the information contained in this book.

Library of Congress Cataloguing in Publication Data

Kim, Sang H.
   Vital point strikes : the art & science of striking vital targets for self-defense and combat sports / Sang H. Kim.
-- 1st ed.
   p. cm.
Includes index.
ISBN 978-1-934903-05-6
1. Martial arts--Training. 2. Self-defense--Training. I. Title.
GV1101.K58 2008
796.8--dc22
                              2008016681

The MOUNTAIN MAN logo and VITAL POINT STRIKES
are trademarked and copyrighted by Turtle Press Corporation.

DEDICATION

*To my father
who persevered and survived WWII, the Korean War
and his own inner war for his dreams
with grace and valor.*

*To my grandmother
who taught me the value of gentle discipline
in martial arts since I was 4.*

ACKNOWLEDGEMENTS

I am deeply grateful to my teachers: Calligraphy Master Jung Dong-shik at Hwawon Elementary School, Taekwondo Master Kim Dae-shik at Dalsung Middle School, Calligraphy Grandmaster Lee Sung-jae at Daegun High School, Grandmaster Kim Do-boo at Taekwondo Yunmukwan in Daegu City, Superintendent Kim Soo-hwan of National Police Agency of Korea, Hapkido Master Kim Jae-hwan and Kim Dong-hwan, Grandmaster Park Yong-tak at Taekwondo Jungmu Dojang in Daegu City, Kumdo Master Lee S. Won, Grandmaster Kim Ho-je, Dean Emeritus at Kukki-won in Seoul, Dr. Kim Sung-bae for Acupuncture knowledge, Dr. Arthur Joseph McTaggart of USIS in Daegu City, John R. Sano of US Embassy in Seoul, Ambassador Dr. Chang Dong-hee, Professor Han Young-choon and Professor Park Sung-han of Yeungnam University, Dr. Lee Kyu-hyung of Kyemyung University, CID officers at Camp Walker in Daegu City, Athletic Director Rick Hazelton of Trinity College in Connecticut, Dr. Ken Min at UC Berkeley, Dr. Hwang In-soo at Yale University, Dr. James Agli of Southern Connecticut State University, Commissioner Ralph Carpenter, Colonel Edward Lynch and Officer Eric Murray of Connecticut State Police; to my commanders: President Park CH, General Chun DH, special agent Lee BH; to my friends: Professor Chung Kuk-hyun of Korean National Physical Education University and 4 time Olympic champion, Grandmaster Yun Jun-chul, Dr. Chung Jin-bae of Yeonsei University, Dr. Stephen Harrigan; to my former colleagues who gave their lives in their missions and those whom I have trained with and learned from.

My enlightenment in the art of survival came from classes under special agent instructor TK Kim in the Counter Intelligence Academy in South Korea. He taught us how to reinvent an invincible self to survive captivity in enemy territories. Twice, I had the honor to remember him as my mentor for life.

My special thanks goes to Alan Tafoya, a seasoned actor and martial artist, for assisting me in this project and his sheer passion to enhance our arts. It was my great pleasure to work with him.

I also would like to thank my parents Kim Byung-soo and Oh Wol-ki for preparing me to travel around the world without losing my identity; and to William and Judith Mager for having faith in my dreams.

Finally, I have to admit that without the support and editorial collaboration with my wife Cynthia and love and encouragement from our daughter Jessica, this work could never be completed.

-Sang H. Kim

TABLE OF CONTENTS

CHAPTER 9: Vital Points on the Leg & Foot   223

BOOK 3: VITAL POINT APPLICATIONS   259

CHAPTER 10: Vital Point Striking Drills   261

CHAPTER 11: Standing Fight Applications   275

CHAPTER 12: Ground Fight Applications   321

CHAPTER 13: Knife Defense Applications   339

CHAPTER 14: Gun Defense Applications   371

NOTES ON TRANSLATION

In translating the original Chinese characters for acupoint names, the author uses Pinyin (also known as Hanyu Pinyin). Pinyin is similar to the English alphabet despite certain limitations. For those who have further interest in studying meridians, the Pinyin system can be of help in learning the terms correctly.

For the translation of words into English and Korean, the author has borne in mind the following principles:

1. Each Chinese character was translated literally.

2. If the literal translation failed, interpretation as closely as possible to the meaning of the context was applied.

3. The same Chinese character was repeatedly translated as the same English or Korean word for the ease of reading.

4. Referring to existing translations of the Chinese characters by the traditional Chinese medicine texts, the author tried to enhance the structure of the words for universal comprehension, preferring meaningfulness and contextual relevance to literal correctness.

PREFACE

Looking back, the beginning of this book was conceived in a military tent in 1981. I was an undercover agent living with over 1,200 top criminals who had been arrested during a tough sweep by the newly installed government. One of my missions was to investigate the causes of a half dozen deaths involving internal abdominal hemorrhaging among the prisoners. My discovery was that most of the dead were brutally struck in the infraanterior pelvic region prior to death. In all of the cases, there were signs of extreme suffering that had lasted from a few minutes to a few hours. Since the location of the prison camp was isolated near the demilitarized zone and the medical facilities in the camp were poorly equipped, the available treatment was not adequate to save the lives of the prisoners. In addition to capturing the killers, what interested me, since I was an ardent martial art practitioner, was the discovery of the relationship between the injuries and the causes of death. Blows to the neck, damage to the Solar Plexus, and kicks to the lower abdomen all caused internal bleeding in the abdomen which resulted in death.

Prior to this posting, my martial arts experience had been marked by competition experience in Taekwondo and hand-to-hand combat training in the military. I had witnessed many competitors receive bruises and broken bones and get knocked out by blows to the head but I had never seen the brutal effects that could result from a kick or strike to a vital point such as the blows the prisoners had suffered in the camp.

During this time, as an officer in the camp, I was also the target of daily assault attempts by prisoners, including attacks by prisoners with makeshift weapons fashioned from objects like toothbrushes. Over the months that I was posted at the camp, I had many opportunities to defend myself and learned valuable lessons about the type of techniques that work in a physical confrontation and about the mental fortitude required to confront an assailant who had nothing to lose and was intent on killing.

That was nearly 3 decades ago but the lessons of that hellish time have stayed with me and I have always wanted to create a practical reference for martial artists that integrates Eastern acupoint theory, Western science and anatomy, and effective martial arts techniques. This book is not intended to be a comprehensive reference but to be the book that I wished I had access to when I was a young martial artist. My focus is on illustrating the relationships between Eastern and Western theories and demystifying some of the myths surrounding pressure point techniques, making the concepts accessible to the average martial artist. However, at the same time, I strongly recommend that interested readers seek out a skilled and knowledgeable instructor.

Vital Point Strikes is not a complete art or science. Vital point striking is a complex and potentially dangerous subject of study and certainly not one you can learn from a book. This book is intended to be a supplement to study with an instructor.

It has been 30 years in the making but my hope is that each reader will see this book as a stepping-stone to developing the ideas illustrated here for those who follow our footsteps.

-Sang H. Kim
from Santa Fe, Spring 2008

VITAL POINT STRIKES

THE ART & SCIENCE OF STRIKING VITAL TARGETS FOR SELF-DEFENSE AND COMBAT SPORTS

BOOK
1

VITAL POINT
FUNDAMENTALS

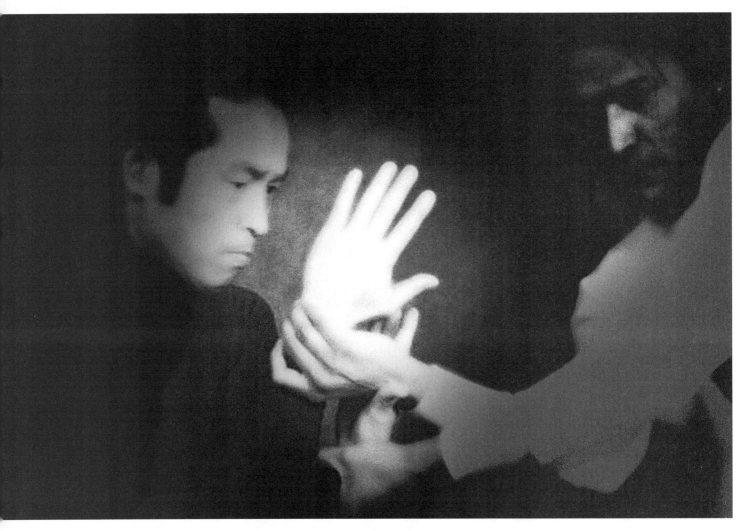

"Knowledge is a most vital element in combat. Your ability to take action depends on it."

Sang H. Kim, *Combat Strategy*

CHAPTER 1

INTRODUCTION TO
VITAL POINTS

WHAT IS A VITAL POINT?

Vital Pain Points (急所 : Keupso or Kyusho)

A vital point is a pressure sensitive point on or near the surface of the human body. Vital points function like gateways to the nervous system, the main controller of the body, allowing you to use pain to influence the actions and reactions of an opponent. Even a single strike can cause serious damage, unconsciousness or, in rare cases, death.

For example, a forceful strike into the Wind Mansion (GV16) at the base of the brain can result in instant death. The gallbladder (on the right side of the trunk, below the liver) and the Sauce Receptacle (CV24) on the tip of the chin are targets for potential knockout blows in boxing. The carotid artery, temple and Philtrum are common targets for striking in a self-defense situation.

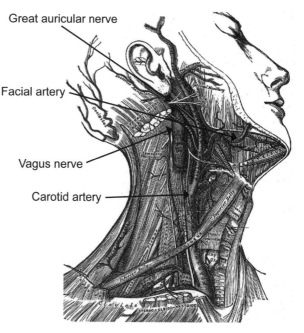

Figure 1.2 Examples of vital areas on the neck.

The rear and sides of the neck and head are rich with vital points due to the presence of nerves and arteries. For example, a forceful strike to the carotid artery on the neck can cause a loss of consciousness because the shock of impact disturbs the flow of blood and oxygen to the brain, causing a blackout. But also note the other major arteries and nerves in close proximity to the carotid artery which provide viable alternate targets.

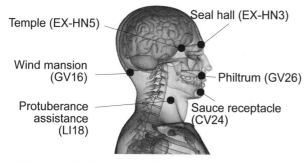

Figure 1.1 Examples of major vital points.

Vital Points Can Shut Down the System

Because the human body is a highly complicated interconnected system, it is vulnerable to attacks that disable key points of the system, thereby causing systemwide failure. By attacking one of the vital regions of the body, you can paralyze the entire system. Particularly damaging are attacks on the nervous system. When the nervous system becomes disabled, so does the rest of the body. Injuries to the brain and spinal cord are among the most lethal. A relatively minor injury, like a concussion causes a temporary loss of mental faculties while a serious injury, like a severance of the spinal cord can cause permanent paralysis or death. Because it attacks a key area of the human system with a specific objective, a vital point strike can turn a physical brawl into a tactical fight and render an opponent powerless.

Self-defense and Vital Points

Generally in fighting, size, power, speed, and aggression matter. In order to survive, you need to have something that makes you superior to your opponent. Physically, it is nearly impossible to always be the bigger, stronger fighter. Size is relative. If you are 5 feet tall, you may encounter an opponent who is 6 feet tall or 4 feet tall so your size and power can only be effective relative to a situation. Your knowledge and fighting strategy, however, are constant.

By practicing and understanding vital point strikes, your striking power can be 3 to 5 times more effective than randomly striking an opponent.

The key to successful vital point striking is combining technical knowledge of the human body with physical precision. For example, a strike to the carotid artery in the neck can knock out an opponent in a matter of seconds. Vital point striking can help you overcome a deficit in size and power.

The question then is how accurately and forcefully you can strike a lunging, moving, resisting opponent. With practice and knowledge, you can improve your speed and accuracy, increasing the possibility that in a real confrontation you could strike a successful vital point blow.

Figure 1.3 10 primary vital regions.

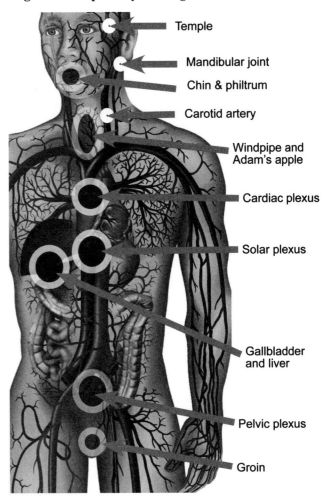

- Temple
- Mandibular joint
- Chin & philtrum
- Carotid artery
- Windpipe and Adam's apple
- Cardiac plexus
- Solar plexus
- Gallbladder and liver
- Pelvic plexus
- Groin

Systematic attacks on the plexus of vital points can progressively shut down the body's system. With knowledge of vital point strikes, you can turn a physical brawl into a tactical fight.

Vital Points by the Numbers		
Total named vital points:		**409**
Vital points located along the centerline:		**52**
Vital points located on 12 meridians on the left side of the body:		**309**
Vital points located on 12 meridians on the right side of the body:		**309**
Extra points:		**48**

The Origin of Vital Points

Traditionally, there are approximately 409 named vital points located along 12 meridians and 2 vessels of the human body. Because there are 12 meridians on the right side of the body and 12 meridians on the left side of the body, there are a total of 24 meridians. Alternatively, the 12 meridians and 2 vessels are sometimes simply referred to as 14 meridians.

Originally, vital points (acupoints) were used for medical purposes. In time, martial art masters began to incorporate this medical knowledge into their training. They recorded what they discovered in secret books and handed the knowledge down to trustworthy disciples. Traditionally secret techniques included Hwalbup (resuscitation methods), Salbup (killing methods), and Hoshinbup (self-defense methods).

Vital Point Applications

There are approximately 202 named vital points on the body that can be used practically in fighting, including 19 lethal points, 49 paralyzing points, and 36 tactical points.

Since vital point striking is an efficient way of defeating an opponent, it is widely used in full contact sport fighting, military hand-to-hand or hand-to-weapon combat, police work, and personal self-protection. In police work, vital points are effectively used to subdue and control criminals without using excessive force. In combat sports like boxing, jujitsu, taekwondo and MMA, competitors exploit vital points to knock an opponent out or force him to submit.

Two Supervising Meridians

The **Governing Vessel** runs along the midline of the back, ascending to the head and descending to the face. It connects with and governs all the Yang meridians and is called the Sea of the Yang Meridians.

The **Conception Vessel** runs along the midline of the abdomen and chest, ascending to the chin. It connects with all of the Yin meridians. It receives the energy from the Yin meridians and conceives new energy to distribute to the entire body. It is called the Sea of the Yin Meridians.

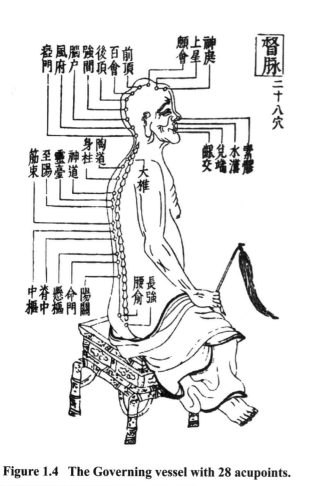

Figure 1.4 The Governing vessel with 28 acupoints.

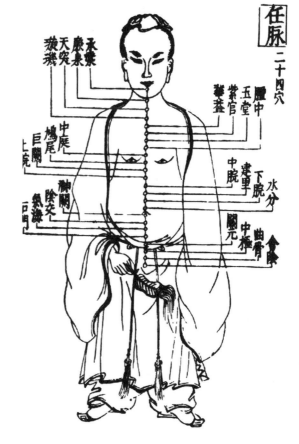

Figure 1.5 The Conception vessel with 24 acupoints.

TYPES OF VITAL POINTS

Lethal Points

When martial artists think of vital point attacking, they often focus on the "death touch" aspect of vital point arts. However, while killing a person with a single empty-handed strike is possible, it is highly unlikely, especially when striking a moving opponent. Death is more likely to result from a vital point attack using a weapon, like a knife or blade, a skill that is often taught in military training.

It is important to understand that striking, pressing or penetrating lethal points with sufficient force can damage the Central Nervous System or Cardiovascular System with fatal consequences. The most vulnerable vital points are located on the head, neck, chest and abdomen and severe injury to these points can result in death. The primary causes of death from vital point attacks are related to hemorrhaging caused by blunt or penetrating trauma, irreversible shock, multiple traumatic injuries and organ failure.

Paralyzing Points

Although some vital points are not lethal, when struck accurately at the proper angle with sufficient force, a strike can cause unconsciousness, temporary paralysis of an area of the body or incapacitating trauma. Striking these points can end a confrontation, render an assailant helpless or provide a window of time during which you can escape to safety. For example, a solid hook or uppercut punch to the Gallbladder (AD-T2) can temporarily cause the liver to stop functioning correctly. It may also momentarily take away the ability to breathe, creating the feeling of a complete loss of power. Striking paralyzing points can temporarily or even permanently damage the Central Nervous System, therefore these points should not be used without justification.

Tactical Points

Some vital points are tactically important. For example, pinching the thigh muscles will make your opponent move away from you to escape the pain. This gives you time to escape or counterattack. Attacking tactical points on the legs takes away an opponent's mobility; attacking the arms takes away his striking and grabbing power. Tactical point attacks reduce your opponent's capacity or stamina or force him to react in ways that are advantageous for you. Because they are nonlethal, tactical points are preferable in most situations to the more permanently damaging paralyzing and lethal points.

Most of the lethal points are located on the head, neck, chest and abdomen. Primary causes of death from attacking these points are related to hemorrhaging caused by blunt or penetrating trauma, irreversible shock, multiple traumatic injuries and organ failure.

A shin kick to the Bend Center (BL40) in the back of the knee can paralyze the tibial nerve. It stops the function of one quarter of the body (the leg that is kicked), reducing your opponent's mobility and opening up the upper body for a choke or elbow strike.

Practical Application

Pain Tolerance Factors

Pain tolerance is a measure of the amount of pain that a person can endure before breaking down emotionally and/or physically and giving up. Studies show that there are definite relationships between psychological factors and the body's physiological pain responses. There are also complex interactions of biological and cultural variables in dealing with pain; a child raised in a physically harsh environment will grow into adulthood with a higher level of pain tolerance than a child with a "softer" upbringing.

It is not possible to quantify how much of a person's pain tolerance is influenced by physiological factors and how much is "mind over matter," but it is clear that psychological factors can have a significant effect on a person's physiological responses. Some people are good at self-denial, including the denial of physical and emotional pain. Ultimately, because pain is sensed in the brain, it is the brain that determines how painful the stimulus is. The reality of pain becomes real only when the brain quantifies it.

Pain tolerance also fluctuates with your physical and mental condition. Pain seems to be tolerated less well during an illness, especially when fever is present. Emotional uncertainty causes anxiety, which in turn lowers pain tolerance. When the mind or body is weakened, pain is generally felt more acutely.

Many martial arts and military training programs include methods aimed at increasing a trainee's pain tolerance levels. These training programs include both physical techniques like using deep breathing to lower the heart rate and blood pressure, thereby elevating the body's pain tolerance, and psychological techniques like mental distraction to move the mind's attention away from the pain. In martial arts training, it has long been believed that using the mind to overcome physical pain is a path to enlightenment.

Pain Threshold

A person's pain threshold is the minimum intensity or duration of a sensory stimulus needed to produce pain. It's important to understand the difference between pain tolerance and pain threshold. The pain threshold is the minimum amount of stimulus required to cause pain. For example, how far someone has to bend your finger backward to cause the first sensation of pain. Pain tolerance is the degree of pain you can tolerate. For example, you can stand the pain of someone bending your finger backward 20 degrees but no more.

While many techniques are available to attempt to increase your pain tolerance, your pain threshold is fairly constant. It may be temporarily lowered by a localized inflammation. If you sprain your finger, bending it even 5 degrees backward may elicit pain due to the swelling or bruising of the injury. Taking medication that reduces the pain and inflammation may change your pain threshold while your body is under the influence of the medication, but when the effects of the medication wear off, your pain threshold will return to its previous level.

Understanding the relationship of a person's pain threshold and pain tolerance is important in the use of vital point striking. To have an effect, your techniques must at a minimum trigger an opponent's pain threshold. From that point, you'll have a range of pain to work within, as indicated by the gray area in Figure 1.6, until the opponent reaches the limit of his pain tolerance. This range of pain can be used to gain compliance from an opponent in a self-defense or law enforcement situation or to submit an opponent in sport fighting.

Varying the level of pain according to the opponent's response is a valuable tool, not only to gain physical compliance but also to intimidate the opponent. By increasing pain when an opponent resists and, conversely, decreasing it when he complies, you establish psychological dominance. This can be particularly valuable in law enforcement, when you need to handcuff a suspect and walk him to your car. A suspect who knows that he can avoid further pain by complying with your instructions is less likely to put up a fight.

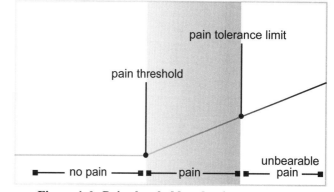

Figure 1.6 Pain threshold and pain tolerance

19 LETHAL POINTS

Striking lethal points can cause permanent damage and may cause unintended death.
(Points exist on both sides of the body except * marked points.)

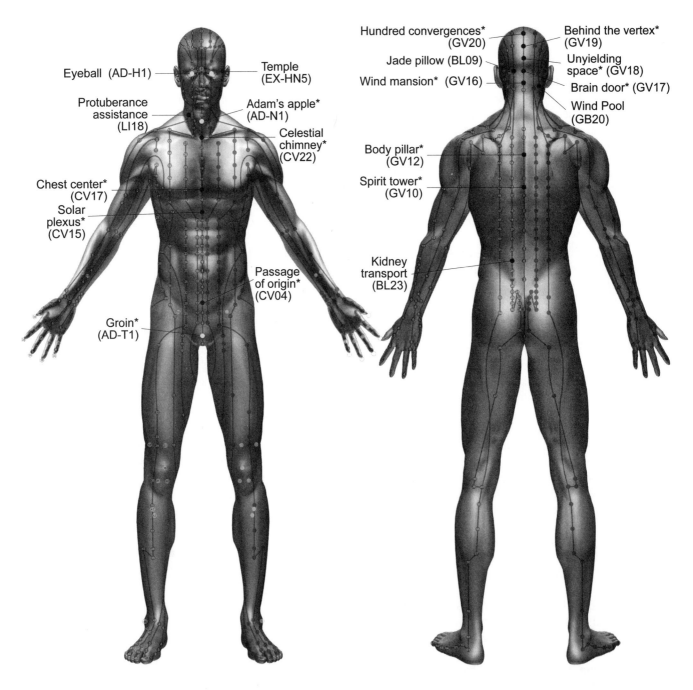

Figure 1.7   Anterior view of 9 lethal points.   **Figure 1.8   Posterior view of 10 lethal points.**

49 PARALYZING POINTS

Accurately striking paralyzing points can cause unconsciousness and incapacitation.
*(Points exist on both sides of the body except * marked points.)*

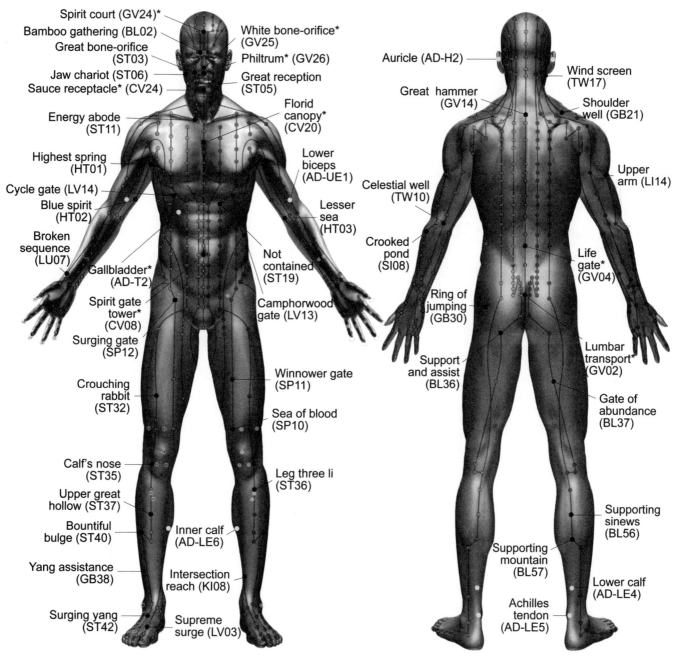

Figure 1.9   Anterior view of 33 paralyzing points.

Figure 1.10   Posterior view of 16 paralyzing points.

36 TACTICAL POINTS

Tactical point strikes provide you with significant strategic advantages.
*(Points exist on both sides of the body except * marked points.)*

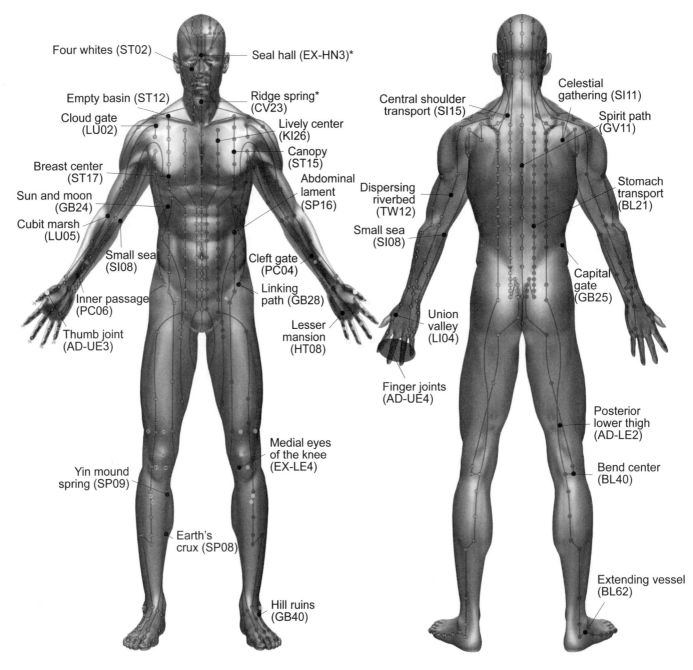

Figure 1.11   Anterior view of 21 tactical points.

Figure 1.12   Posterior view of 15 tactical points.

WHY VITAL POINTS?

Visceral Pain

Knowledge is vital for self-protection: how to evade, intercept, counterattack, and cope with the realities of a physical fight.

Are you prepared if someone punches you in the stomach and you suddenly cannot breathe? What about a kick to the groin or knifehand chop to your Adam's apple, both strikes that can temporarily disable you? How about a finger jab into your eyes that leaves you blind? What about a rear naked choke that leaves you on the verge of passing out?

More importantly, are you prepared for the psychological aspects of a fight? Being physically assaulted is destructive and disorienting. The brutality of unexpected circumstance takes your mind away instantly, especially when you are unprepared. It can make you furious or frightened, due to the pain and your inability to cope with the situation.

When facing a sudden assault, the mind goes blank momentarily, even for those who are highly trained in combat arts. Yet in the midst of this shock and confusion, a trained mind finds ways to respond to the situation. Your knowledge of vital points and striking techniques can be a valuable tool in overcoming the initial panicked moments of a fight.

Because vital point strikes are solid fighting methods that you can depend on, you'll come to think of them as your "secret weapon" and when you have a secret weapon, your attitude changes. You'll be firmer in your stance, and you'll have definitive guidelines for dealing with specific situations. You'll have a plan that allows you to work methodically to demoralize an opponent.

Figure 1.13   Vital points on meridians.

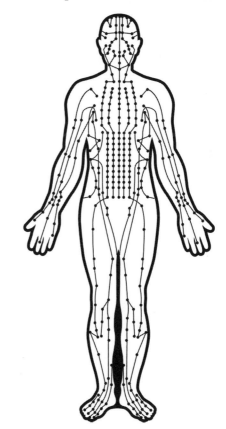

Having a specific target for each strike makes you a more effective fighter.

The impact of targeting vital points is strikingly powerful. You can cause the same type of fear and pain in your opponent that you are most fearful of. By striking external pain spots, you can cause visceral pain internally. By striking areas rich with nerves, you can impact several of the body's most important systems with one blow.

First you must know where those vital points are and how to strike them, and for your own survival, you should understand how to protect your vital weaknesses while exploiting the vital points of your opponent.

Nociceptors Sense Pain

Nerve cells play a large role in vital point striking. Nerve endings known as nociceptors are found in any area of the body that can sense pain either externally or internally. When these nociceptors are stimulated by an external threat, they transmit an electrical impulse to the brain, which is translated into the feeling of pain at the site of the stimulus. Because nociceptors are the origin of pain sensation, most vital points are located along the nervous system in the human body.

By striking the carotid artery on the neck, you can also impact several nerves such as the supraclavicular, cutaneous, auricular, occipital and accessory nerves.

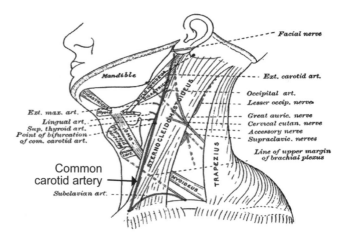

Figure 1.13   Nerve hub around the carotid artery.

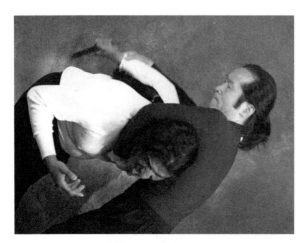

A choke that cuts off the circulation of blood and oxygen by pressing the carotid artery and the windpipe is deadly.

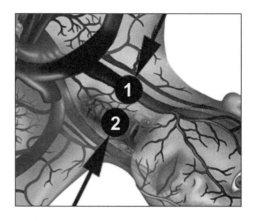

Figure 1.14 Interior view of a simultaneous choke on the carotid artery (1) and windpipe (2).

Specific Results

In fighting, it is important to strike specific targets with a specific goal in mind. Randomly striking an opponent wastes energy and opens you to potential counterattacks. By understanding the impact of each strike and the possible reactions a strike can provoke in an opponent, you can plan your next move.

For example, when an assailant grabs your collar, your first target would be his arm. As he closes in, depending on his height, you can strike his eyes or neck, punch his Solar Plexus or kick him in the groin.

With every move your opponent makes, in fact, he is exposing vital areas right in front of you. The key is to strike the exposed vital points before the opponent recovers and makes his next move.

One Rule That Rules

Vital point strikes are essential for self-defense, law enforcement, military hand-to-hand combat and sport fighting. Once you are engaged in a fight, only one rule prevails: strike the most vulnerable targets in the shortest time to cause maximum damage to the opponent.

For self-protection, strike the targets that are closest to you or most exposed. For police work, control the suspect's leverage points. In hand-to-hand combat, strike the most damaging areas. In competition, first go to the chin and temple, then to the body. Be stealthy and surprise your opponent.

Pain Works

No one likes pain. Although people vary greatly in the way they respond to pain, the intensity of stimuli needed to trigger the pain threshold is almost the same for every person. When you strike a vital point, the stimulus travels through pain receptors to the brain. Then the brain begins to work on a solution to get rid of the source of the pain: usually this involves avoiding the source of the stimulus or covering the area of the body where the pain is sensed.

This is an essential principle of vital point striking. Attacking a vital point will cause your opponent to try to move away from the source of the pain (you), to comply with your demands to relieve the pain or to cover the area of the body where the pain is occurring. Keeping this in mind can help you estimate how an opponent will react to a specific type of attack.

"Once you are engaged in a fight, only one rule prevails: strike the most vulnerable targets in the shortest time to cause maximum damage to the opponent."

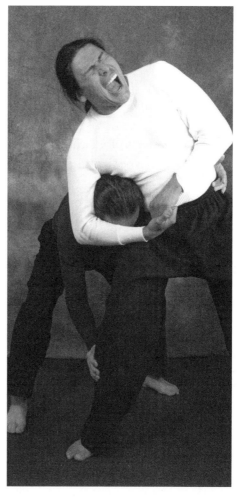

Even a larger and more muscular opponent is as sensitive as a smaller person to pain caused by an attack on the nervous system.

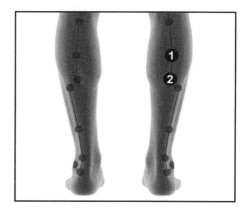

Figure 1.15 (1) The Supporting Sinews (BL56) point. (2) The Supporting Mountain (BL57) point. Both points pass the tibial nerve and the medial sural cutaneous nerve.

CAUTIONS

1. Understand the principles of vital points and the consequences of striking specific targets.

2. Begin to practice on easy to find areas on your hands and arms.

3. Begin with light pressure and monitor the effects carefully.

4. Inhale before pressing or striking. Exhale while applying pressure.

5. Be aware that a vital point strike can render a person unconscious, paralyze some parts of the body and even cause death. Never practice full power or full pressure strikes on a partner and always use common sense when practicing.

6. Have at least 72 hours rest between practicing on the same points.

7. When you are tired, wait until you fully recover before practicing.

8. After practice, rub the vital points gently with oil or lotion. For bruises, apply an ice pack for 15 minute intervals and keep the body part elevated above the heart level.

CHAPTER 2

VITAL POINT THEORIES

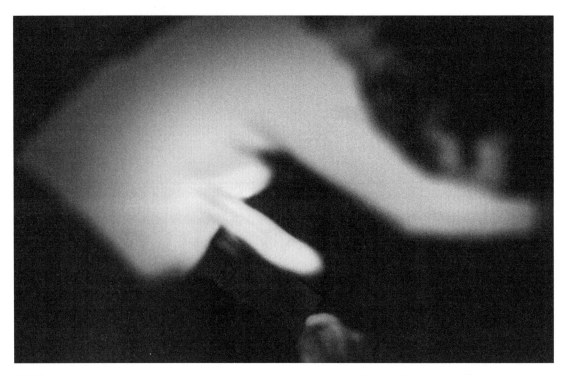

"With dexterity, no one can equal you in your maneuvers; and even the most eminent masters can hardly fathom your concealed knowledge. Expecting east, you go west. North yields to South. One concedes to the other to complete the whole."

Sang H. Kim, in *The Secret of Junsado*

Classic Eastern Theory

12 Meridians and 8 Vessels

According to ancient Chinese medical theory, the human body is interwoven with webs of meridians, through which life energy called Ki (or Chi, Qi) flows. The Ki completes a cycle from one meridian to another every 24 hours. It is believed that Ki connects human organs with cosmic energy through the 12 meridians, which are connected to 8 vessels.

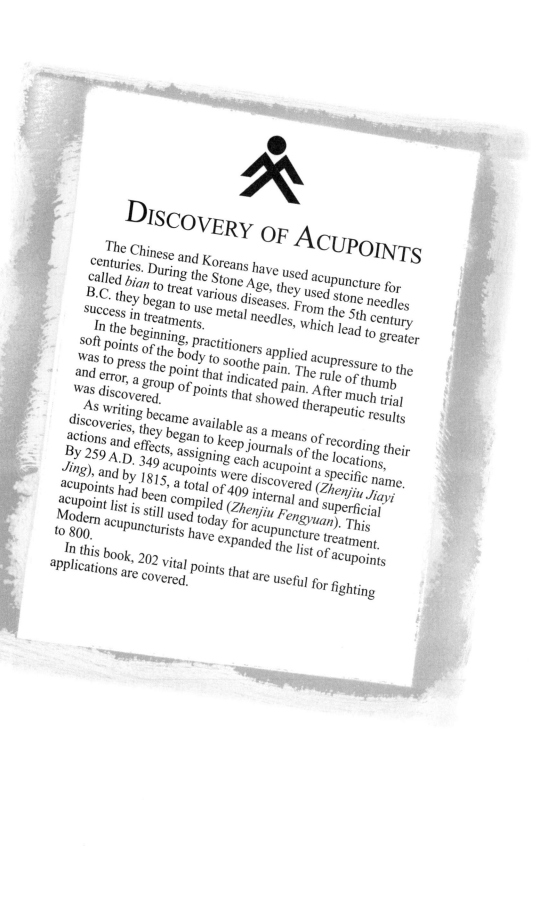

DISCOVERY OF ACUPOINTS

The Chinese and Koreans have used acupuncture for centuries. During the Stone Age, they used stone needles called *bian* to treat various diseases. From the 5th century B.C. they began to use metal needles, which lead to greater success in treatments.

In the beginning, practitioners applied acupressure to the soft points of the body to soothe pain. The rule of thumb was to press the point that indicated pain. After much trial and error, a group of points that showed therapeutic results was discovered.

As writing became available as a means of recording their discoveries, they began to keep journals of the locations, actions and effects, assigning each acupoint a specific name. By 259 A.D. 349 acupoints were discovered (*Zhenjiu Jiayi Jing*), and by 1815, a total of 409 internal and superficial acupoints had been compiled (*Zhenjiu Fengyuan*). This acupoint list is still used today for acupuncture treatment. Modern acupuncturists have expanded the list of acupoints to 800.

In this book, 202 vital points that are useful for fighting applications are covered.

12 MERIDIANS AND 8 VESSELS

Distribution of the Meridians

The twelve meridians are located symmetrically on the right and left sides of the body. There are six meridians on each of the hands and feet: the three Yin meridians of the hand run from the chest to the hand (Interior Meridians); the three Yang Meridians of the hand run from the hand to the head (Exterior Meridians); the three Yang Meridians of the foot run from the head to the foot (Exterior Meridians); the three Yin Meridians of the foot run from the foot to the abdomen and chest (Interior Meridians).

The Conception Vessel and the Governing Vessel begin from the perineum and arise along the anterior and the posterior midline of the body respectively, ending at the anterior head.

Twelve Meridians

Meridians are energy paths that connect to the organs internally and to the limbs externally. On the surface of the meridians, there are accessible vital points that are connected to the brain, chest and stomach.

The 12 Meridians are the Lung Meridian, the Large Intestine Meridian, the Stomach Meridian, the Spleen Meridian, the Heart Meridian, the Small Intestine Meridian, the Bladder Meridian, the Kidney Meridian, the Pericardium Meridian, the Triple Warmer Meridian, the Gallbladder Meridian, and the Liver Meridian.

Eight Vessels

Vessels are energy paths that connect to the meridians without a direct connection to the organs. There are no accessible vital points on the vessels except on the Governing Vessel and the Conception Vessel. In this book, therefore, only the two vessels with vital points are included. Some Chinese scientists classify these two vessels as meridians, making 14 meridians.

The 8 vessels are: Governing Vessel, Conception Vessel, Thrusting Vessel, Girdle Vessel, Yang-Activation Vessel, Yin-Activation Vessel, Yang-Maintenance Vessel, and Yin-Maintenance Vessel.

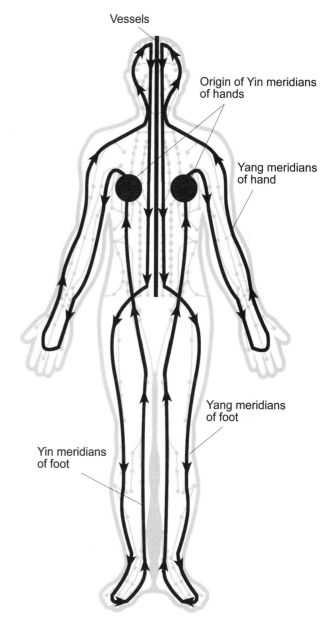

Figure 2.1 The flow of yin-yang meridians.

12 MERIDIANS

The Lung Meridian (11 acupoints)

Location: Begins near the stomach and ends at the thumb.
Function: Interacts with the lung and communicates with the large intestine; connects to the Liver Meridian and the Large Intestine Meridian.

The Large Intestine Meridian (20 acupoints)

Location: Starts from the index fingernail and ends at the corner of the nose.
Function: Interacts with the large intestine and communicates with the lung; connects to the Lung Meridian and the Stomach Meridian.

The Stomach Meridian (45 acupoints)

Location: Starts from the side of the nose and ends at the lower medial side of the big toe.
Function: Interacts with the stomach and communicates with the spleen; connects to the Large Intestine Meridian and the Spleen Meridian.

The Spleen Meridian (21 acupoints)

Location: Starts from the lower medial side of the big toenail and ends under the armpit.
Function: Interacts with the spleen and communicates with the stomach; connects to the Stomach Meridian and the Heart Meridian.

The Heart Meridian (9 acupoints)

Location: Starts from the heart and ends at the lower medial corner of the small fingernail.
Function: Interacts with the heart and communicates with the small intestine; connects to the Spleen Meridian and the Small Intestine Meridian.

The Small Intestine Meridian (19 acupoints)

Location: Starts from the lateral side of the tip of the small fingernail and ends at the medial corner of the eye.
Function: Interacts with the small intestine and communicates with the heart; connects to the Heart Meridian and the Bladder Meridian.

The Bladder Meridian (67 acupoints)

Location: Starts from the corner of the eye and ends at the lower lateral corner of the small toenail.
Function: Interacts with the urinary bladder and communicates with the kidney; connects to the Small Intestine Meridian and the Kidney Meridian.

The Kidney Meridian (27 acupoints)

Location: Starts from the small toe and ends at the pericardium.
Function: Interacts with the kidney and communicates with the urinary bladder; connects to the Bladder Meridian and the Pericardium Meridian.

The Pericardium Meridian (9 acupoints)

Location: Starts from the pericardium and ends in the center of the tip of the middle finger.
Function: Interacts with the pericardium and communicates with the Triple Warmer; connects to the Kidney Meridian and the Triple Warmer Meridian.

The Triple Warmer Meridian (23 acupoints)

Location: Starts from the lower lateral corner of the fourth fingernail and ends at the lateral side of the eye.
Function: Interacts with the Triple Warmer and communicates with the pericardium; connects to the Pericardium Meridian and the Gallbladder Meridian.

The Gallbladder Meridian (44 acupoints)

Location: Starts from the side of the eye and ends at the lower lateral corner of the big toenail.
Function: Interacts with the gallbladder and communicates with the liver; connects to the Triple Warmer Meridian and the Liver Meridian.

The Liver Meridian (14 acupoints)

Location: Starts from the big toenail and ends at the lungs.
Function: Interacts with the liver and communicates with the gallbladder; connects to the Gallbladder Meridian and the Lung Meridian.

Figure 2.2   Anterior view of 12 meridians (6 each side).   **Figure 2.3   Posterior view of 12 meridians (6 each side).**

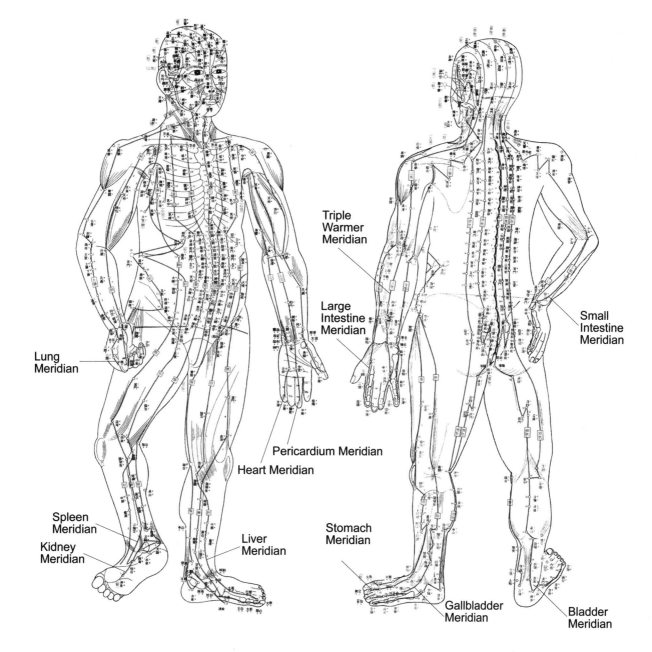

Triple Warmer Meridian

Large Intestine Meridian

Small Intestine Meridian

Lung Meridian

Pericardium Meridian

Heart Meridian

Spleen Meridian

Kidney Meridian

Liver Meridian

Stomach Meridian

Gallbladder Meridian

Bladder Meridian

TWO PRIMARY VESSELS (52 ACUPOINTS)

Conception Vessel (24 acupoints)

Location: Begins from the lower abdomen, runs along the midline through the throat to the chin, curves around the lips passing through the cheek, and ends in the infraorbital area.
Function: Communicates with the mouth, lips, eyes and eyelids.

Governing Vessel (28 acupoints)

Location: Begins at the pelvic cavity and ends at the Philtrum.
Function: Communicates with the brain, spinal cord, kidneys, uterus, nose, eyes, mouth, and lips.

Figure 2.4   24 vital points in the Conception Vessel.

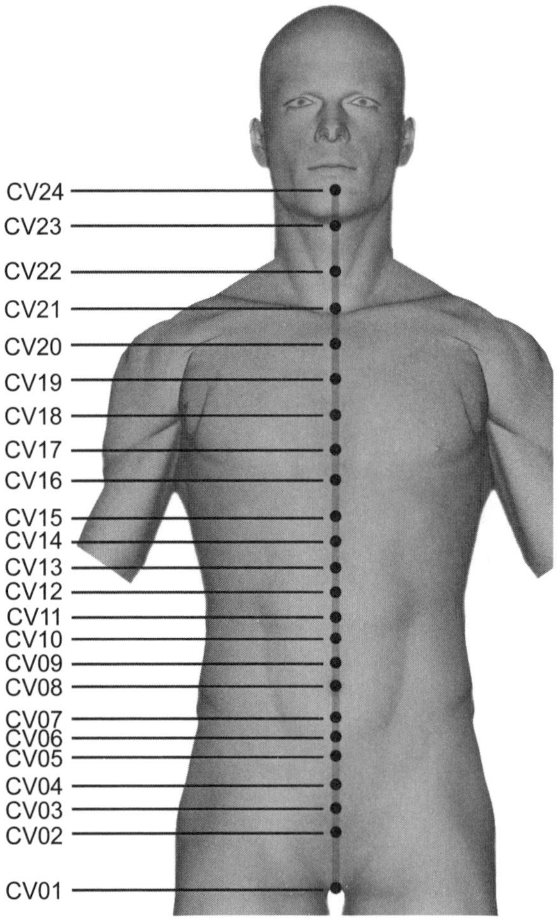

Figure 2.5   28 vital points in the Governing Vessel.

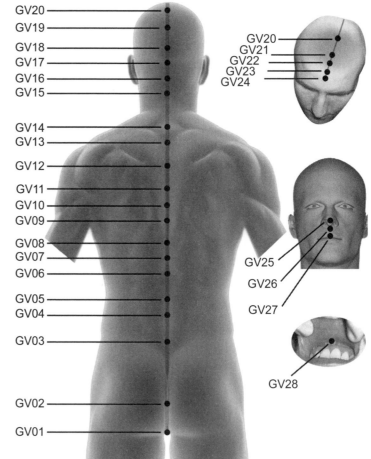

Behind Ki Theory

Yin-Yang and the Five Elements

In an attempt to explain cosmic phenomena, ancient Eastern philosophers and scientists created the Yin and Yang diagram and the Five Element Theory. They proposed that every change in the universe is the result of an interaction between two opposing yet complementary energies called Yin-ki (negative energy) and Yang-ki (positive energy). The Yin and Yang principle describes the opposing yet interdependent and ceaselessly transforming nature of the universe.

The Five Element Theory defines the five essential elements of the universe - Wood, Fire, Earth, Metal, and Water - and explains their relationships based on two possible interactions: mutual nourishment and mutual restraint. The theory proposes that these interactions can take the form of two normal and three adverse patterns. The normal patterns are energy generating and energy regulating; the adverse patterns are over-restraint, overacting, and counteracting.

An energy generating relationship is one in which an element nourishes the next element in the cycle to promote growth. For example, water nourishes a tree (wood). An energy regulating relationship is one in which an element keeps another in check, balancing and neutralizing its energy. For example, water extinguishes fire. The energy generating and energy regulating relationships appear to be opposite in nature but, in fact, they are interdependent and need each other to be whole. In traditional Chinese medicine, the Five Element Theory is extended to explain the interrelationship of the body's internal organs and to diagnose imbalances.

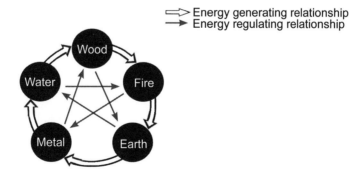

Figure 2.6 The five element diagram.

CHAIN REACTIONS

According to Eastern theory, based in part on the Five Element Theory, health is maintained by balancing the energy in the body. When the equilibrium is broken, disease occurs. Seemingly unrelated parts of the body are interdependent. Nerve damage in one part of the body can cause illness in a remote area, far from the original trauma. Similarly, in many cases, this is how acupuncture treatment works: a stimulus in one part of the body causes a reaction in another that promotes healing.

In the Western sport of boxing, a powerful punch to the chin deprives blood and oxygen from the brain causing an instant knockout. Since the nerves in the mandible (jaw) are connected to the mouth and digestive system, when the chin is struck, it sparks a chain reaction in the digestive system causing blood to rush away from the brain. As a result, the brain gets much less oxygen and unconsciousness occurs.

A destructive stimulus in one part of the nervous system can cause deadly results in seemingly unrelated parts of the body.

Classic Western Theory

The Nervous System

Despite some differences, there are many similarities between the Eastern meridian system and the Western nervous and circulatory systems. For example, in their respective systems, the meridians and nerves function to regulate the organs to maintain the overall health of the body. Additionally, the meridians follow the path of the blood vessels or vice versa. In Eastern belief, Ki (inner energy, Chi, or Qi) and blood are closely related in production, circulation, and distribution. Ki is regarded as the commander of blood; blood the mother of Ki. In Western anatomy, the blood vessels and nerves go hand in hand. In the posterior spinal cord, for instance, arteries and nerves travel down the spinal cord branching out through the vertebrae and connecting to various parts of the body. The position of the Governing Transport (BL16) coincides with the position of the branch of the posterior intercostal arteries and the 6th intercostal nerve under the 6th thoracic vertebra. These examples manifest the common purpose of both systems. That being said, this chapter focuses on overall study of human anatomy and physiology to synthesize useful elements of both systems for practical application in martial art training.

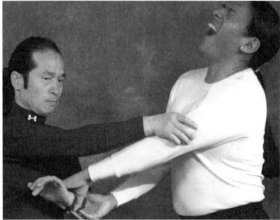

急所

NERVOUS SYSTEM

Nervous System

The master controller of the human body is the nervous system. It is the lightest part of the body, yet it is the most complex and versatile system. The nervous system is a network of nerve cells, called neurons, which regulate the body's responses to stimuli by processing information, determining responses, and sending out signals that trigger actions. The Central Nervous System (CNS), made up of the brain and spinal cord, represents the largest part of the nervous system while the Peripheral Nervous System (PNS) comprises the remaining elements of the nervous system.

Central Nervous System (CNS)

The CNS is the command center of the body. It interprets incoming sensory information, and then sends out instructions telling the body how to react. The CNS consists of two major parts: the brain, which primarily processes and analyzes information and sends out signals that trigger actions, and the spinal cord, which transmits signals between the brain and the rest of the body.

Peripheral Nervous System (PNS)

The PNS is made up of the part of the nervous system that lies outside of the brain and spinal cord (CNS) and serves the limbs and organs. The PNS is further made up of two systems: the somatic nervous system and the autonomic nervous system.

The somatic nervous system controls voluntary movements of the skeletal muscles to regulate activities that are under our conscious control, like walking, running, or punching and receives external stimuli.

The autonomic nervous system (ANS) is responsible for maintenance activities in the body, which generally take place without our conscious effort. The ANS is further divided into the parasympathetic nervous system and the enteric nervous system, both responsible for the "rest and digest" functions, and the sympathetic nervous system, which is responsible for the "fight or flight" response experienced during stress or danger.

Because somatic and autonomic nerves originate in close proximity from the spinal cord, they communicate with each other, so sensory information from somatic nerves can trigger responses in autonomic nerves and vice versa.

What does this mean? When a somatic nerve senses

Figure 2.7 Central and peripheral nervous systems.

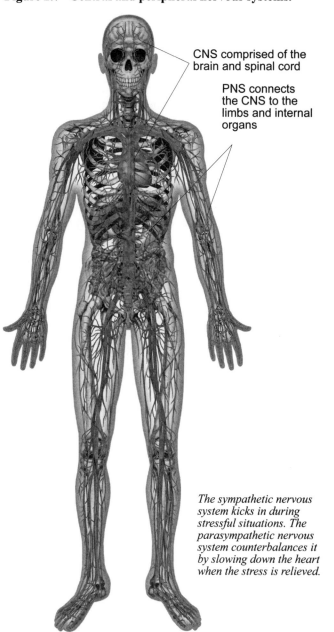

CNS comprised of the brain and spinal cord

PNS connects the CNS to the limbs and internal organs

The sympathetic nervous system kicks in during stressful situations. The parasympathetic nervous system counterbalances it by slowing down the heart when the stress is relieved.

pain in a muscle, it can trigger a response in related autonomic nerves, causing corresponding organs to shut down or shift into high gear, often without the input of the brain. This is why striking a point on the leg, arm, shoulder or other muscular area can impact the function of the heart, kidneys, liver or stomach.

45

Neurons

Neurons are the cells that make up the brain, spinal cord, and nerves. They are highly specialized for processing and transmission of cellular signals, and because they are found throughout the body, they vary greatly in size, shape and electrochemical properties.

There are three types of neurons. Sensory neurons carry sensory impulses from receptors on the skin to the CNS. Motor neurons carry impulses from the CNS to the muscles and glands. Interneurons conduct impulses between sensory neurons and motor neurons.

This information travels in the form of nerve impulses that are conducted along axons. A nerve impulse can travel between 1.5 feet (unmyelinated axons) and about 325 feet (myelinated axons) per second.

Nerves

A nerve is a cable-like bundle of axons (the long, slender projections of neurons) wrapped in delicate connective tissue. As part of the peripheral nervous system, nerves, like neurons, conduct impulses. Afferent nerves deliver signals to the CNS and efferent nerves relay impulses from the CNS to the muscles and glands.

Most nerves connect to the CNS through the spinal cord, except for the twelve cranial nerves which connect directly to the brain and primarily serve the motor and sensory systems of the head and neck region.

Pain, in vital point striking, is the result of compressing a nerve against a bone or a striking a nerve that is located close to the surface of the skin.

At rest, the parasympathetic nervous system is at work. When faced with a life-threatening situation, the sympathetic nervous system comes into play, preparing the body to respond to the threat by fighting or fleeing.

Figure 2.8   The functions of nervous systems.

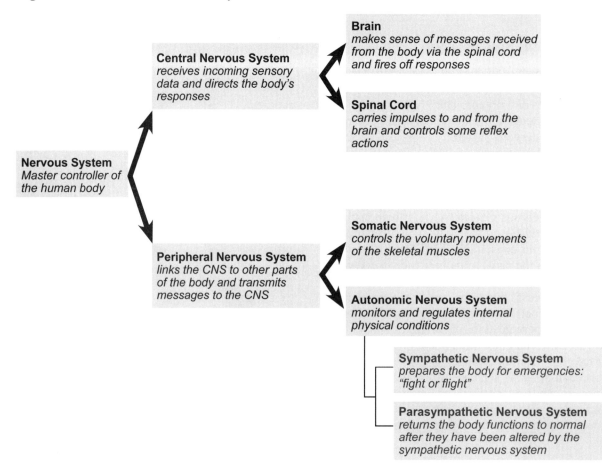

Figure 2.9 12 pairs of cranial nerves. *(The brain, human cranial nerves by Patrick J. Lynch, medical illustrator; C. Carl Jaffe, MD, cardiologist, 2006.)*

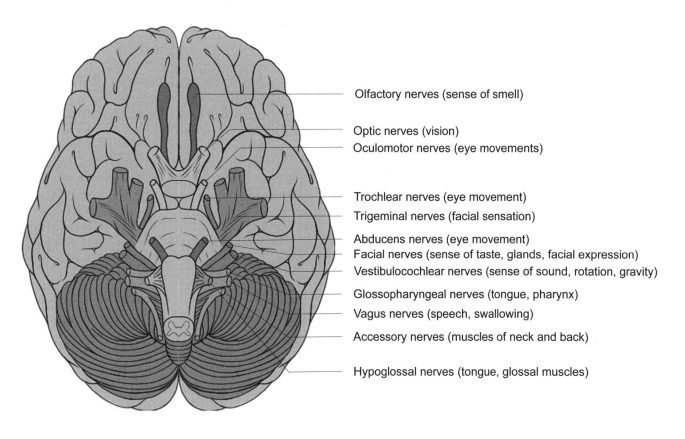

Olfactory nerves (sense of smell)

Optic nerves (vision)
Oculomotor nerves (eye movements)

Trochlear nerves (eye movement)
Trigeminal nerves (facial sensation)
Abducens nerves (eye movement)
Facial nerves (sense of taste, glands, facial expression)
Vestibulocochlear nerves (sense of sound, rotation, gravity)
Glossopharyngeal nerves (tongue, pharynx)
Vagus nerves (speech, swallowing)
Accessory nerves (muscles of neck and back)

Hypoglossal nerves (tongue, glossal muscles)

Practical Application

Major Cranial Nerves as Vital Points

Trigeminal nerves

Location: The trigeminal nerves are the largest of the cranial nerves. There are three branches: the ophthalmic (eyes and forehead area), maxillary (upper mouth area), and mandibular divisions (behind the ear, lower mouth area). They receive sensation from the face.

Significance: Most of the vital points in the head are on one of the branches of the trigeminal nerves.

Vagus nerves

Location: The vagus nerves start from the lower portion of the brainstem and pass downward through the neck into the chest and abdomen. They transmit impulses from the pharynx, larynx, viscera of the thorax and abdomen to the brain. They are responsible for speech and swallowing.

Significance: Most of the vital points on the neck and lower posterior sides of the face are on one of the branches of the vagus nerves.

Facial nerves

Location: The facial nerves emerge from the lower part of the pons and spread over the sides of the face and the occipital region. They are responsible for facial expression, sense of taste, and the salivary lacrimal glands.

Significance: Most of the vital points in the head are on one of the branches of the facial nerves.

Accessory nerves

Location: The accessory nerves originate from the lower portion of the brainstem. There are two branches: cranial and spinal. The cranial branch merges with the vagus nerve and transmits impulses to muscles of pharynx and larynx. The spinal branch extends downward into the neck and carries impulses to the shoulder muscles.

Significance: Many vital points on the neck and shoulders are on one of the branches of the accessory nerves.

Figure 2.10   31 pairs of spinal nerves plus major nerves on the posterior leg.

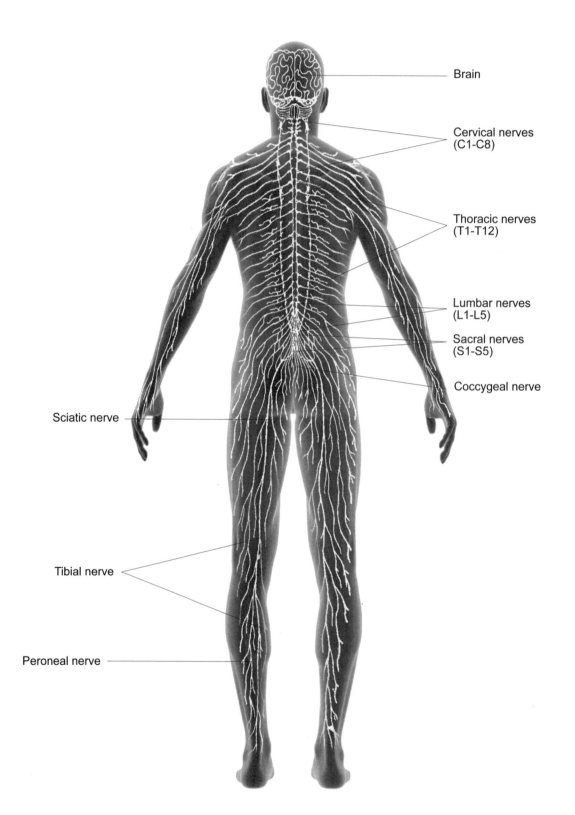

Brain

Cervical nerves
(C1-C8)

Thoracic nerves
(T1-T12)

Lumbar nerves
(L1-L5)

Sacral nerves
(S1-S5)

Coccygeal nerve

Sciatic nerve

Tibial nerve

Peroneal nerve

The Brain

The human brain is composed of up to 1 trillion nerve cells, of which 100 billion are neurons. The brain is protected by the skull and enveloped by three layers of membranes. The outermost layer, the cerebral cortex, is responsible for higher brain functions, such as sensation, voluntary muscle movement, reasoning, memory and the expression of individuality. The cerebral cortex receives incoming sensory information from the spinal cord via the thalamus.

The thalamus functions as a central relay center for sensory impulses, processing and relaying data from the spinal cord to the appropriate regions of the cortex for interpretation. The thalamus also interprets sensations of pain, pressure, temperature, touch, emotions and memory, translating the raw data received from the rest of the body into a form that is "readable" by the cerebral cortex.

The Spinal Cord

The spinal cord, which is made up of approximately 13.5 million neurons, is a part of the brain stem. It carries impulses to and from the brain and controls some reflex actions. The spinal cord is protected and cushioned by vertebrae and membranes. It has two primary pathways: one that is responsible for transmitting information related to touch, proprioception (sense of relative position of your body parts) and vibration, and one that is responsible for transmitting information related to pain and temperature.

The spinal cord is also responsible for managing the reflex arc, which allows reflex actions to occur more quickly by activating spinal motor neurons directly rather than sending information to the brain and waiting for a reply. The brain receives information about the reflex action while it is occurring rather than directing the action, as it does in more complex situations.

An example of the reflex arc in action is the pin prick reflex. If someone sharply jabs your hand with a pin, you will immediately pull your hand away from the source of the pain. The sensory input of pain in your hand travels to your spinal cord, is processed there and triggers a response that travels back to the hand, instructing it to rapidly withdraw.

A more complex example of the reflex arc occurs when you need to make multiple physical adjustments at once. For example, if someone kicks you in the shin, you will not only retract your leg from the kicker, but also you will shift your weight to your other leg to maintain balance and perhaps drop your hands to the wounded area to cover it, all under the direction of the spinal cord.

Figure 2.11   Function chart of spinal cord.

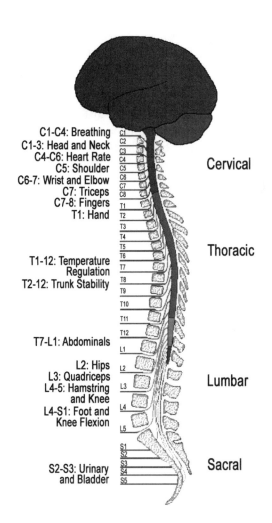

C1-C4: Breathing
C1-3: Head and Neck
C4-C6: Heart Rate
C5: Shoulder
C6-7: Wrist and Elbow
C7: Triceps
C7-8: Fingers
T1: Hand

Cervical

T1-12: Temperature Regulation
T2-12: Trunk Stability

Thoracic

T7-L1: Abdominals

L2: Hips
L3: Quadriceps
L4-5: Hamstring and Knee
L4-S1: Foot and Knee Flexion

Lumbar

S2-S3: Urinary and Bladder

Sacral

Spinal Injuries

Spinal nerves are the pathways of our life force. They are extremely sensitive and vulnerable. Most spinal injuries incurred in a fight are caused by falling, twisting, or throwing. Primary nerve injuries are caused by punctures, incisions, or blunt trauma to the spinal cord such as herniated discs, pinched nerves, and fractured vertebrae. In the event of this type of injury, the victim may suffer an instant loss of motor, sensory, or autonomic function. Secondary injuries, which tend to be chronic conditions such as paralysis, are usually the result untreated or irreparable primary injuries.

ON PAIN

Biologically speaking, pain is the body's defensive warning system designed to trigger the mental and/or physical behavior that will terminate the painful experience. It enables the body to react quickly to minimize damage to the organs and the nervous system.

Pain

Pain is physical and emotional suffering associated with actual or potential bodily damage. In fighting, pain generally results from damage to the musculoskeletal system and nervous system, and in some cases to the internal organs. Biologically speaking, pain is the body's defensive warning system: pain triggers the mental and physical behavior necessary to terminate the painful experience. It is both a critical function that enables the body to react quickly to minimize damage to the body and a learning mechanism that seeks ways to reduce or avoid the repetition of the painful situation in the future. For example, pain tells you not only to remove your hand from a hot stove, but it also teaches you not to touch the stove again.

Pain Detectors

Pain results from activation of specific receptors called nociceptors, which are small nerve endings in the skin and other tissues that respond to "threatening" stimulation and send signals to the brain. Noci means noxious, and this refers to the way that nociceptors are designed to respond to strong tissue-damaging stimuli such as a pinch or a cut.

When vital points are struck, nociceptors are activated and nerve impulses are relayed to the brain and translated as pain. If stimulation is repeatedly applied to the same area, the nociceptors there become increasingly sensitive, reacting even to mild stimuli.

Perception of Pain

Pain was once thought as a subjective experience based on emotional reactions rather than concrete physical sensations. However, recent studies reveal that pain is physically perceived in the anterior cingulate cortex (ACC). The ACC is located in the frontal part of the cingulate cortex, which is in the middle of the brain. The ACC is responsible for problem solving, error detection, anticipation of tasks, motivation, and emotional responses. It's a central station for processing information and assigning control to other areas in the brain. It is also involved with various autonomic functions such as motor and digestive functions, the regulation of blood pressure and heart rate.

Figure 2.12   Left cerebral hemisphere.

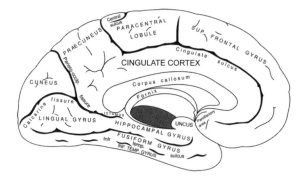

Pain is perceived in the anterior cingulate cortex (ACC). The ACC is located in the frontal part of the cingulate cortex in the middle of the brain.

Figure 2.13   Pain detectors.

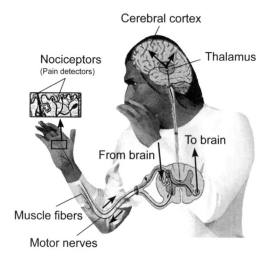

Pain in the Brain

The nervous system is your body's communication center. The Central Nervous System (CNS) consists of the brain and the spinal cord. The Peripheral Nervous System (PNS) is made up of the nerves outside of the CNS. Together they control every part of your life, from breathing and memory to the pain in your back.

Nerves extend from your brain to your face, ears, eyes, chin, temples, toes, and spinal cord, and from your spinal cord to the rest of your body. The spinal cord functions like your body's superhighway, relaying messages to and from the brain at lightning speed.

When you are injured, your sensory nerves gather information from the site of the injury and send it to the spinal cord, which then transmits the message to the brain. The brain interprets that message and discharges a response to the affected area of the body by way of the motor neurons which directly or indirectly control your muscles.

Vital Point Pain

In vital point striking, pain is measured not merely by the force applied against the target but by changes in pressure at the center of the point. A powerful but untargeted strike can result in waste of energy whereas a precise snappy strike at the bullseye of a vital point can paralyze an opponent instantly. Since the ultimate goal in fighting is to control the opponent, a precise strike follows the law of economy in the use of energy.

To understand the importance of precision, think about hitting a baseball. No matter how hard you swing, if you miss the ball completely, it will simply fall to the ground behind you. If you hit the ball hard, but inaccurately, you'll end up with a ball that goes far, but has little effect on the game because it will end up out of bounds, resulting in a foul ball. In order to hit a home run, you need to hit the ball not only hard, but on the "sweet spot" of the bat at precisely the right time.

Vital point striking is the same: you have to strike the target point precisely and with sufficient force to "hit a home run" and cause pain in your opponent. If you have to choose, precision is preferable to power.

Power vs. Precision

Power comes from precise penetrating strikes. Attention must be focused on the movement, distance, angle and timing of the strike. Note below how a blunt powerful strike may not reach the intended target point while a precise penetrating strike hits its target.

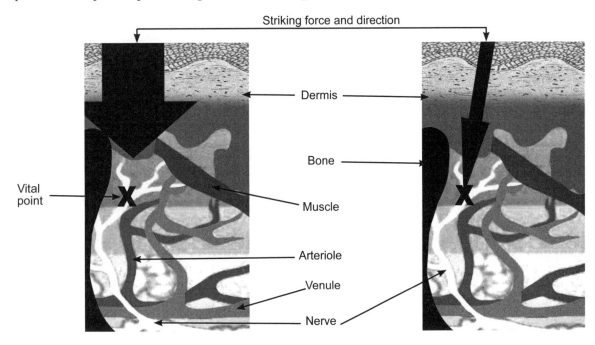

Figure 2.14 Diagram of inaccurate power strike.   **Figure 2.15 Diagram of a precise angular strike.**

PAIN AND REFLEXES

The body has a pain withdrawal reflex, where it reacts to pain by moving away from it. This is useful knowledge in fighting, particularly in anticipating what an opponent's reaction might be to a particular attack.

Reflexes

Reflexes are automatic, unconscious, neuromuscular responses to changes occurring inside or outside the body. Reflex actions are involuntary, rapid, and predictable because they are controlled by the reflex arc. To save "travel time," the reflex arc allows reflex actions to occur quickly by activating spinal motor neurons without routing signals through the brain.

A reflex action occurs when a stimulus generates an impulse in a sensory neuron. The impulse travels to the spinal cord, where it passes from a sensory neuron into a motor neuron via an interneuron. Then, the motor neuron transmits the impulse through other motor neurons to a muscle for a proper response.

Speed & Reflexes

Many martial artists are eager to improve their reflexes as way to shorten their response time. While you can't actually improve the speed at which messages are transmitted between your nerves, spinal cord and brain, you can improve your ability to process and react to situations through repetition and practice.

Perception and reaction speed in fighting rely on the quick response of your visual and nervous systems. First, your eyes or in some cases your ears perceive the need for a response. Next, they rapidly and accurately transmit the nature of the event requiring a response to the brain. The brain compares this event with similar, previously experienced circumstances and searches for an appropriate response.

Once a response is selected, the brain sends out signals to the body via the nervous system and the body responds to these intricate commands. During the execution period, the brain and body communicate to make minute adjustments in every phase of the movement. This entire process can take place hundreds of times a minute as your body reads and adapts to its changing environment. The key element in this chain of events is the brain's ability to quickly locate a similar previous event and formulate a response.

Through repetition in training, you experience a situation hundreds or thousands of times, making your brain very familiar with the situation and with possible appropriate responses. This is similar to learning to drive. You may have to think about slamming on the

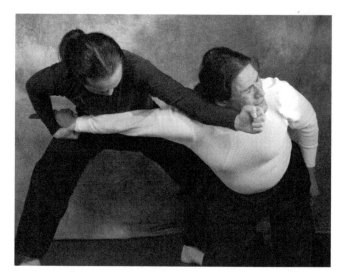

Some points are painful because of the prevalence of nerves in the area. The body's pain withdrawal reflex causes it to react to pain by moving away from it.

Through training and repetition, you can improve your response time by increasing your brain's efficiency in evaluating and responding to your opponent's actions.

brakes the first time you encounter something unexpected in the road, but eventually, braking becomes a reaction that you perform almost before you've realized that your foot has moved from the gas to the brake pedal. Similarly, your reaction speed can be improved significantly by proper training. For specific training methods, refer to *Ultimate Fitness Through Martial Arts* (Turtle Press).

Pain Withdrawal Reflex

The pain withdrawal reflex is an involuntary action in which the body reacts to pain by moving itself away from the source of the pain, to prevent excessive damage to the tissues, or to reduce or even eliminate that pain.

For example, when you apply pressure to the biceps of the opponent his body will move away from you. Why does this happen? When you press a vital spot, skin receptors are activated and sensory impulses travel to the spinal cord. These impulses are processed and a response is delivered to the appropriate motor neurons, which transmit the impulses to flexor muscles in the arm, telling them to contract and pull the arm away from the source of the pain.

Fighting Application

Vital point striking is an ideal way to trigger the pain withdrawal reflex. By striking or pressing certain points, you can anticipate your opponent's movement patterns and effectively devise your next movement to strengthen your position. When you combine vital point strikes and grappling techniques that maximize that pain withdrawal reflex, your range of fighting options becomes greater.

For example, applying pressure into the windpipe will cause your opponent to move downward. Pushing up on the mandibular joints with tips of your thumbs will make your opponent move upward. Poking the rib cage with your middle knuckles will make your opponent move back.

Limitations

Although the pain withdrawal reflex sounds like a magical method, its effects will be limited against certain opponents including an opponent who is wearing a thick leather jacket and motorcycle helmet, a highly trained martial artist who can override the pain, a drunk or drugged person, or an enraged or deranged person. In these cases, alternative tactics will be necessary to subdue or defeat the opponent.

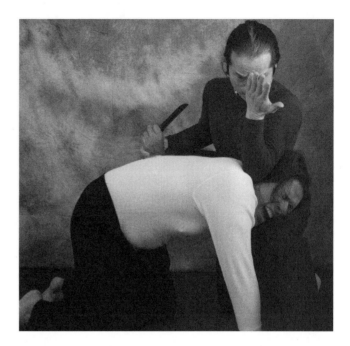

A knee strike to the side of the head causes the opponent to try to raise his head, presenting the perfect opportunity for a downward elbow strike to the opposite side of his head.

The carotid artery choke shown here can cause sufficient pain to make an opponent drop his weapon as he seeks to avoid or eliminate the pain in his arm, shoulder and neck.

On Fear of Pain

Fear is an innate or learned emotional response to factual and imagined threats. Fear is a survival mechanism, and is usually connected to pain.

Fear in the Brain

Fear is a chain reaction in the brain that involves several of the brain's processing centers and is highly dependent on stored memories of past fear-related events and their outcomes. Fear is processed in both the more "primitive" areas of the brain (brainstem, midbrain and thalamus) and the more complex processing centers of the prefrontal cortex and amygdala. The fear associations in the brainstem are simple and categorical and they are the "first line of defense." The associations in the amygdala are more complex, allowing for the interpretation of emotional signals and cues, including facial expressions, and the intentions that they convey. The associations in the cortex are the most complex, facilitating interpretation of abstract cues, including the analysis of sensory information that does not have an existing association in the brain (i.e. a new experience).

In some cases, a pattern of incoming sensory data will be interpreted by the brainstem, midbrain and thalamus as "danger" and then quickly determined to be harmless by the cortex.

For example, you hear a loud bang and reflexively jump and look around but then realize that it was simply the sound of a door slamming, so you relax. Your initial startle reflex was triggered by the brainstem, midbrain and thalamus. The realization that a slamming door does not present a threat was the result of further processing by the cortex and amygdala.

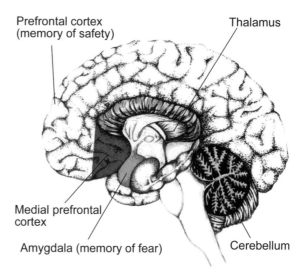

Prefrontal cortex (memory of safety)

Thalamus

Medial prefrontal cortex

Amygdala (memory of fear)

Cerebellum

Figure 2.16   Brain for memory of fear and safety.

Conversely, if the loud sound had been a car exploding nearby, your cortex would have processed the additional sensory inputs such as fire, exploding projectiles or people around you panicking and instructed your body to flee.

Fear Response

Fear is a complex reaction that arises without conscious effort in an attempt to deal with a real or imaginary threat. It involves experiential, behavioral, physiological and psychological elements. However, when faced with fear, the physical and physiological responses of humans are remarkably similar across cultures: heightened heartbeat, freezing response, muscle tension, increased perspiration, and secretion of adrenalin. This capacity to respond immediately is critical to a rapid response to potentially-threatening sensory signals. Fear is an emotional state that triggers a rapid and automatic physical response to initiate the appropriate actions for coping with a threat.

Fear can trigger a rapid response to initiate the appropriate actions for coping with a threat.

Practical Application

Physical Manifestations of Fear

There are many signs of fear that can be observed physically in an opponent including:

Change in facial expression
- a fixed stare
- raised or lowered eyebrows
- clenched teeth
- squinting
- tightly drawn lips

Change in posture
- clenched fists
- raised arms
- hunched shoulders
- tense posture
- expanded chest

Even in a person who is good at concealing fear, there will be involuntary changes taking place in the body that are nearly impossible to conceal. Watch for the following telltale signs:

- *increased sweating*, even in a cool or cold environment

- *rapid shallow breathing* as the body oxygenates the blood to supply the muscles for action

- *pale face and extremities* as blood is rerouted to critical organs

- *excessive lick lipping or swallowing* due to a decrease in saliva

Fear Heightens Focus

When a potential assailant approaches you, rising fear and anxiety command your brain to take actions to ensure your survival such as looking for an exit or grabbing a weapon and to eliminate all of the other actions you could be doing such as checking your phone messages or enjoying the scenery, while at the same time analyzing the visual and auditory cues that the assailant is presenting.

Initially, your brainstem, midbrain and thalamus will sound the alarm - someone is encroaching on your personal space - and your body will begin to respond with the first signs of the fight or flight response.

As your heart rate and breathing increase, your cortex and amygdala are working to interpret the intentions of the potential assailant including his facial expressions, body language, speech and demeanor. Is the assailant smiling, frowning, grimacing? Are his hands up in a gesture of surrender, concealed in his pockets, balled into fists, holding a weapon? Is he running, walking, strolling, sprinting, weaving erratically? Is he shouting, laughing, crying, speaking softly, silent?

Even as you read these descriptions, you probably found yourself associating each with an assumption about the person's intent and a potential response. You may have even felt your heart rate speeding up or your breathing change slightly as your brain revisited similar situations that you've experienced in the past and visualized your responses. There are a wide variety of reasons why a person might suddenly and unexpectedly approach you in a public place: an injured person seeking assistance, a homeless person looking for spare change, a police officer intent on questioning you or a mugger intending to steal your wallet. Without your cortex and amygdala to compare the approaching person with memories of people who approached you in the past, you would react to every approaching person as either threatening or benign.

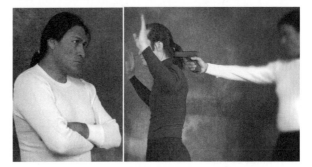

The cortex and amygdala in the brain interpret the intentions of the potential assailant based on your past experience.

The processing of sensory data in the cortex and amygdala allow you to increase or decrease your fear response appropriately. However, this highly complex system of analysis and response can also backfire and cause unwarranted anxiety, such as in the case of Post Traumatic Stress Disorder. When very strong fear memories become associated with specific cues, such as the sound of a helicopter or a gunshot, these memories can be triggered over and over by benign sensory cues (such as a loud noise) in inappropriate situations, leading to hypervigilance and anxiety even in safe situations. Because the brain's response to fear can be distorted, it is susceptible to being exploited.

Fear and Behavior Modification

Fear is not only a survival tool, it is one of the most powerful methods of influencing another person socially and psychologically. Fear changes a person's attitude by establishing undesirable consequences for failing to agree or comply with a given demand. Because we normally seek to avoid fear, fear and threats are two of the most effective methods to change the attitudes and behaviors of human beings.

Think of something you are afraid of, for example walking across a narrow beam that is suspended one hundred feet above the ground or being trapped in a room with dozens of snakes. What would you do to avoid being placed in this situation? Because of your fear, you are willing to alter your behavior, perhaps significantly.

This knowledge can be used in a fight, whether a self-defense situation or competitive match, to influence your opponent, even before the first punch is thrown. Boxers and other professional fighters have long understood the value of posturing before a fight. Barroom brawlers are even more acutely aware of how effective a good "game face" can be in intimidating an opponent. And once you engage with an opponent, fear can be used in a wide variety of ways to force your opponent to submit or surrender.

For example, because the brain stores each fear related experience and uses it as a basis for responding to similar future experiences, when you inflict a painful elbow strike on your opponent's temple, whenever you make a similar movement, he will associate that with the painful previous strike and react accordingly. By landing a few painful blows early, you can condition your opponent to fear your strikes and gain a psychological edge.

Conversely, don't fall prey to this kind of intimidation tactic if your opponent attempts to use it against you. When you get hit, react by strengthening your

Act confidently. Refuse to submit. Inflict pain on the opponent. Turn fear into bravado.

defenses and counterattacking strongly. Make your opponent associate his striking with your strong counterattack, turning the tables on him. For example, if your opponent throws a good jab and you immediately counter with a hard front leg kick to the lower abdomen, he will be reluctant to use the jab again. By countering hard and fast, you cause him to associate his jab with pain in his stomach.

Putting Fear to Use

In terms of fear responses, one size does not fit all. Different people respond at different levels to the same threat. However, there is an optimal level of fear that produces a change in attitude or behavior. If you do not create enough fear, your opponent will be unaffected. Your opponent's perception of how competent you are to deal with a situation plays a large part in his reactions to you. If you appear to be highly competent and unafraid of your opponent, his fear and self-doubt will increase. Fear can also be created through body language, commitment to your actions, an unwillingness to submit and the ability to inflict pain on the opponent effectively and repeatedly.

However, if you do not trigger an opponent's fear response strongly enough, he will have less fear, and consequentially, your fear may increase. This is an important factor in fighting because it dictates your ability to deal with both your own fear and your circumstances. The more personally involved you become with an opponent, the more fear that can be generated both by you and your opponent. A personal direct threat creates the strongest fear response.

The fear and adrenalin rush that you experience in a confrontation give you an unmatched surge of energy and bravado. When you learn to harness fear rather than being overwhelmed by it, you can use it to good advantage.

THE CIRCULATORY SYSTEM

The Circulatory System carries the blood and oxygen that are the life force of the human body.

The Circulatory System is composed of the heart, blood vessels and blood. Its function is to transport nutrients, gases, and wastes to and from cells, help fight diseases and help stabilize body temperature and pH to maintain homeostasis. A healthy circulatory system is essential to the health of the body.

Blood Vessels

Among the major types of blood vessels are the arteries, veins and capillaries. The capillaries are microscopic vessels which enable the exchange of water and chemicals between the blood and the tissues. The arteries carry blood from the heart to the capillaries and the veins return the blood from the capillaries to the heart. The heart, in turn, regulates the flow of blood through the blood vessels through regular rhythmic contractions. The average human heart beats (contracts) about 72 times per minute.

Vital Points and the Circulatory System

While the effects of vital point strikes on the nervous system are primarily pain related, the effects of vital point strikes on the circulatory system include dizziness, loss of consciousness, disorientation, bruising, blood clots, and in extreme cases fatal conditions like stroke, cardiac arrest, hemorrhage, and brain damage. Vital point strikes to the nerves tend to have immediate and obvious outcomes. The effects on the circulatory system can be immediate, like dizziness or loss of consciousness, or they can take hours or days to manifest themselves, like in the case of a blood clot that forms in the leg and travels to the heart.

Vital points related to the circulatory system, therefore, sometimes hold less value as targets and can be more dangerous to attack. A strike might appear to have little or no immediate effect, but unseen damage to the circulatory system could lead to serious complications if left untreated. In addition to striking, there are points related to the circulatory system that can be compressed to starve a region of the body of blood and oxygen, similar to what happens when your arm or leg "falls asleep" if you sit or lie on it for an extended period of time. Limiting the circulation to a limb might be an annoyance to an opponent, making it temporarily difficult for him to use his hand or leg, but cutting off the circulation to the brain can end a fight in seconds. Compressing the arteries in the neck is not only a sure way to subdue an assailant but can be fatal.

For all of these reasons, extreme caution should always be used when attacking points that are related to the major arteries and the heart.

Baroreceptors

Baroreceptors are sampling areas in the arteries and blood vessels that detect the pressure of blood flowing through them and can send messages to the Central Nervous System to increase or decrease the cardiac output and thereby quickly raise or lower the blood pressure. There are baroreceptors in the aorta and the carotid sinuses of the carotid arteries. While the aorta is protected by the chest wall, the carotid sinuses are exposed in the soft tissue of the neck. Striking the carotid sinus can cause a temporary increase in pressure in the carotid artery. The baroreceptor will then send a message to the brain directing it to lower the pressure in the artery, causing a sudden drop in blood pressure and heart rate which can lead to loss of consciousness and, in some cases, death. Because striking the carotid sinus relies simply on triggering this reaction, even a light strike can result in a knockout.

Striking or choking the Protuberance Assistance (LI18) can cause dizziness, loss of consciousness or death.

Synthesis of East and West

Eastern masters have a holistic approach to the human body whereas Western scientists have developed analytical and experimental approaches. However, the value of meridians versus the nervous system is not something we need to argue about to prove which is superior. Both the martial arts and medical fields present critical decisions, often dealing with life and death, that require practical and precise applications of knowledge with an open mind. When it comes to the human body, there is no path that is perfectly paved. Every decision and action is a stepping stone on a journey.

That being said, if you closely look at the meridians and nervous system charts below, there are more similarities than differences. By combining knowledge from the both systems of thought, you will discover a far richer treasure than presented by either system alone.

Figure 2.17 Meridians.

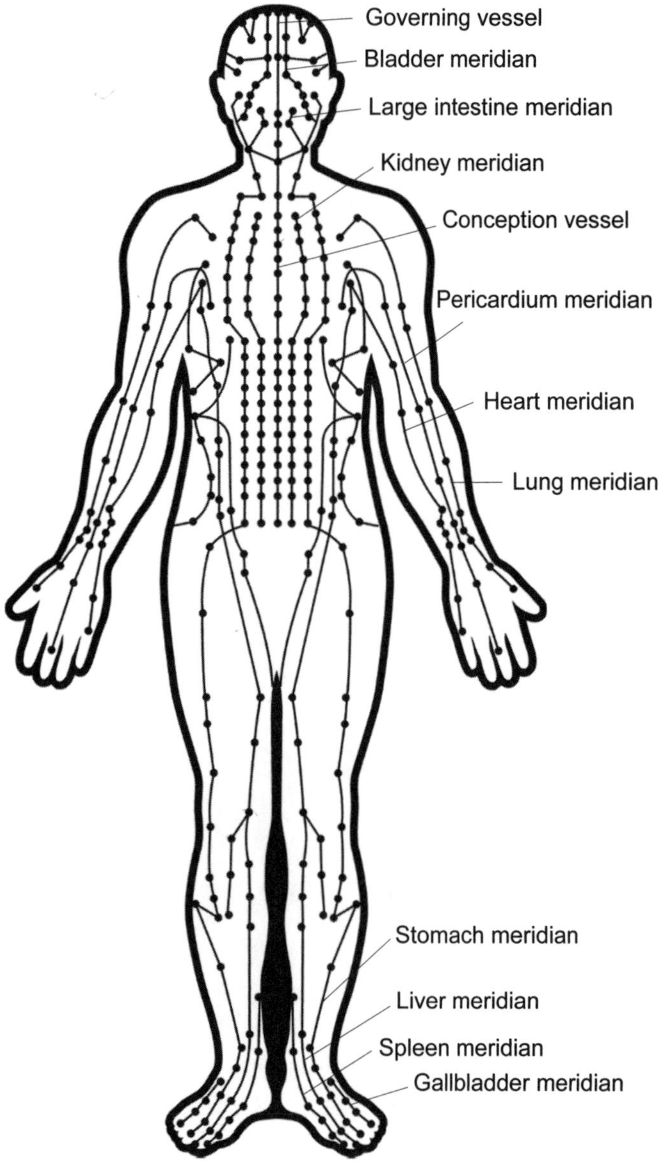
Governing vessel
Bladder meridian
Large intestine meridian
Kidney meridian
Conception vessel
Pericardium meridian
Heart meridian
Lung meridian
Stomach meridian
Liver meridian
Spleen meridian
Gallbladder meridian

Figure 2.18 Nervous System.

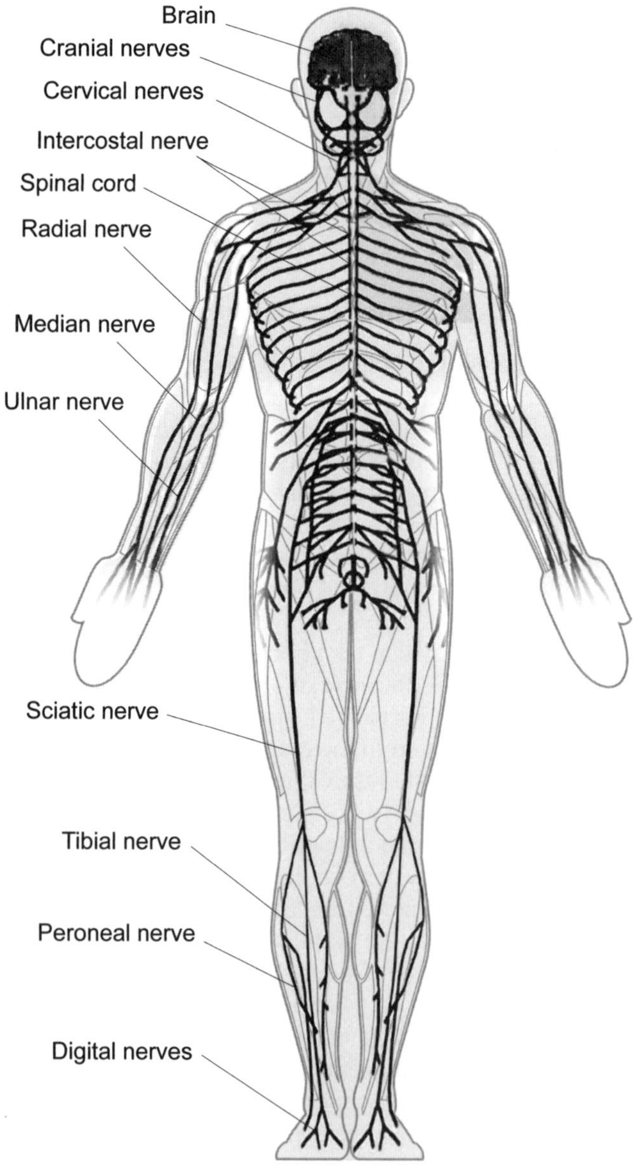
Brain
Cranial nerves
Cervical nerves
Intercostal nerve
Spinal cord
Radial nerve
Median nerve
Ulnar nerve
Sciatic nerve
Tibial nerve
Peroneal nerve
Digital nerves

CHAPTER KEY POINTS

1. The purpose of striking vital points is to defeat an opponent. There are four ways to accomplish this: attack the nervous system to cause pain and paralysis, attack the arteries to disrupt the blood flow to the brain or major organs, attack the respiratory system to disrupt the breathing or attack the major organs to cause pain and distress.

2. There are 409 named vital points located on 12 meridians and 2 vessels in the human body. Most of these points are located near nerve endings which are connected to the Central Nervous System. When the Central Nervous System perceives pain, a change of behavior occurs. By studying those changes, you can anticipate and manipulate an opponent's reactions.

3. The head is the central command center and the most vital area of the human body. The neck is the second most vital area, because it is the site of key arteries and respiratory system components as well as a portion of the spinal cord. Striking or constricting specific areas of the neck can be lethal. You must exercise the utmost care and caution in the practice and application of any techniques to the head and neck.

4. One of the most effective ways to end a confrontation is to create such fear, either real or imagined, in the opponent's mind that he no longer wants to fight you. Real fear comes from physical pain and imagined fear comes from your opponent's perception of your competence and confidence. By utilizing your knowledge of vital point strikes, you can hasten or intensify your opponent's fear and anxiety.

5. Because the use of vital point strikes in a confrontation can cause permanent damage or even death, it is important that you understand the potential effects of every technique and to always use only the minimum justified amount of force necessary to end a confrontation and escape to safety. In some cases, if you've caused enough fear in the opponent's mind, you may be able to safely walk away from the situation much sooner than if you had to resort to physically fighting to a resolution. Be decisive and brave in escaping to safety at your earliest opportunity.

"A technique must be sufficiently tested and a fighter sufficiently disciplined to ensure success."

Sang H. Kim, on *Fighting*

CHAPTER 3

FIGHTING FUNDAMENTALS

5 POTENTIAL OUTCOMES OF A FIGHT

The fundamental goal in fighting is to defeat the opponent by making him physically submit or allowing you to escape. Here are the possible outcomes of a fight:

Knockout

A knockout is the inability to continue fighting due to fatigue, injury, or a loss of consciousness. It is usually caused by trauma to the brain from powerful strikes like an elbow strike to the temple, knee kick to the groin or head-butt to the nose.

Tap-out

A tap-out is a refusal to continue to fight in a sport fighting situation. It usually occurs because of a joint lock or choke that leads to a submission, or a complete loss of fighting will or capacity due to a severe injury. Examples of injuries that might lead to a tap-out are a thumb to the eye, arm bar or an opponent using a ground-and-pound strategy from the mount.

Choke-out

A choke-out is the act of strangling or choking the opponent to unconsciousness. Taken to the extreme, a choke-out can lead to death. There are three ways a choke-out can occur: stoppage of the oxygen flow in the brain by compressing the airways, stoppage of the blood circulation to the brain by constricting the carotid artery, or a combination of the two.

Death

Killing is the deprivation of life, a complete destruction of a person's right to live. In situations of justified self-defense, law enforcement or military combat, you may have to take someone's life. It is, however, extremely difficult to take the life of a fellow human being even when your own life is threatened. The consequences of killing, for good or bad, are traumatic. For most of us, it is easier to spare a life than take it, not because of cowardice but because of the way we are created as human beings. Taking a life should always be the last resort and should always be justified.

Escape

Escape is getting away from the danger of a confrontation. In self-defense situations, you can escape through smart tactics or tricks, physical force, or outrunning the opponent.

FIGHTING ZONES AND RANGES

For vital point strikes, it is crucial that you physically contact the target. Your intentions and planning are only useful when you execute them on an opponent. Understanding the field of engagement and the concept of fighting zones is, therefore, critical in choosing techniques that are appropriate to a situation. The knowledge of fighting regions is critical in understanding what weapon to use against a given target. By combining the concepts of zone and range, you will improve your ability to manipulate a fighting situation in order to use your preferred weapons and techniques to your advantage.

FIGHTING ZONES

Field of Engagement

The field of engagement is the area in which a fight takes place. In a one-on-one fight, the field of engagement can be divided into four zones and multiple points of engagement.

The four zones are the neutral zone, your zone, your opponent's zone and the fighting zone. In a one-on-two fight, there is an additional zone called the trap zone, which two opponents can lure you into and attack from both directions.

The point of engagement is the place at which first contact between you and your opponent is established. At this point, for the first time, you can sense the power and skill level of your opponent.

Neutral Zone

This is an imaginary area that covers the distance between you and the opponent, which either of you can seize to take the control of the fight. At one or more points in the neutral zone, the point of engagement will occur. Initially the neutral zone is nobody's zone.

It may appear to be static but according to the tactics and positions of the fighters, the neutral zone con-stantly shifts its shape. An observer may not see the changes but the fighters know and feel the shifting.

The neutral zone is also relative in size according to the speed of either fighter and the types of weapons used by one or both fighters. A reckless attack or an absentminded defense can lead to trouble, so be sure to thoroughly test the neutral zone before stepping in.

Your Zone

Your zone is where you can control the fight most effectively. This is the space you want to lure your opponent into, so you can trap and defeat him. The size of your fighting zone depends on the degree of mastery you have over your striking distance.

Remember, there are two types of fighting distances: absolute and relative. Absolute distance is geneti-cally predetermined for each individual. The length of your arms and legs determines your absolute distance. Relative distance is an imaginary space between you and the opponent that is determined by the speed, skill levels and experience of both fighters. The ability to take advantage of relative distance is partially in-born and partially acquired through training.

In fighting, smart use of relative distance is what separates superior martial artists from average fighters. When you attack, you have to move in with a force that affects the perception of your opponent. When your force is well condensed and strong, it will destroy the security of his zone. If your attack is weak, you will become trapped in your opponent's zone. If you become trapped in your opponent's zone and cannot use force to dominate your opponent, you can try to lure him into making a mistake or into acting in a way that allows you to use his strength against him to regain the advantage.

Opponent's Zone

This is where your opponent controls the fight or has an advantage. Your goal is to break into this space and keep your opponent on the defensive. The more of his space you control, the more focused your attack will be.

When your opponent attacks, you see his punches and kicks but what you don't see is his intention of using the weapons he has concealed in his zone. When you least expect it, he will try to use these weapons. Your goal is, therefore, to deprive him of as many options as possible by disrupting his space even while he's attacking you. In a self-defense situation, focus your attacks on the opponent's eyes and limbs.

⊚VITAL TIPS

• For vital point striking, purposeful physical contact is crucial. Be aware of the fighting ranges and master at least one technique that works best for you at each range.

• Perfecting one technique for each situation often works better than knowing many techniques but not understanding which one to use at a key point in the fight.

• The first strike, if solidly landed, often causes shock and confusion. Studies show that simple, direct and effective techniques work best for self-defense.

Figure 3.1 Field of engagement in 1-on-1 fight.

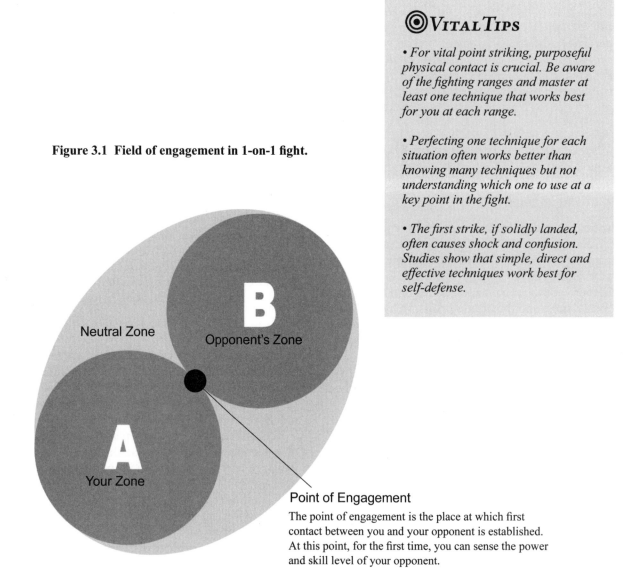

Neutral Zone

B

Opponent's Zone

A

Your Zone

Point of Engagement

The point of engagement is the place at which first contact between you and your opponent is established. At this point, for the first time, you can sense the power and skill level of your opponent.

Fighting Zone

The fighting zone is the area where a fight takes place. The attacker closes in and the defender retreats, stalls or jams. The shape of the fighting zone constantly fluctuates from a single point of contact to full-scale engagement.

The attacker's goal is to penetrate the defense of his opponent. An experienced fighter will instantaneously counterattack while an inexperienced fighter gives up part of his zone and loses the initiative. The more aggressive fighter usually takes control of the fighting zone.

The fighting zone can expand and contract depending on psychological circumstances. When you are confident you can contract your zone with the intent of luring your opponent in for a counterattack. When you are tired or need time for further assessment of the situation, you can expand your zone simply by keeping your distance.

In general, the shape of the fighting zone reveals the morale of the fighters. A proficient fighter has a tendency to invade the opponent's zone from the start. This aggressive attitude manifests a decisive fighting spirit, which drives the opponent into a corner. Inexperienced or equally matched fighters will have less change in the shape of the fighting zone whereas good fighters constantly change their positions and move forward, backward, laterally and angularly to maintain the initiative, keeping the shape of the fighting zone in constant flux. You should attack immediately after you change your position before he counters your action.

Figure 3.2   Initial fighting zone in 1-on-1 fight.

Figure 3.3   Dynamic fighting zone in 1-on-1 fight.

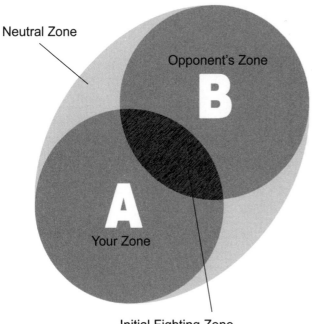

Initial Fighting Zone
From the neutral zone, A and B clash in the initial fighting zone, feeling out each others' capacity. At this point Force A is equal to Force B.

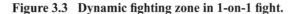

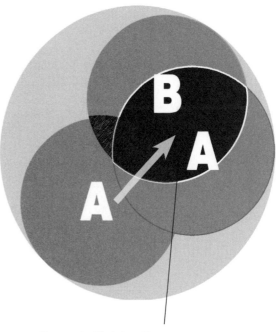

Dynamic Fighting Zone
A immediately attacks B's left side and controls the fight, shifting the force dynamics. Now, Force A is greater than Force B.

Trap Zone in a One-On-Two Fight

In a one-on-two fight, there is an additional zone called the trap zone into which two opponents can lure and attack you from both directions. This is one of those situations that you should avoid at all costs. Instead, utilize one of them (B in the diagram below) as a shield while striking any available target on B and manipulating his position to block attacks from C. By doing so you can frustrate both opponents. Once you take control of B, you can attempt to fight C, run away or search for a better option such as an environmental weapon or help from a bystander.

Against two opponents, pace yourself. You'll get tired a lot faster than fighting one person. Time is also crucial in one-on-two fight. Do not hesitate.

If you get caught in the trap zone, guard your face and vital points and move laterally to utilize one of the opponents as a shield. Grab B or C by the shoulder or arm and position yourself behind or to the side of him.

Vital point strikes are effective tactics when you are trapped. Strike points on the windpipe (fingertip press), Adam's apple (arc hand), nose (headbutt), and groin (knee kick), then strike or push lateral targets to unbalance the opponent, allowing you to move to a more advantageous position or escape. For example, temporarily blind the opponent with your palm from behind and throw a knee kick to the side of his thigh, then push him toward the other opponent.

Conversely, you can attack lateral targets first to open up your opponent's guard for strikes along his centerline. As soon as you have the chance, run to safety.

Figure 3.4   Trap zone in 1-on-2 fight.

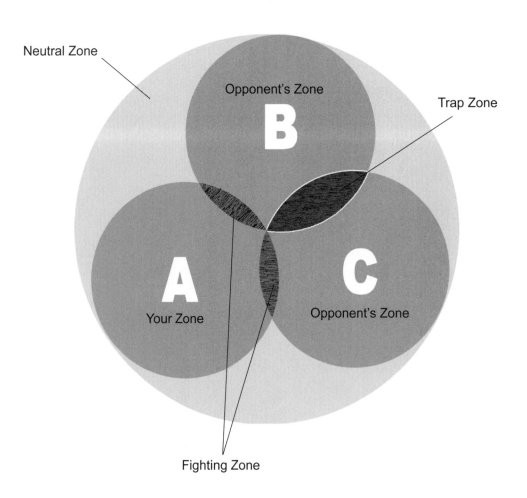

FIGHTING RANGE

What is Fighting Range?

Range is the distance between the weapon you intend to use (your fist, foot, etc.) and the closest target of the opponent. Based on your estimation of the distance, you have to decide what type of weapon to use and then attack and defend, not only in that initial range, but in the constantly changing ranges as the fight progresses. While the fighting zone is a strategic concept to dominate an opponent, fighting range is a tactical method of gaining superiority by choosing the right techniques at the right distance.

For vital point strikes, it is crucial that you physically contact the target. Your intention and planning are only as good as the implementation of your plan. The knowledge of fighting ranges will help you understand what weapon to use at what distance, allowing you to conserve energy while maximizing the impact of each strike, kick or grappling technique you employ.

Standing Fighting Range

There are three ranges in a stand-up fight: long, medium and short range.

Long range is where most lead hand techniques are used. At this range, you can move in with quick footwork and throw a punch or kick to the closest target such as the chin or kneecap. You can utilize your body weight to accelerate the force of your attack.

Medium range is where the fiercest exchanges of techniques take place. You do not need to step in at this range. Your opponent is within your hitting distance and you are within his. Your focus should be on hitting and dodging and hitting again.

Short range is close quarters fighting where head-to-head standoffs usually occur. You can use elbow strikes, uppercuts, and, in self-defense situations, even hair pulling. Footwork is almost impossible at this range and you will have to shorten your punches and kicks by bending your elbows and knees to strike at a sharp angle. At short range, grappling is the best option for taking an opponent to the ground and continuing to shoot precise vital point strikes to the head and trunk. Short range is also the best range to effectively apply locking, arresting, control and immobilization techniques through the use of vital point manipulation.

Effective techniques at long range are weapons, punches, and kicks. At medium range, elbow strikes, shin and knee kicks, and arm locks work well. At short range, short knee kicks, headbutts, eye gouging, hair pulling and vital point pressing are effective.

Transitional Range

Transitional range is where standing fighting moves to groundfighting. One fighter throws and the other falls. Initially, gravity takes over, then minute adjustments of the more skillful fighter, and then back to gravity. A dexterous fighter can manipulate the angle of falling to gain superiority on landing.

There are two stages in transitional range: pre-landing and post-landing. In the pre-landing stage, the fighter who initiated the throw or takedown usually has superiority. In the post-landing stage, the fighter who controls the momentum of the landing controls the fight, which often reverses the situation.

Groundfighting Range

There are two types of ranges in groundfighting: open range and closed range. On the ground, if you are sitting on top of the opponent, you're in open range and you have space to strike with your hands. If you're in the chest-to-chest position, you're in closed range, where you do not have enough space to freely strike your opponent. Effective techniques in open range are punches to the face or elbow strikes to the temple. In closed range short knee kicks to the rib cage or an elbow press on the neck or the bridge of the nose are examples of effective techniques.

Figure 3.5 **Ranges in standing fighting.**

Primary Factors in Range Fighting

Long Range:

Key factors: reach, speed, power
Sub factors: flexibility, mobility
Kinetic factors: extension, striking
Skills required: footwork, kicking, punching
Prime targets: chin, solar plexus, groin, legs
Sensory system: visual

Medium Range

Key factors: power, control
Sub factors: adaptability, coordination
Kinetic factors: extension, pushing, twisting
Skills required: elbow strikes, knee kicks, grappling
Prime targets: chin, temple, ribs, groin, neck
Sensory system: visual, tactile

Short Range

Key factors: leverage, control
Sub factors: strength, coordination
Kinetic factors: torque, pulling
Skills required: short strikes, grappling
Prime targets: chin, eyes, groin, neck, legs
Sensory system: tactile

Transitional Range

Key factors: leverage, control
Sub factors: balance, strength, flexibility
Kinetic factors: gravity, equilibrium
Skills required: falling, sweeping, throwing
Prime Targets: trunk, legs
Sensory system: tactile, proprioception

Open Range on the Ground

Key factors: power, leverage, control
Sub factors: strength, grappling knowledge
Kinetic factors: extension, rotation, torque
Skills required: strikes, grappling
Prime targets: chin, nose, temple, rib cage
Sensory system: visual, tactile

Closed Range on the Ground

Key factors: leverage, strength
Sub factors: ground mobility
Kinetic factors: rotation, torque
Skills required: grappling
Prime targets: face, arms, legs, joints
Sensory system: tactile

Long range

Medium range

Short range

Transitional range

Open range

Closed range

Long Range

Effective techniques in long range are kicks, punches, and weapons.

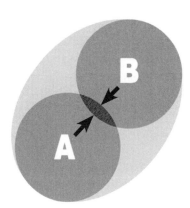

Figure 3.6   Long range diagram.

Punch to the Seal Hall
(EX-HN3)

Palm heel strike
to the Bamboo
Gathering (BL02)

Side kick to the Sun
and Moon (GB24)

Medium Range

In medium range fighting, elbow strikes, backfists, shin and knee kicks, and armlocks work well.

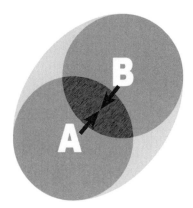

Figure 3.7   Medium range diagram.

Elbow strike to the
Empty Basin (ST12)

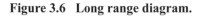

Elbow strike
to the Eyeball
(AD-H1)

Short front kick
to the Groin
(AD-T1)

Short Range

In short range fighting, short knee kicks, headbutts, eye gouging, and hair pulling are effective.

Headbutt to the Sprit Court (GV24)

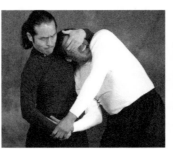

Palm press to the Eyeball (AD-H1) and the White Bone-Orifice (GV25)

Rear chin hook & elbow strike to the Great Bone-Orifice (ST03)

Figure 3.8   Short range diagram.

Groundfighting in Open and Closed Range

In groundfighting, if you are on top of the opponent, you're in open range and you have space to strike with your hands. If you're in the chest-to-chest or chest-to-back position, you're in closed range, where you do not have enough space to strike your opponent. Effective techniques in open range are punches to the face or elbow strikes to the temple. In closed range an elbow press on the neck or bridge of the nose are examples of effective techniques.

Open range arm bar

Closed range in arm lock position

Open range punch

Figure 3.9 Groundfighting range diagram.

REGION STRATEGY

What is a Region?

A region is a section of your fighting zone. If a zone is a house, then examples of regions are the living room, kitchen and basement. This concept is important in fighting because you can protect against intruders by using specific weapons in each room. If you have only one room to hide in or protect, your chances of winning or losing are 50/50. If you have one more room to protect or lure your opponent into, your safety plan becomes more complex. You'll need to have multiple weapons and multiple plans, one that suits each room. But, if you have a gun hidden in your basement, you have a much better chance of winning. In the same way, in a fight you should not only have a specific plan using specific weapons for each region of your fighting zone, but you need to have that "gun in the basement" to strike a decisive blow.

Why Regions?

When you know where your opponent is attacking from, you can block or counterattack with a higher rate of success. If your defensive posture has no openings, your opponent will be hesitant to engage. If you intentionally open one or two gaps in your defense, he'll attempt to exploit them. When you have mentally divided your fighting zone into smaller regions, you can intentionally create a gap in one region with the intent of luring your opponent into your strongest area. When your opponent attacks, you will be prepared to block, neutralize, counterattack, or move.

Visualizing Your Regions

When you stand in a fighting posture, your fighting zone extends 360 degrees around you. Assume your fighting posture or stance and then divide your zone into three segments: the anterior, lateral and posterior regions as illustrated below. The anterior region is the area inside your guard and contains most of your vital targets, including your centerline, face and neck. The lateral region is the opposite of the anterior region and covers the area on the external side of your fighting stance that extends from your rear foot to your front foot. The posterior region is the area to the rear of your body, behind your rear foot. If you quickly switched stance, your anterior and lateral regions would be reversed but your posterior region would remain the same.

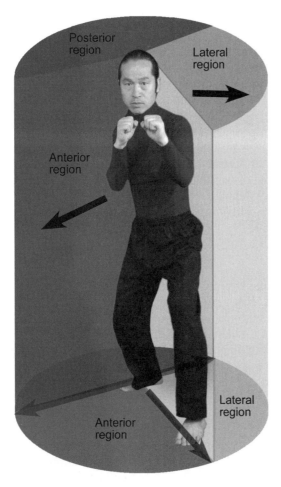

Figure 3.10   Fighting regions in your zone.

How to Use Your Regions

Let's say you are good at palm heel striking, backfist striking and rear elbow striking. If your opponent comes into your anterior region, palm heel strike his chin. If he enters your lateral region, hit his face with a backfist. If he grabs you from behind, thrust your rear elbow strike into his floating ribs.

This is a very simple example of course. You'll need to think about what techniques you'll use at long, medium and short range in each region. For example, what technique is your strongest if your opponent enters your anterior region at medium range? Is there anything you can do to stop an attacker who is at long range in your lateral or posterior region? How about against an attacker who accosts you at short range or transitional range from your posterior region? By considering not only ranges but also regions, you will be forced to think realistically about the many possibilities that you might face in a self-defense, law enforcement or sport fighting situation.

Simply understanding your regions and having specific weapons prepared to cope with specific threats makes you feel more secure.

Breaking Down Your Opponent's Regions

When you're fighting in your opponent's fighting zone, try to figure out what techniques he favors and what his strengths are. Is he a southpaw or righty? Knowing which hand he favors can help you understand which region he will be able to counterattack more strongly to. While the anterior region is generally more dangerous, your opponent's stronger side dictates how you should enter the anterior region. The lateral region is easier to enter, but contains less high-value targets. The posterior region is of course most vulnerable, but harder to enter. If you encounter an opportunity to enter your opponent's posterior region and get his back, don't hesitate.

Use the initial moments of a confrontation to probe your opponent's regions. Does he have areas that he is not comfortable defending? Is he unusually strong at a particular distance in his anterior region but weak at defending his lateral region? By breaking your opponent's fighting zone down into regions and ranges, you can methodically probe for weaknesses to exploit.

⊙ *VITAL TIPS*   # FIGHT YOUR FIGHT

Each region has a unique purpose in a physical confrontation. The anterior region is the primary fighting area where you defend key vital points and attempt to trap your opponent into defeat. The lateral region is where your opponent tests your defenses. The posterior region is a surprise attack area. To become a well rounded martial artist, know what works best for you in each region.

Example 1) Anterior Region Tactics

Your opponent throws a lead hand and rear hand straight combination. If you are a boxer, slip and counter with a hook to the chin. If you want to go to the ground, go for a single leg or double leg takedown.

Example 2) Lateral Region Tactics

Your opponent throws a low section roundhouse kick to the outer thigh of your lead leg. If you are a stand-up fighter, block the kick with your forearm or shin and immediately shoot a rear hand counterpunch to his chin. If you are a grappler, grab the kicking leg and take him to the ground.

Example 3) Posterior Region Tactics

Your opponent has slipped to your back and tries to apply a rear naked choke. If you're a striker, jab his Solar Plexus with your rear elbow, strike his face with an upward rear punch and throw him over your shoulder. If you like to grapple, rotate your body and sweep his body backward then slam your body on top of his when you hit the ground.

Straight counterattack

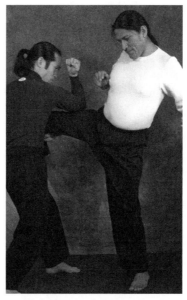
Unbalance the opponent

Pivot and throw

STRATEGY VS. TACTICS

Training in a martial art or combat sport is a process of integrating your strategic and tactical preparations with your physical practice. Action, in the form of physical practice like sparring, heavy bag training or partner drills, is the execution of the sum of your preparation to achieve your objectives. Strategy, tactics and action are the trio that work together to bring about a successful outcome. Your action must meet the requirements of your chosen tactics, and your tactics must be in line with your intended strategy to lead to progress in your training and success in engaging another fighter, whether in self-defense, sport fighting or in the line of duty.

Three Elements of Successful Engagement

1. Strategic understanding
2. Tactical preparation
3. Methodical execution (action)

Strategy vs. Tactics

Strategy is about answering "Why?"
Tactics are about answering "How?"

Strategy and tactics are different in nature. Strategy dictates the direction of your activities while tactics are the individual activities necessary to implement your strategy. Strategy is the higher level concept and tactics are the subcomponents that fall under the umbrella of strategy.

Strategy, Tactics and Action

Without action, strategy is useless. Without tactics, action becomes random. Without strategy, tactics can be aimless, leading to blind action. Strategy, tactics and action must be integrated to achieve your objectives to the fullest.

In fighting, strategy defines the goals to be achieved; tactics determine the methods to achieve those goals. Your strategic goals might be "I want to lose 35 pounds in 6 months", or "I want to defeat XYZ in the next title match." Your tactical decisions to bring about your strategic goals might then be "To lose 35 pounds I'm going to run 25 miles a week" or "To defeat XYZ I'm going to improve my left hook counter."

THE BOTTOM LINE: Strategy is large scale vision that regulates your tactics; tactics are the detailed plans that regulate action; action is the means to accomplish your objectives.

Controlling the Fighting Space

The concept of fighting regions has significant tactical merits in a confrontation. The anterior region is the primary space in which most people fight. This is the region where you should lure an opponent into, trap him and defeat him. The lateral region is a weak spot with limited options. While it is difficult to take advantage of your own lateral region, you can move into your opponent's lateral region to gain a superior position. The posterior region is a blind spot, vulnerable to surprise attacks. Never give an opponent access to your posterior region - doing so can be fatal in self-defense and can lead to a match ending move by your opponent in sport fighting.

Figure 3.11   Regions for right-handed fighters.

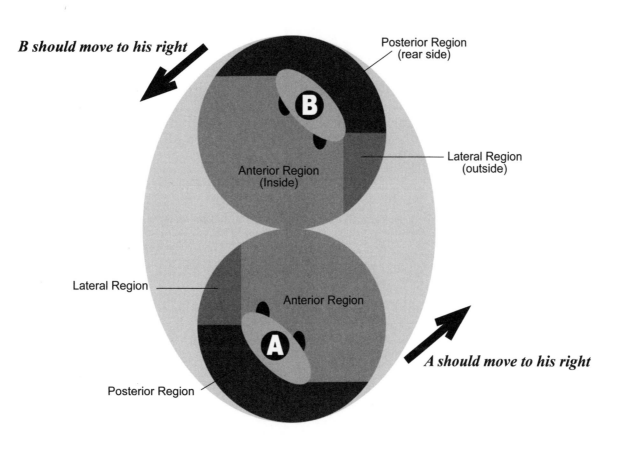

⊙ VITAL TIPS

For a superior position, move to the Lateral Region.

For breaking the opponent's will, penetrate the Anterior Region.

For finishing the fight, position yourself in the Posterior Region.

By luring the opponent into your anterior region, you can trap him in your strongest region and reduce his options. For example, trap the opponent's lead thrust and move into a standing arm bar (left). By attacking the opponent's lateral region you reduce his anterior region and take away the opponent's attacking space while expanding your own space.

Figure 3.12   Strategic initiative of A reduces B's attacking targets (both are right handed).

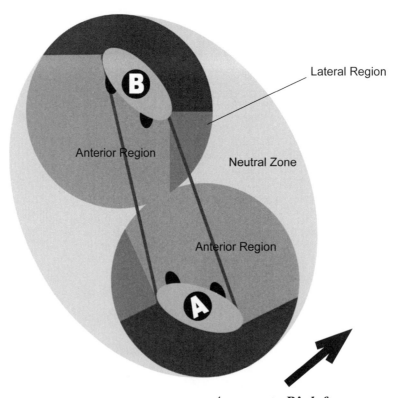

A moves to B's left

By moving to the right, A reduces B's anterior region, taking away B's attacking space. A's anterior region is constant.

Fighting is a physical chess game. When you move, you must secure a superior position. Against a left handed fighter who is attacking your midsection, use your superior position to move into the opponent's lateral region. Position your left foot right next to his ankle, use your right arm to trap the opponent's head and left upper arm, and press down on his back with your left elbow. You now have the superior position because you have blocked your opponent's vision, immobilized his head and one arm and have access to his back. A superior position opens doors to a wider variety of options for your next move.

*CAUTION: When your opponent tackles you, sprawl immediately and lower the center of the gravity for balance. If his throw is already in progress, get ready for the post-landing tactic for superiority.

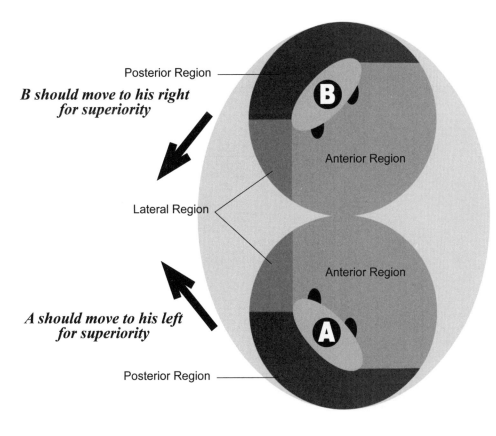

Figure 3.13 Regions for right-handed vs. left-handed fighters.

Moving to the opponent's lateral region gives you more options for controlling the opponent while reducing his options. For example, at right, by controlling the opponent's wrist and turning his body, you gain leverage to hyper-extend the opponent's elbow. This works especially well if you are the shorter fighter, because you can get your shoulder under the opponent's armpit to straighten out his elbow and gain better control.

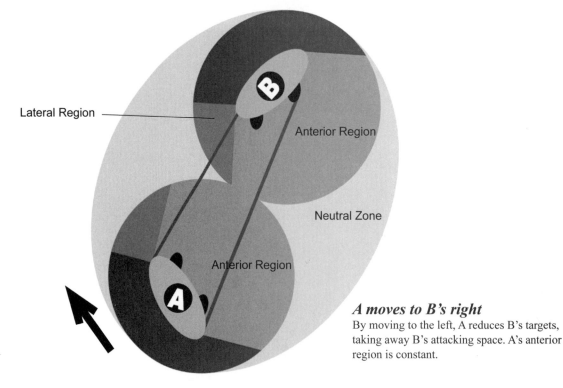

Lateral Region

Anterior Region

Neutral Zone

Anterior Region

A moves to B's right
By moving to the left, A reduces B's targets, taking away B's attacking space. A's anterior region is constant.

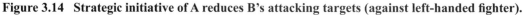

Figure 3.14   Strategic initiative of A reduces B's attacking targets (against left-handed fighter).

FIGHTING STANCE AND FOOTWORK

THE FIRST IMPRESSION

The first things that your opponent sees about you are your expression, posture and stance. Your expression reveals your confidence, your posture reveals your strength, and your stance reveals your mobility. Through these elements, he can see all or parts of your readiness. Your expression is the result of your thought process about the present situation and your competence, which affects the way you stand. Your fighting stance is a combination of foot placement and posture. It shows your ability to guard the primary targets of your body and to fire your weapons as needed. Stance is critical in fighting for three reasons: it determines the direction, amount, and speed of the force of your techniques. When a good stance is combined with quick and smooth footwork, your performance should be efficient and effective.

FIGHTING STANCE

Stance

Stance is the placement of your feet. Stance is critical in fighting for three reasons: it determines the direction, amount, and speed of the force of your techniques. For example, a narrow stance is good for mobility whereas a wide strong stance is powerful. A forward stance is good for attacking; a side stance favors a counterattack. From stance alone, you can discover a great deal about what your opponent has in mind.

When it comes to your own stance, your body's size and your favorite fighting style should define your stance. Above all, your stance should be functional and versatile. First, position yourself so that you can protect yourself by covering your face and centerline meridians. Turning your body slightly to the side reduces the exposure of your vital targets. When you find a comfortable stance, set your feet free for smooth transitions and quick attacks.

Posture

Posture is the position of your arms and legs, the alignment of your body and the placement of your center of gravity.

From your opponent's arm position, you can detect the imminence of an attack. From his leg position you can estimate the angle of an attack. From his body alignment, you can discover whether he prefers attacking or counterattacking. From the placement of his center of gravity, you can detect the type of engagement.

Left-handed or Right-handed

If you feel more comfortable with your right foot in the rear, you are right-handed. If you prefer a stance with your left foot in the rear, you are left-handed, aka a southpaw. Some fighters like to put their stronger leg forward, reversing this traditional approach. Experiment with your right and left side forward in sparring to discover your stronger stance.

The Eyes

Your eyes are the primary source of information about your environment. Based on what you see, you decide what to do and how. You must monitor your opponent at all times by carefully observing his movements, posture, stance and body language. Conversely, you should try not to telegraph what you intend to do

by using your stance to conceal your intentions.

If you're confident, stare into the eyes of your opponent while using your peripheral vision to observe your opponent's whole body and your environment.

If multiple opponents surround you, choose one to focus on while using your peripheral vision to monitor the others. For example, focus your attention on the most dangerous opponent (i.e. a man with a knife) and monitor the others. Move to position yourself so that you can see as many of the multiple attackers as possible in your immediate field of vision. Good positioning skills can save your life.

The eyes are the primary source of information about your environment.

Body alignment reveals the fighting style: attacking or counterattacking.

The arms reveal the imminence of an attack.

The legs reveal the angle of an attack.

Stance determines the direction, amount, and the speed of the force of your techniques.

80

Feet Position

You have three options in positioning your feet depending on the situation: facing forward, sideways or diagonally. If you are a boxer or a good striker, a forward stance, with your front knee facing forward and your rear foot turned out 45 degrees, will allow you to use footwork to set up your strikes. If you are a good counter kicker, you may want to use a side stance, with both feet and your trunk facing sideways, for powerful rear leg kicking. For versatility, you can use a diagonal stance with your front foot turned 15 degrees inward and your rear foot turned less than 90 degrees outward.

Shoulders

When your footing is secure, your shoulders relax. When your shoulders are tight, your neck becomes stiff making your upper body heavy. In a vicious cycle this heaviness trickles down into your mind, making you conscious of the discomfort in your stance. To move naturally and powerfully, you need to lower the center of the gravity, which begins with relaxing your shoulders. When you need to attack or defend, tighten the muscles to create power, then immediately relax to prepare for your next movement. If you are always tense, you'll get tired easily and your stance will be counterproductive.

Knee Position

To keep your body relaxed and alert, bend your knees slightly. Move naturally; do not lock your joints. Flexible knees enable rhythmic movement and speedy reflexes, and prevent injuries.

Elbow Position

When your feet, shoulders and knees are in the right position, bring your elbows close to your body. Your elbows are important for guarding your ribcage and priming your striking techniques for power.

Hand Position

Your hands are the closest weapon to the opponent. They are also the first line of defense that your opponent must break through to get to your vital targets. To serve both of these functions, carefully consider the height and angle of your hands, and the distance of your hands from your torso.

Depending on your personal preference, you may keep your hands open or closed. Keep your arms relaxed and relatively close to your body. Bring up at least one hand to cover your face with the other hand covering the centerline of your body. For example, hold your right hand in front of your right shoulder and your left hand slightly in front of your left shoulder.

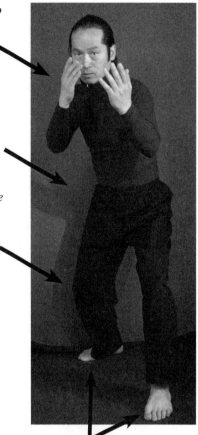

Relax your shoulders and use your hands to protect your face and trunk.

Lower your center of the gravity to increase your power and stability.

Flexible knees enable rhythmic movement and speedy reflexes, and prevent injuries.

For versatility, use a diagonal stance with your front foot turned 15 degrees inward and your rear foot turned less than 90 degrees outward.

The hands are the closest weapon to the opponent and the first line of defense.

Your elbows guard your ribcage and increase the power of your strikes.

81

Three Vital Areas to Protect

Your chin is the first vital area you need to protect. It is one of the most projected targets on the face and most knockouts in stand-up fights are caused by a powerful punch to the chin. Keep one hand up to cover your chin, and your face, at all times. This hand can also be used to protect your throat.

The second vital area you need to protect is your Solar Plexus. Keep your elbows close to your trunk so you can easily protect the area between your neck and Solar Plexus. With your elbow as the center of circular blocks, use your hand to guard your middle and low sections, including your third vital area: your groin.

Be Flexible

Stance is not a static concept but a practical vehicle that can change to accommodate various situations. Prior to attacking, your stance should not telegraph your intentions. Once you engage an opponent, your stance should adapt to changes that occur. Remember, there is no one perfect stance. Experiment with various stances to discover the purpose and function of each.

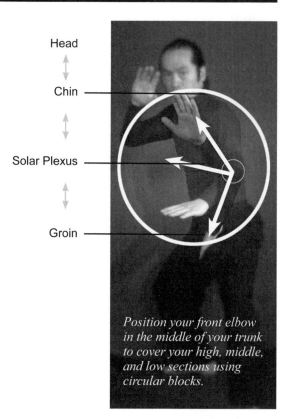

Position your front elbow in the middle of your trunk to cover your high, middle, and low sections using circular blocks.

Figure 3.15   Three vital areas to protect at all times.

Offensive Stance

Defensive Stance

FOOTWORK

Footwork is the vehicle that transports your weapons and keeps you away from your opponent. The objective of footwork is to control the distance between you and your opponent at all times. For quick footwork, your weight should be evenly distributed and your feet should be firmly grounded, yet flexible enough to move in any direction.

Functions of Footwork

There are two functions of footwork: protecting yourself and attacking the opponent. In order to protect yourself, you need to maintain a safe distance: your front leg should be at least the distance of the length of your opponent's leg away from your opponent's front foot. However, to attack, you need to be within striking distance of your opponent. You can accomplish this through footwork. Good footwork enables you to make contact with a target, to strike with power and to defend yourself effectively. It's the most fundamental element in outmaneuvering your opponent.

Smoothness

Your foot movements should be smooth and rhythmical. Keep the balls of your feet close to the ground and slide when you move. Sliding allows you to improve your speed and make easy transitions.

Footwork Principles

When you move the left foot forward, the right foot follows. When the right foot moves backward, the left foot follows. When the left foot moves to the left, the right follows.

Exception: For power punching, move your rear foot toward your front foot, and then move your front foot forward with the punch. Move your feet like a wave that transfers energy deep below the surface, never breaking until it reaches the target. Your footwork carries the force that will knock down your opponent.

Footwork and Balance

Whether you fight or run away, footwork is your lifeline. If you overextend your body to reach a target, your opponent can easily knock you off balance. During transitions, if you lose your balance, you'll be on the ground with your opponent on top of you in no time. In a street fight, this mistake could cost you your life.

Footwork is critical in maintaining your balance. You should always move your feet first before striking. If you don't, it's hard to hit the target and worse, you may expose your weaknesses and get taken down. So, always move with your center in balance.

Two functions of footwork: protect yourself and attack the opponent. In order to attack, you need to stay within striking distance.

Types of Footwork

Offensive Footwork

1. **Forward:** The lead leg moves straight forward and the rear leg follows.
2. **Leftward:** The lead leg moves forward and then to the left. The rear leg follows.
3. **Rightward:** The lead leg moves forward and then the rear leg moves to the right at a 45-degree angle.

Defensive Footwork

4. **Backward:** The rear leg moves backward and the lead leg follows.
5. **Left Backward:** The rear leg moves backward and the lead leg follows. Then the left leg moves backward to the left at a 45-degree angle. The lead leg follows.
6. **Right Backward:** The rear leg moves backward and the lead leg follows. Then the right leg moves to the right at a 45-degree angle. The lead leg follows.
7. **Right Side Step:** The right foot moves to the right side and the left foot follows.
8. **Left Side Step:** The left foot moves to the left side and the right foot follows.

Figure 3.18 Fundamental footwork chart.

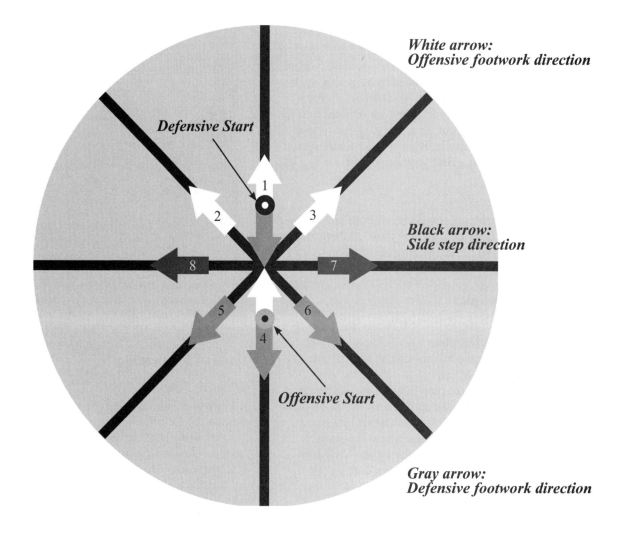

○ *Offensive start point is outside the neutral zone. You are ready to break into the opponent's zone.*
◉ *Defensive start point is within the opponent's zone. You've already stepped into his zone or he has invaded your zone.*
● *Side step start point is in the middle of the fight zone. You have been caught in the middle of your preparation for action.*

Figure 3.19   Fundamental footwork diagram.

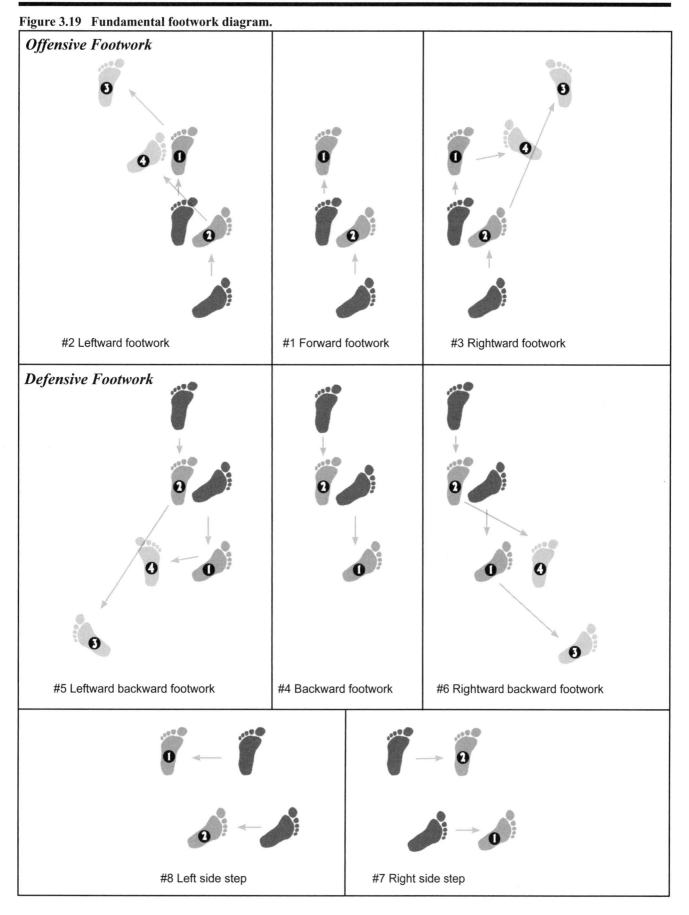

Offensive Footwork

#2 Leftward footwork

#1 Forward footwork

#3 Rightward footwork

Defensive Footwork

#5 Leftward backward footwork

#4 Backward footwork

#6 Rightward backward footwork

#8 Left side step

#7 Right side step

◎VITAL TIPS

Footwork is a Wave of Force

When the speed of your footwork is greater, the net force of the impact of your techniques becomes greater.

In distance fighting, there are three major elements that affect your power: distance, speed, and torque. The more distance your body travels across, the more accelerated your momentum becomes. The faster your body moves, the more power it carries to transfer to the target. The greater torque your muscles generate, the more power your technique has.

Based on this concept, for a knockout strike you should move your rear foot toward your front foot to set your body in motion, then move your front foot forward to let your body drive forward into the opponent. Finally, just as a wave breaks on a rock, strike your opponent with full force.

Once you make contact with your opponent, use torque to generate power in your close combat techniques.

Torque for breaking

Drive for impact

Cover distance for force

STRIKING DIRECTIONS AND ANGLES

The direction of a strike depends on where your opponent stands, what he is doing at the moment, and what target on his body you want to hit. There are five sections of the body that you can attack: head, hands and arms, trunk, thighs, and lower legs. There are three components to consider before launching a strike: distance to the available targets, angle of the surface of the target, and timing of the opponent's movement.

STRIKING DIRECTION

Strike the Closest Target First

Generally speaking, your opponent's lead hand and lead foot are the closest to you, followed by the lead arm and lead leg, with the trunk and head farthest away. Although the hand and foot are the closest targets, they are easy for your opponent to move out of range and hard for you to catch. However, the forearm and lower leg are good targets due to the availability of vital points in both areas. Once you penetrate your opponent's defense, you can attack the face and trunk including the vital points on the nose, eyes, temples, throat, floating ribs, kidneys, and Solar Plexus. If these targets are not available, attack the lower section including vital points on the groin, outer thighs, kneecaps, shins, calves, and ankles to take away your opponent's mobility. Once you have impaired his ability to move, you can go back to the head and trunk.

Distance and Direction

Distance dictates what weapon to use and how to deploy it. The first target to strike is the closest one. If a target is right in front of you, hit it on the most direct line. If the target is to the side, attack in a circular motion. Avoid using circular techniques at long distance, because you may lose your balance or reveal your weaknesses. If the target is beyond your reach, close in first with footwork and strike with a direct attack.

Angles

There are two considerations when it comes to using angles in fighting: striking angle and positioning angle.

The striking angle is the degree of the contact your technique makes on the skin or surface of the opponent's body. The most idealistic striking is perpendicular to the target surface. However, fighting is a dynamic struggle for superiority and things change constantly, so the perfect opportunity may never come. You need to be fast enough to seize the opportunity or put yourself be in the right position at the right time by setting up your opponent.

The positioning angle is the degree of your attacking line against the opponent's position. From a superior position, you have more choices for surprise attacks. For instance, when your opponent kicks your groin, instead of moving straight backward, you are better off moving diagonally in a lateral direction. If you end up in your opponent's anterior region, you can strike his centerline; if you land in his lateral region, you can attack his back or choke him out.

Your opponent's actions can determine the best target for your strike. Above, striking the forearm or hand first is a superior choice to attacking the opponent's centerline, which is normally the best.

The best option is always to attack the centerline of the body at a perpendicular angle. The second best option is to strike a region adjacent to a meridian, such as the floating ribs and temple. As you progress, you'll be able to spot these opportunities instinctively.

Speed and Timing

How fast and in which direction your opponent moves affects your striking direction. If you reach out too early or too late or in the wrong direction, you end up missing the target. Striking at just the right moment is the result of good timing.

Timing is the act of adjusting your tempo of movement in relation with your opponent's tempo of movement. The goal is to strike the intended target with precision to maximize the power of your strike. By controlling your speed, your technique can reach its maximum power upon impact. By choosing the right moment to strike, your technique will hit the intended target, even if your opponent is in motion.

Figure 3.16 Striking directions in a standing fight.

Attack the closest and most sensitive targets first. Once you get through the opponent's defenses, attack the face and trunk including vital points on the nose, eyes, temples, throat, floating ribs, kidneys, and Solar Plexus. Then, attack low section vital points on the groin, outer thighs, knee-caps, shins, calves, and ankles. When you take your opponent's mobility away, the fight will become one-sided.

Figure 3.17 Options for striking directions in a standing fight.

Which Way to Strike

1. Strike directly at the closest target.
The most effective attack is to strike directly to the closest target. In the situation above:
    a. If the opponent thrusts with the knife, the hand holding the knife is the first target (#1).
    b. If his head moves in first, hit his nose (#2) with your knifehand. If you are an excellent kicker,
        boldly, shoot your roundhouse kick to the Protuberance Assistance (LI18).
    c. If his legs are moving first, attack the lead leg with low roundhouse kick to the ankle (#4), or
        the inner thigh (#5). When he is in the medium range, kick his groin (#6) with a front kick.

2. Be versatile.
If your opponent closes in one step toward you then changes his mind and retreats one step, choose whatever weapon suits the distance best. If he moves to your left, kick or strike leftward into his centerline. If he moves to your right, strike rightward into his centerline. If he moves toward you, slide back and pivot and hit. When the direction of your attack has the right speed and timing, your strike will have an powerful impact on the opponent.

CHAPTER 4

BODILY WEAPONS AND TECHNIQUES

Death Touch: Fact or Fiction

The Death Touch or Delayed Death Touch is often the first concept that comes to mind when vital point striking is mentioned. But does it really exist? Can a single strike lead to instant death or cause an opponent to die days later?

As we've seen in the previous chapters, vital point striking can be dangerous and even deadly, but there is no "magic" strike that will kill an opponent instantly every time or cause an opponent to die some predictable number of hours or days later. A single strike with sufficient force, delivered at the proper angle can result in death. Points on the neck, throat and head are particularly vulnerable because any injury that damages the brain directly or impairs the flow of blood and oxygen to the brain can be lethal. For example, constricting the carotid artery can cut off the flow of blood to the brain, resulting in unconsciousness and death.

Similarly, the delayed death touch of legend - stories of mysterious strikes that have seemingly no effect until days later when the victim suddenly dies of unexplained causes - is just that, a legend. However, there may be some scientific basis for the legend.

Consider the condition we now know as Second Impact Syndrome (SIS), a rare condition in which the brain swells rapidly and catastrophically after a victim suffers a second concussion before symptoms from an earlier concussion have subsided. The two successive concussions don't need to be severe and the second impact can be something as minor as a slap that causes the victim's head to jerk suddenly. An opponent might seem to survive such a blow to the head without significant damage, only to collapse and die suddenly hours later. Although there are no immediate outward indications that something is wrong, as soon as the second blow to the head is landed, the brain begins swelling. When the victim falls unconscious the next day, someone with no knowledge of SIS might attribute the condition to a magic strike rather than the cumulative effects of the swelling that was triggered by a series of brain injuries.

Similar conditions that can result in a delayed death directly resulting from a traumatic injury are a subdural hematoma where there is bleeding in the brain or a coronary embolism where a blood clot forms somewhere in the body (for example from damage to a blood vessel in the leg) and travels to the heart. The difference between these conditions and a magic death touch is that these conditions are often treatable if recognized and while they may result in death, there is no way to inflict them with certainty by a single empty hand strike and no way to determine the number of hours or days later that a victim will die. However, before the advent of modern medicine, victims who died as a result of such conditions may indeed have appeared to die from a mysterious delayed reaction.

BODILY WEAPONS & TECHNIQUES

There is no part of the human body that is not designed to be a weapon for survival.

Strategic weapons *are the nose, ears, neck, and eyes: the nose for smelling dangerous chemicals or poisons, the ears for hearing an invader, the neck for rotating the head to the object, and the eyes for observing the activities of the opponent. All of these body parts are critical for information collection so you can make decisions and then act on them.*

Tactical weapons *are the body parts we more commonly think of as bodily weapons such as the joints and bones of the arms, hands, legs and feet. When these parts are toughened and used with speed and power, the impact can be devastating.*

The body takes the body down, the arms control the arms, then the hands finalize the technique, taking complete control. Hands are like the foot soldiers in the infantry, searching vacant buildings.

HANDS

The hands are essential to vital point striking. They can be formed into many configurations to strike, poke, press, pinch, jab, twist, pull, push, punch, slap and grab every vital point on the opponent's body. Among the bodily weapons, the hands are the fastest, most dexterous and easiest to deploy. They act and react naturally, often without conscious thought. As children, without even knowing that martial arts existed, we naturally used our hands to defend ourselves when needed. To be effective in fighting, it is important to recover our natural responses. When your hands are free to move instinctively, you can be spontaneous in blocking, striking and grappling.

FINGERTIPS

Tip of the Index Finger

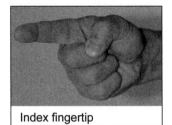

Index fingertip

Function: The tip of the index finger is a sharp weapon that can be used to press the Celestial Chimney (CV22) and other soft vital points.

Method: Straighten your index finger and bend it slightly. Close the rest of your hand into a fist. Through the fingertip, transmit the force of your hand, wrist, arm and body.

Major Targets: Eyeball (AD-H1), Celestial Chimney (CV22), Energy Abode (ST11), Wind Screen (TW17)

Scissors Fingertips

Scissors fingertips

Function: The scissors fingertips are useful in attacking the eyes.

Method: Straighten your index and middle fingers and bend them slightly. Split your fingers apart; the distance will vary according to the target. Use your thumb to hold your other two fingers against your palm.

Major Targets: Eyeballs (AD-H1)

Pinching Fingertips

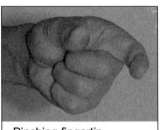

Pinching fingertip

Function: Pinching fingertips are effective in attacking soft tissue areas where vital points are located close to the surface of the skin, for example the biceps or cheek.

Method: Hook your thumb and index finger slightly. To pinch, bend your index finger to form the base of the pinching and press downward onto the radial side of your index finger with your thumb, squeezing the skin between the two.

Major Targets: Auricle (AD-H2), Blue Spirit (HT02)

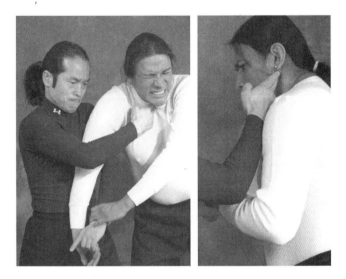

The tip of the finger can penetrate deeply into the cavity between bones causing tormenting pain. Target examples are the Energy Abode (ST11) and the Wind Screen (TW17).

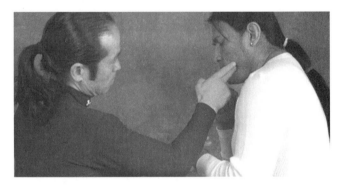

A fingertip thrust to the Great Reception (ST05) keeps the opponent's face away from you.

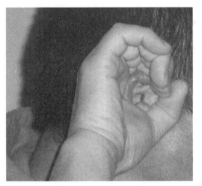

Pinching the Auricle (AD-H2) causes unpleasant pain in the ear.

Four Fingertips

Function: All four fingertips are effective in attacking the eyes, mandibular joint, and temple, as well as pressing the Brachial Plexus and the Shoulder Well (GB21). You can snap the tips or thrust deeply into the target.

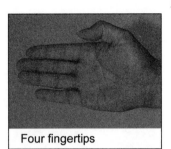

Four fingertips

Method: Straighten the fingers and bend them slightly. For snapping, bend your wrist backward and snap toward the target. For thrusting, straighten your wrist, collect your energy in your fingertips and thrust into the target. Strike or thrust horizontally against a horizontally exposed target such as supraclavicular fossa. Strike or thrust vertically against a vertically exposed target such as the Solar Plexus.

Major Targets: Celestial Chimney (CV22), Wind Pool (GB20), Protuberance Assistance (LI18), Empty Basin (ST12), Shoulder Well (GB21), Turtledove Tail (CV15), Great Horizontal (SP15), Return and Arrive (ST29)

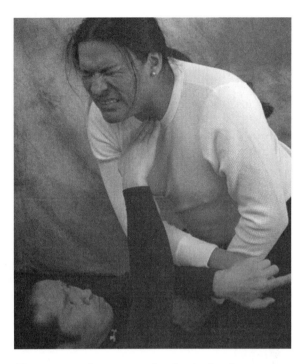

Fingertips make your reach a few inches longer than a closed fist. They make a great surprise attack against a distant target. From the ground, thrust to the Celestial Chimney (CV22) with your fingers.

Fingertips can be used in combination with choking or locking techniques to maximize the effect. Here a diagonal fingertip thrust to the Wind Pool (GB20) is used to break the opponent's will to fight back.

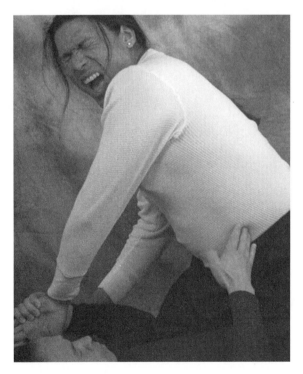

Fingertips penetrate the soft skin deeper than a punch to inflict pain in the viscera. Against a tall opponent, you can thrust to the Great Horizontal (SP15).

Thumb Tip

Function: A thumb tip is effective for pressing nerve cavities because it is a powerful, penetrating, easy to use weapon. Thumb tips can be used to press the eyeballs or to open the mouth laterally.

Method: Open your hands with your fingers outstretched. Bend your thumb slightly less than 90 degrees with the tip pointing at the target. Using the force of the forearm, thrust the tip of your thumb into the target. Once your thumb is planted on the vital point, transfer your body weight through your forearm into the target to maximize the impact.

Major Targets: Eyeball (AD-H1), Protuberance Assistance (LI18), Lower Biceps (AD-UE1), Union Valley (LI04), Dorsal Center (AD-UE5), Great Bone-Orifice (ST03), Pool at the Bend (LI11), Blue Spirit (HT02), Guarding White (LU04), Small Sea (SI08), Lesser Sea (HT03), Lesser Mansion (HT08), Wind Screen (TW17), Wind Pool (GB20), Celestial Pillar (BL10), Supporting Sinews (BL56), Supporting Mountain (BL57)

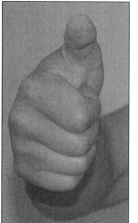

Single thumb tip

Double thumb tips can be used to press the Great Bone-Orifice (ST03).

Above: A thumb tip thrust to the Supporting Sinews (BL56) is useful to escape from a side headlock.

Below: A thumb tip press to the Ridge Spring (CV23) is a surprise to an on-coming opponent.

A thumb tip press technique can be used in combination with various striking techniques to intensify the effects.

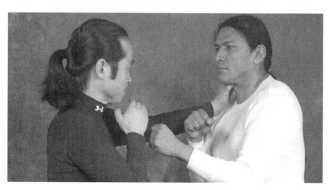

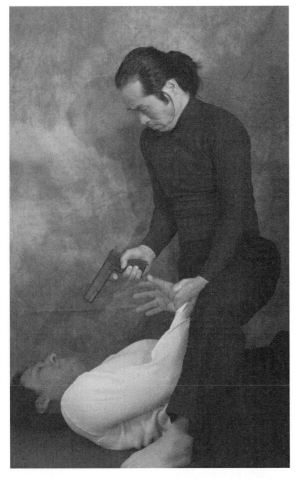

A thumb tip press to the Lumbar Pain Point (EX-UE7) on the back of the hand helps you control the opponent efficiently.

To get out of a double hand grip on your wrist, instead of punching his face, press the Guarding White (LU04). This may be a better option for subduing the opponent whereas if you punch him the situation may develop into brawl rather than self-defense.

If your opponent attempts to get out of your thumb tip press, strike a more pain susceptible target such as Florid Canopy (CV20).

A double thumb tip press intensifies the impact: left thumb press to the Lumbar Pain Point (EX-UE7), right thumb tip press to the Lesser Sea (HT03).

KNUCKLE PUNCH/PRESS

Single Knuckle

Function: For striking soft cavities, single knuckles are effective weapons. Due to the sharp focused edge and support of the other fingers, a single knuckle strike generates condensed force that penetrates deeply into the nerves and blood vessels. Striking should be precise and fast to cause sharp shocking pain. Rotation of the knuckle after impact adds pain as well as further damage to the deeper tissue. For thrusting, a prolonged deep thrust generates an unpleasant sensation that can be used to move or manipulate the opponent. There are three common knuckles for vital point strikes: the middle, index and thumb knuckles.

Single Middle Knuckle

Middle knuckle

Method: Open your hand and make a fist with the middle knuckle protruding. Press the top of the first knuckle of the index finger with the first knuckle of the thumb.

Major Targets: Temple (EX-HN5), Eyeball (AD-H1), Wind Pool (GB20), Jade Pillow (BL09), Philtrum (GV26), Ring of Jumping (GB30), Surging Yang (ST42)

Single Index Knuckle

Index knuckle

Method: Open your hand and make a fist with the index knuckle protruding. Support the index finger, with the tip of the thumb and the middle finger.

Major Targets: Temple (EX-HN5), Eyeball (AD-H1), Wind Pool (GB20), Jade Pillow (BL09), Protuberance Assistance (LI18), Philtrum (GV26)

Single Thumb Knuckle

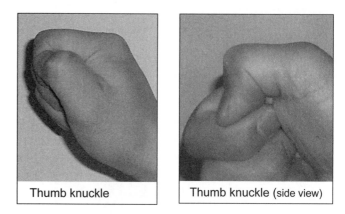

Thumb knuckle

Thumb knuckle (side view)

Method: Open your hand, make a fist, and put the tip of the thumb on the crease of the first and second knuckle of the index finger.

Major Targets: Temple (EX-HN5), Eyeball (AD-H1), Wind Pool (GB20), Jade Pillow (BL09), Philtrum (GV26), Ring of Jumping (GB30)

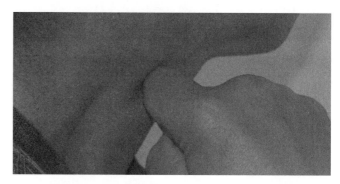

Above: Single index knuckle thrust to the common carotid artery.

Below: Single middle knuckle thrust to the Surging Yang (ST42).

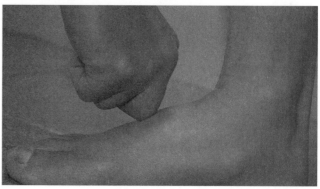

Four Knuckles

Function: The four knuckles are useful for striking narrow, long targets such as the vertical line around the Solar Plexus, side of the neck, and under the floating ribs. This type of strike produces complex pain by impacting multiple targets surrounding a particular vital point or points. For example, striking the Solar Plexus not only causes pain in the cavity but also in the neighboring region due to the network of nerves in the area. The four knuckles can be used to strike horizontally, thrust vertically or as an uppercut according to the target.

Method: Bend your four fingers at the first two joints, as in the first step of making a fist. Keep your thumb bent along the side of your palm.

Major Targets: Turtledove Tail (CV15), Wind Screen (TW17), Abdominal Lament (SP16), Protuberance Assistance (LI18), Spirit Door (BL42), Cycle Gate (LV14)

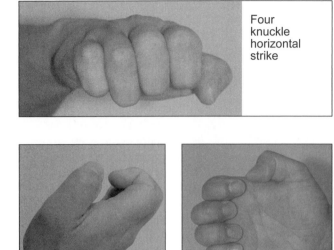

Four knuckle horizontal strike

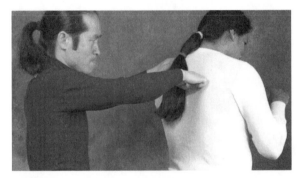

Four knuckle uppercut

Four knuckle vertical thrust

A double knuckle punch to the Spirit Door (BL42) can cause a stoppage of breath and paralysis of the upper body.

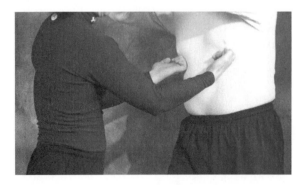

A knuckle punch to the Turtledove Tail (CV15) inflicts pain throughout the Solar Plexus region.

A double knuckle punch to the Four Whites (ST02) can paralyze the facial area. When done quickly, it shocks the opponent.

Strike the Cycle Gate (LV14) while the opponent inhales. His body will buckle for your uppercut or knee kick.

FIST

Straight Punch Fist

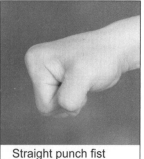

Straight punch fist
(side view)

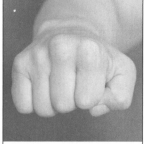

Straight punch fist
(front view)

Function: A fist is one of the most powerful weapons that your body is equipped with. The power of a fist does not come from your size and muscular development alone; it comes from a combination of many elements such as fitness, technique, speed, precision, timing, momentum, and mental conditioning. An overly tight fist is counterproductive, resulting in injury and imprecision. Keep your fingers, wrists, elbows and shoulders aligned and relaxed. Squeeze your fist at the moment of impact to deliver focused power generated from the center of your body.

Method: 1) Open your hand and fold your four fingers securely into your palm. 2) Put your thumb on the second knuckles of the index and middle fingers and press them firmly. 3) Hold the fingers firmly together so that each bone augments the one next to it forming a unit of integrated force. Align the bones of your wrist to deliver your bodily force. Keep your hand firm enough to deliver the force of the punch yet supple enough to relax the muscles until the point of impact.

Major Targets: Sauce Receptacle (CV24), Temple (EX-HN5), Great Reception (ST05), Philtrum (GV26), Turtledove Tail (CV15), Abdominal Lament (SP16), Spirit Tower (GV10)

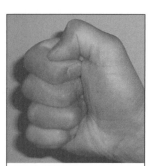

Fist with thumb up

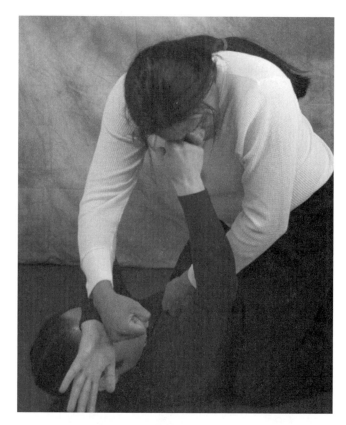

Against a punch, cover your face and shoot your fist to the Four Whites (ST02) or the Great Bone-Orifice (ST03).

A straight punch to the Temple (EX-HN5) can shock the brain and cause severe headache and dizziness.

The Great Reception (ST05) and the Jaw Chariot (ST06) are most popular targets for a knockout.

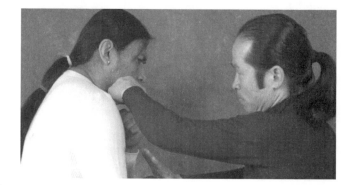

Vertical Punch Fist

Function: Vertical punching is used against a vertically weak target such as the Solar Plexus or a target when the muscles or other underlying structure are aligned vertically. Before hitting, relax your hand. At the moment of impact, squeeze your hand firmly and nail the target like a hammer. When you hit a hard target, keep your hand supple. When you punch a soft target strike it deeply. The important qualities of a punch are accuracy, agility, and concentration of power.

Method: 1) Open your hand and fold your four fingers securely into your palm. 2) Put the tip of your thumb on the crease of the first and second knuckle of the index finger. 3) Hold the fingers firmly together so that each bone augments the one next to it forming a unit of integrated force. 4) Align your fist with the striking surface perpendicular to the ground.

Major Targets: Great Reception (ST05), Protuberance Assistance (LI18), Turtledove Tail (CV15), Abdominal Lament (SP16), Spirit Hall (BL44), Spirit Tower (GV10), Capital Gate (GB25)

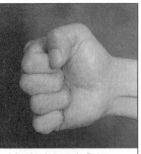

Vertical punch fist
(side view)

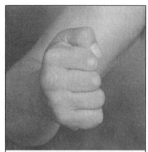

Vertical punch fist
(front view)

In combination with a wrist lock, a modified vertical punch to the Great Reception (ST05) is shockingly powerful.

As the opponent inhales in response to your wrist lock throw, punch to the Abdominal Lament (SP16).

Uppercut Punch Fist

Uppercut fist

Function: An uppercut punch is used in close or medium distance to transfer the total bodily force upward.

Method: 1) Make a fist and assume a fighting position. 2) From your fighting position, lower your punching hand slightly. 3) Rotate the hips forward while pushing off the ball of the rear foot and punching straight up into the target, and then quickly bring your hand back to your original position.

Major Targets: Ridge Spring (CV23), Turtledove Tail (CV15), Not Contained (ST19), Abdominal Lament (SP16), Central Venter (CV12)

An uppercut punch is most effective when the opponent inhales in preparation for the next attack.

Backfist

Function: A backfist utilizes the back knuckles of the hand for striking. It is primarily used as a surprise attack, counterattack, or to close the distance from the front, side or rear. In general, it is most useful at medium range. At close range, you can pull the opponent's head toward you to add more power to a backfist strike. The power of a backfist comes from the snapping action, forearm muscle torque, and deceptive execution. For maximum surprise and power, begin to move your hand as closely to the center of the body as possible and snap it very quickly to the target. The striking directions are forward, horizontal, vertically downward or spinning. To make the backfist even more practical, you can move on to elbow strike or choking techniques as soon as your fist lands on a target on the face.

Vertical (Downward) Backfist

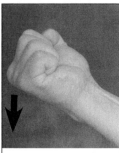

Downward backfist

Method: Make a fist as described in the straight backfist method. For a vertical strike, snap the fist vertically downward to the target.

Major Targets: Marsh at the Bend (PC03), Cubit Marsh (LU05), Lower Biceps (AD-UE1), Shoulder Well (GB21), Spirit Tower (GV10)

Spinning Backfist

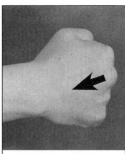

Horizontal backfist

Method: Make a fist as described in the straight backfist method. For a spinning strike, turn while moving your rear foot forward toward the target and coiling your body. As you complete your turn, uncoil your body and release your fist into the target.

Major Targets: Temple (EX-HN5), Protuberance Assistance (LI18), Jaw Chariot (ST06), Auditory Convergence (GB02), Auricle (AD-H2)

Straight Backfist

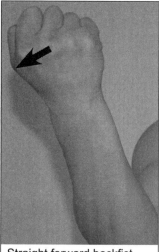

Straight forward backfist

Method: Fold your four fingers tightly into your palm. Put your thumb on the second knuckles of the index and middle fingers and press them firmly. Bring the fist under your armpit or in front of your chest with your elbow bent as tightly as possible. Snap the backfist toward the target in front of you.

Major Targets: Bamboo Gathering (BL02), Sauce Receptacle (CV24), Temple (EX-HN5)
Seal Hall (EX-HN3), Eyeball (AD-H1)

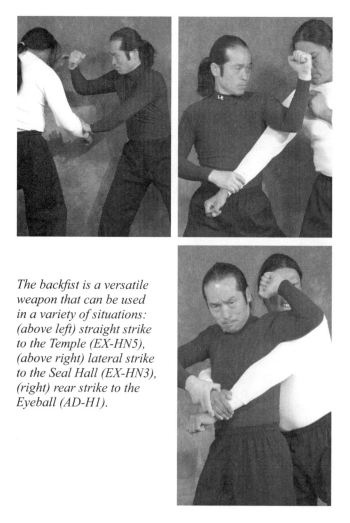

The backfist is a versatile weapon that can be used in a variety of situations: (above left) straight strike to the Temple (EX-HN5), (above right) lateral strike to the Seal Hall (EX-HN3), (right) rear strike to the Eyeball (AD-H1).

Hammer Fist

Function: A hammer fist is a technique that utilizes the bottom of the fist to strike a target like a hammer. It can be applied from all angles. It is powerful and deceptive, if used properly. In general, the trajectory of the strike is circular.

Method: Squeeze the four fingers tightly in the palm. Put your thumb on the second knuckles of the index and middle fingers and press them firmly. For a forward strike, bring the fist close to your body with your elbow bent as tightly as possible, and snap the bottom of the fist to the front. For a downward strike, raise your elbow, snap the forearm downward. For a horizontal strike, bring your elbow and hand close to the centerline with the palm facing your body, then snap your hammer fist at shoulder height outward with the palm facing downward. For a rear strike, drop your fist to hip height and strike backward to a target such as the groin.

Major Targets: Unyielding Space (GV18), Groin (AD-T1), Jade Hall (CV18), Extremity of Yang (GV09), Spirit Door (BL42), Spirit Hall (BL44), Spirit Path (GV11), Spirit Tower (GV10), Behind the Vertex (GV19)

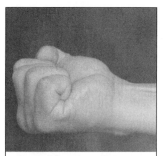

Inward hammer fist

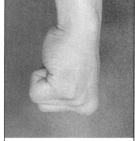

Backward hammer fist

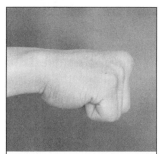

Outward hammer fist

Below left: Hammer fist strike to the Behind the Vertex (GV19).

Below right: Downward hammer fist strike to the Jade Hall (CV18).

Lateral rear hammer fist strike to the Groin (AD-T1) against rear bear hug.

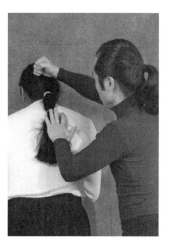

Lateral downward hammer fist to the Groin (AD-T1) in combination with wrist lock against a knife attack.

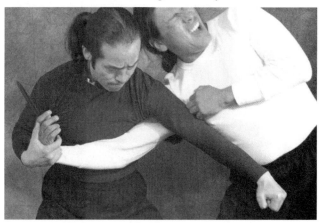

OPEN HAND

Knifehand

Function: A knifehand (aka hand blade) is widely used for offense and defense. It is an effective weapon to strike vertical targets such as the neck and upper arms. The impact can impair the blood circulation and damage nerves and the skeletal system. The trajectory of the strike is circular.

Method: Open your hand with your fingers held straight. Press your fingers tightly together. Focus the force firmly in your fingers to the degree that the palm side arches slightly forward. Curl your thumb into the palm and bend the thumb knuckle downward. The bottom of the bone near the wrist is the striking area. For an inward strike, bring the knifehand in front of your same side shoulder with your palm facing forward and snap it out inwardly toward a target. For an outward strike, bring the knifehand in front of the opposite side of your chest with the palm facing the body and snap it outward toward a target. For a downward strike, raise your arm in the air and swing it down toward a target in a chopping motion. For maximum power, transfer the internal force from your lower abdomen to your arms by twisting your hips and synchronizing the entire body as a unit with the strike.

Major Targets: Philtrum (GV26), Pool at the Bend (LI11), Protuberance Assistance (LI18), Temple (EX-HN5), Shoulder Well (GB21), Small Sea (SI08), Supporting Sinews (BL56)

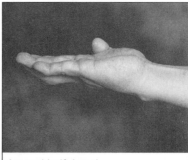

Inward knifehand

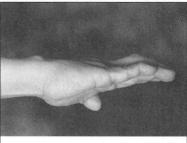

Outward knifehand

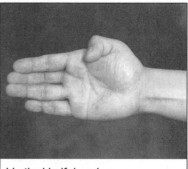

Vertical knifehand

Left: A knifehand strike to the Protuberance Assistance (LI18) can cause a knockout or even death due to a sudden, precipitous drop in blood pressure.

Right: The knifehand is a flexible weapon. As the shape or position of the target changes, you can change your hand shape for a palm heel or hammer fist strike.

Palm Heel

Function: A palm heel is used for striking, blocking or pressing using the metacarpal bones of the hand. It is an effective weapon for striking protruding targets such as the nose, ear or chin.

Method: Open your hand. Bend your fingers slightly and expose the bony area of your hand. Focus the force firmly in the heel of your palm. The bone near the wrist is the striking area but the middle part of the hand is also useful for striking the ear and nose. Do not limit yourself to one size or type of hand shape. Be flexible in changing the shape of your hand to fit different targets: small and projecting, widespread, deep and hollow.

Major Targets: White Bone-Orifice (GV25), Great Reception (ST05), Ridge Spring (CV23), Sauce

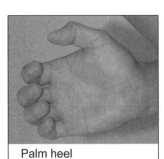

Palm heel

Receptacle (CV24), Temple (EX-HN5), Seal Hall (EX-HN3), Eyeball (AD-H1), Auricle (AD-H2), Great Bone-Orifice (ST03), Celestial Well (TW10), Philtrum (GV26), Jaw Chariot (ST06)

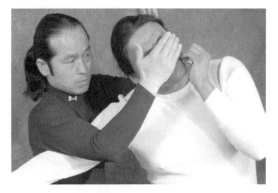

A palm strike to the White Bone-Orifice (GV25) can impede the vision of the opponent.

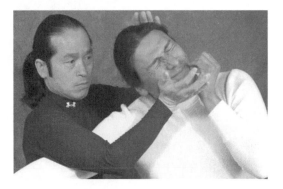

Palm heel strike to the Great Reception (ST05) and head twist.

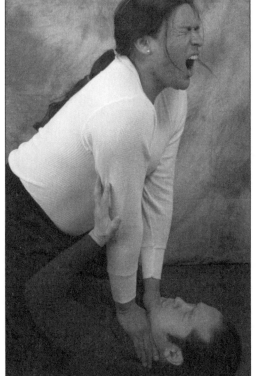

Left: Double palm heel strike to the Celestial Well (TW10) to topple the opponent over your head.

Right: Palm heel strike to the Ridge Spring (CV23) and under the Sauce Receptacle (CV24).

Self-defense is a matter of choice, distraction, pain and attitude. Against an empty hand attack, if you pull out a gun, you may not even have to use it as most people run away from it or freeze at first sight. Against a wrist grab, strike the attacker's neck with your elbow. By striking an entirely different part of the body, you can distract your opponent, giving you a psychological and strategic gap to beat him or escape. Finally, your attitude is critical. It is evident in the way you position yourself and assume a posture appropriate to the situation. Your attitude expresses many undone actions and your emotional fortitude.

ELBOW

The elbows and forearms are bigger in size than the hands. They are not as fast as the hands but have more power and can break the will of an opponent. They can smash bones and knock down an opponent with sheer force. In close quarter fighting, your elbows and forearms can be as fast as your hands depending on the level of your training. You can shoot your elbow from all different angles and surprise the opponent. To be effective in defense, keep your elbows slightly bent at all times. In attacking, keep your elbow as sharp as the tip of an arrow, and the forearm as cutting as a sword.

Elbow

Function: An elbow strike is done by the sharp end of the ulna and the hard lower end of the humerus. It causes cuts, head injuries, broken ribs, and knockouts. It is an effective weapon for close fighting. Generally it is used in combination with kicks, punches and grappling techniques. The directions of attack are forward, rearward, upward, downward, inward, outward, and diagonal. Elbow striking is particularly effective from the top in groundfighting since the ground traps the head allowing the full force of the strike to pound the skull.

Method: 1) For a horizontal elbow strike, bend your elbow and bring your fist in front of your same side shoulder with your palm facing inward. Raise your elbow in front of you horizontally with your palm facing downward. 2) For a vertical upward elbow strike, bend your elbow and bring your fist in front of your same side shoulder with your palm facing inward. Raise your elbow in front of you vertically with your palm facing your ear. 3) For a vertical downward elbow strike, raise your arm and drop the elbow vertically with the palm facing you. 4) For a rear elbow strike, bend your elbow and bring your fist in front of your same side shoulder with your palm facing inward. Move your elbow backward with your palm facing upward (mid section) or with the palm downward (high section). 5) For a diagonal elbow strike, bend your elbow and bring your fist in front of your same side shoulder with your palm facing inward. Move your elbow diagonally inward on an up-to-down path.

Major Targets: Bamboo Gathering (BL02), Philtrum (GV26), Protuberance Assistance (LI18), Temple (EX-HN5), Leading Valley (GB08), Auditory Convergence (GB02), Wind Pool (GB20), Shoulder Well (GB21), Eyeball (AD-H1), White Bone-Orifice (GV25), Sauce Receptacle (CV24), Great Reception (ST05), Jade Pillow (BL09), Jaw Chariot (ST06), Turtledove Tail (CV15), Outer Mound (ST26), Spirit Tower (GV10), Crouching Rabbit (ST32), Upper Arm (LI14)

Rear elbow strike to the Outer Mound (ST26).

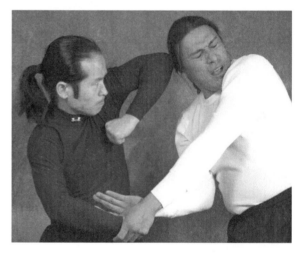

Horizontal elbow strike to the Leading Valley (GB08).

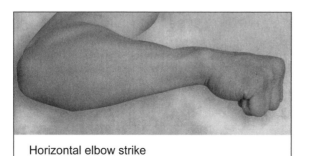

Horizontal elbow strike

Diagonal elbow strike to the Eyeball (AD-H1).

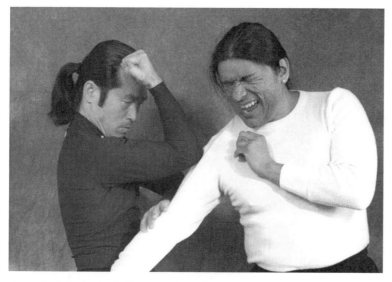

A vertical downward elbow strike to the Upper Arm (LI14) can paralyze the opponent's arm.

Cut-in elbow strike to the Wind Pool (GB20).

A vertical downward elbow strike to the Spirit Tower (GV10) can be used to augment a wrist lock.

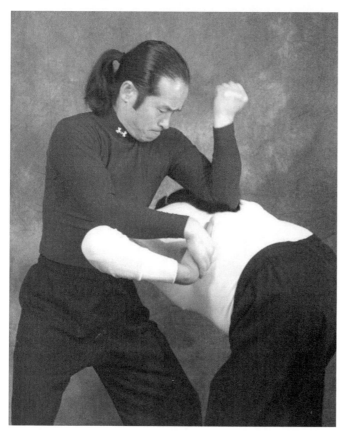

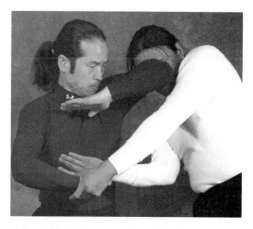

A backward elbow strike to the Great Bone-Orifice (ST03) to escape from a grab.

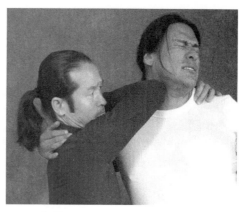

Inward elbow strike to the Protuberance Assistance (LI18) can defeat a larger attacker.

Forearm

Function: The forearm is a blunt weapon that can be used for defensive and offensive purposes. You can move it vertically, horizontally, diagonally and other ways as situations arise. An inner forearm is a good way to trap the head, neck, arm or leg. The outer forearm can generate a powerful blow to the head, arm or torso. Be careful when striking hard targets, because the radius and ulna bones can be fractured.

Method: Bend your elbow and make a fist. 1) For a vertical forearm strike, raise your elbow and bring the outer forearm down toward the target like a sword. 2) For a horizontal forearm strike, bring your arm outward slightly, then move your forearm toward target. 3) For a diagonal forearm strike, bring your arm to your ear with your palm facing forward, then move your outer forearm toward the target at a forty-five degree angle. 4) For a forearm V-block, bend your arm in a V-shape and position your elbow at an angle to receive the blow with minimum friction. 5) For other forearm blocks, use the ulna side of the forearm or the back of the forearm for safety.

Major Targets: Protuberance Assistance (LI18), White Bone-Orifice (GV25), Shoulder Well (GB21), Marsh at the Bend (PC03), Lower Biceps (AD-UE1), Small Sea (SI08), Lower Calf (AD-LE4)

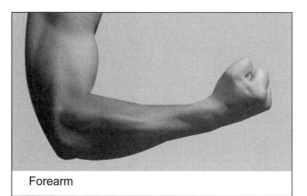

Forearm

V-block with your forearm against a knife thrust at close range.

Raise your forearm in a turning block against a gun pointed at you from the rear.

When choking, use your forearm to press the Protuberance Assistance (LI18).

Forearm control of the neck and arm.

Forearm control of the head.

Forearm control of the neck while subduing an attacker.

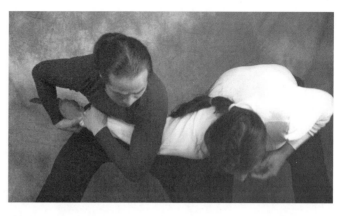

Above: Use your forearm to trap the opponent's arm against a knife thrust.

Below: Push the opponent's head with your forearm to block his vision and control his body.

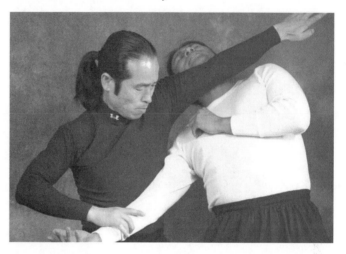

Forearm choke while trapping the knife hand.

Invisible weapons catch the opponent by surprise, delivering added fear.

KNEE

The knee is a blunt weapon. It moves slower than any other bodily weapon, but its impact is devastating. A round knee kick to the Central River (GB32) on the thigh can disable the leg momentarily. A knee kick to the Lumbar Transport (GV02) on the tailbone can paralyze the body. The knee is a weapon of power, surprise, and demolition.

Knee Kick

Function: Your knees are your most powerful weapons in a close quarter fight. You can jab the knee to the groin, outer thigh, lower stomach, and drop it on the head when an opponent goes down. There are five types of knee kicks that are useful for self-protection: straight, circular, jump, stomp, and ground knee kick.

Method: 1) For a straight knee kick: From fighting stance, raise your knee and bend it sharply, then kick with the center of the patella. You can kick forward to a target such as the groin or lower stomach and upward to a target such as the opponent's head when you pull it down. At the moment of impact, keep your standing knee slightly bent for balance. 2) For a circular knee kick, from fighting stance, bend your knee sharply and swing it into the target in a circular motion. Keep your standing knee slightly bent and your torso balanced. 3) For a jump knee kick, from fighting stance, hop with your kicking knee sharply bent, both hands up and your torso upright for balance. Bury your knee into the center of the opponent's body. 4) For a stomp knee kick, from a standing position, bring your sharply bent knee up and drop it vertically onto the target on the ground. 5) For a ground knee kick, from the side mount position, kneeling on one knee, hold the opponent with both hands. Bring your kicking knee straight or diagonally backward according to the angle of your strike. Keep your eyes on the target at all times. Slam the target with your knee while holding the opponent firmly.

Major Targets: Groin (AD-T1), Curved Bone (CV02), Passage of Origin (CV04) , Outer Mound (ST26), Central River (GB 32), Crouching Rabbit (ST32), Spring at the Bend (LV08), Yin Bladder (LV09), Turtledove Tail (CV15), Chest Center (CV17), Camphorwood Gate (LV13), Capital Gate (GB25), Gallbladder (AD-T2), Lumbar Transport (GV02), Philtrum (GV26), Jaw Chariot (ST06), Bend Center (BL40)

A straight knee kick to the Curved Bone (CV02) can break the opponent's grip.

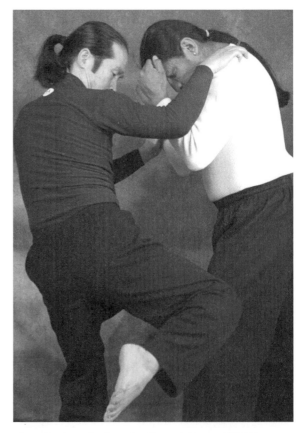

Circular knee kick to the Central River (GB32).

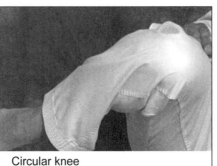

| Straight knee | Circular knee |

116

Circular knee kick to the Turtledove Tail (CV15). For added impact, pull the opponent toward you. If you can time your kick to when he inhales, it can knock him out instantly.

Counter your opponent's grab with a circular knee kick to the Outer Mound (ST26).

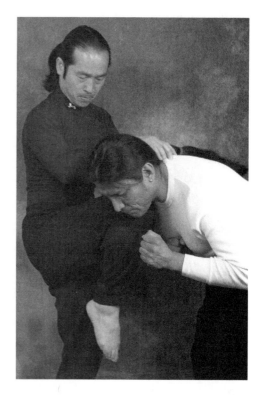

Above: Deliver a straight knee kick to the Adam's Apple (AD-N1) while pulling the opponent's torso down from the side.

Below: A straight knee kick to the White Bone-Orifice (GV25) while pulling his head down from the side.

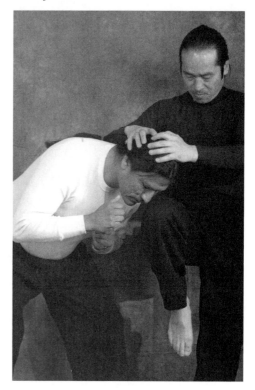

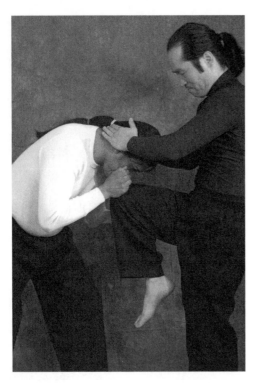

A straight knee kick to the Philtrum (GV26) while pulling his head down from the front.

Above: Straight knee kick to the Chest Center (CV17) against the opponent trying to tackle you.

Below: A circular knee kick to the Jaw Chariot (ST06) against an opponent going for your legs. Step back and kick quickly to avoid getting caught.

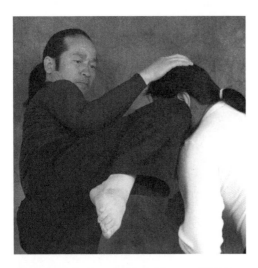

Jump knee kick to the Jaw Chariot (ST06). This technique is done in combination with a left straight punch to the Sauce Receptacle (CV24) on the chin, a right palm heel downward strike to the Upper Star (GV23) on the head, then an in-place short jump knee kick to the head.

A snapping knee kick to the Bend Center (BL40) to take an opponent down to the rear.

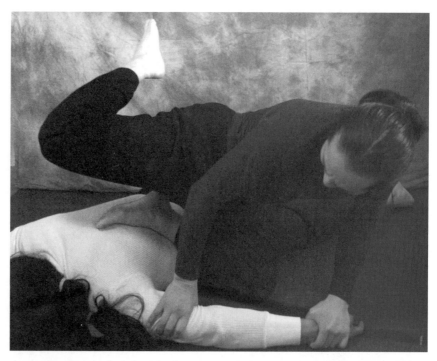

A circular knee kick to the Wind Mansion (GV16) after pinning the opponent on the floor with his face down. Make sure to pin his arm with your two hands before lifting your knee. Lower your torso slightly for balance. If he tries to get out, drop your leg on his arm for an arm bar. Caution: striking the occipital ridge of a downed opponent can be fatal.

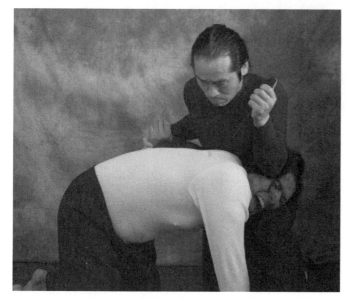

Double strikes to both Temples (EX-HN5). First drop him to the ground with a wrist lock and place your left knee in the direction his head moves. As his head reaches your knee, drop your elbow on the temple. Practice slowly until you can perform the sequence smoothly.

Your knee and upper thigh are also useful in transitions to magnify pain and maintain your initiative.

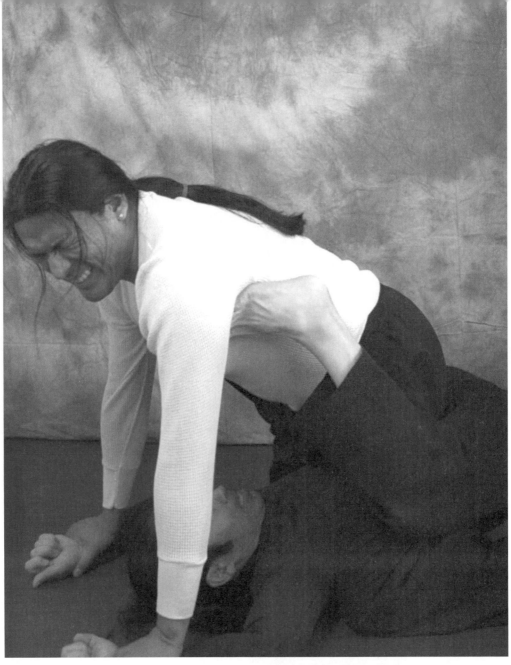

Surprise is the most effective psychological tool in a fight.
The rarely used has the most breathtaking effect.

FOOT

The feet are mainly used for mobility, yet are powerful weapons to attack the limbs, trunk, and head. The legs are longer and much more powerful than the arms, thus the feet can reach where the hands cannot and can smash targets that are too big for hands. To fight against a puncher, use your feet as a surprise attack. With wise usage of the feet, you can defeat any type of opponent at close, medium and long distance.

Kicking

Function: The feet are the wheels of the human body. They provide mobility. When these mobile parts are directed to specific vital points, they turn into deadly weapons. Your feet can reach from the opponent's toes to the top of his head and produce much more force than hand strikes. When precision, speed, and flexibility are combined, your kicking techniques become invaluable in standing and ground fighting. The most commonly used kicks for self-defense are front, roundhouse, side, back kick and kicking on the ground.

Method: 1) For front kick, from fighting stance, lift your sharply bent kicking knee forward. As the knee reaches the proper height, release your foot toward the target. 2) For roundhouse kick, from fighting stance, chamber your knee forward, pivot your standing foot and rotate your hip toward the target, then release the foot toward the target. 3) For side kick, from fighting stance, bring your knee forward and pivot the standing foot toward the target, then throw the blade of your foot, and kick the target. 4) For back kick, from fighting position, chamber your knee and thrust your heel or bottom of the foot into the target. 5) For kicking on the ground, put one of your hands behind you on the ground for leverage, turn your body slightly to the side for protection and mobility, and as the opponent comes closer, throw side kicks or an upward stomp kick with the bottom of your foot at the opponent's shin, knee, thigh, or stomach.

Major Targets: Groin (AD-T1), Curved Bone (CV02), Passage of Origin (CV04) , Outer Mound (ST26), Central River (GB 32), Crouching Rabbit (ST32), Spring at the Bend (LV08), Yin Bladder (LV09), Turtledove Tail (CV15), Chest Center (CV17), Camphorwood Gate (LV13), Abdominal Lament (SP16), Great Horizontal (SP15), Capital Gate (GB25), Protuberance Assistance (LI18), Temple (EX-HN5), Crane's Summit (EX-LE2), Inner Calf (AD-LE6)

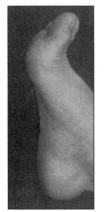

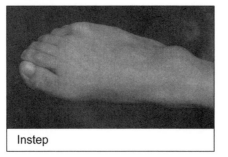

Instep

Left: Ball of the foot

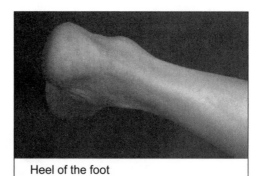

Heel of the foot

Blade of the foot

Use an instep front kick to the Groin (AD-T1) against an opponent grabbing your wrists.

Roundhouse ball kick to the Passage of Origin (CV04).

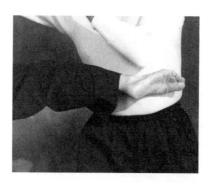

Roundhouse instep kick to the Great Horizontal (SP15).

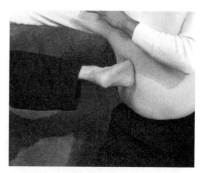

Roundhouse ball kick to the Abdominal Lament (SP16).

Side kick to the Crane's Summit (EX-LE2).

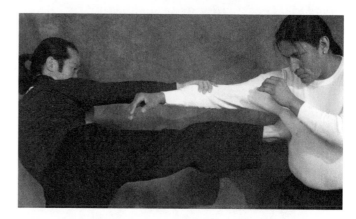

Above: A side kick is useful to stop a puncher since your leg is longer than the opponent's arm. You should be quick and precise. Retract your foot before he grabs it.

Left: Inward heel kick to the Yang Mound Spring (GB34).

Below: Against a rear attack, use the bottom of the heel to kick the Groin (AD-T1), Curved Bone (CV02), or Passage of Origin (CV04).

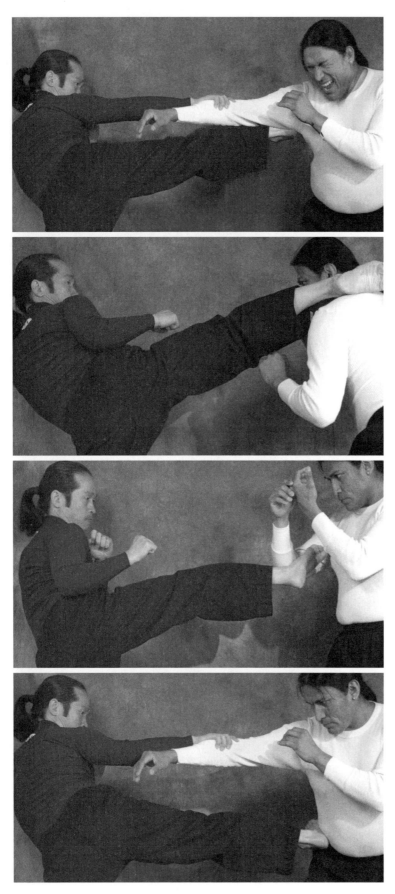

Use the longer reach of your side kick to kick the Highest Spring (HT01).

Roundhouse kick to the Wind Pool (GB20).

Front pushing kick to the Turtledove Tail (CV15).

Against an opponent who rushes in, use a side stop kick to the Great Horizontal (SP15).

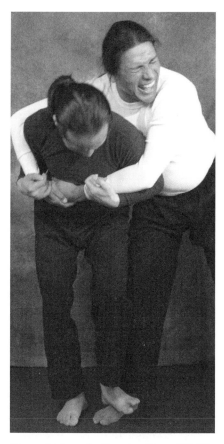

Stomp kick to the Surging Yang (ST42) to distract the opponent.

Avoid striking a hard target (the tip of the chin of the opponent) with your soft vital spot the Surging Yang (ST42).

A non-traditional upward side kick into the Highest Spring (HT01) can surprise an opponent who thinks you are defenseless.

When there is a sudden totally unexpected change in the environment, we have a tendency to inhale. When the opponent grabs your wrist, relax your muscles initially, then suddenly rotate your wrists inward and open the gap. As he inhales, strike the Turtledove Tail (CV15, Solar Plexus) with your head. A well placed headbutt can stop his breathing.

HEADBUTT

As a weapon, the head is better used for thinking than for striking, however when you have no other options, a headbutt can be a lifesaving technique. The element of surprise is critical to headbutting. The headbutt is a technique that you can use once in a fight, so if you choose to use it, make it count.

Headbutt

Function: The head is the most vulnerable target and thus a headbutt is dangerous to use in fighting. However, due to the hardness of the skull, when applied correctly, a headbutt is a powerful technique that may stop an aggressive opponent in a desperate situation. The key is to close the distance and to use the hard part of the forehead to strike a soft target such as the nose.

Method: From a natural stance, tuck your chin down, clench your teeth, and stiffen the neck muscles. Aim and snap your head toward the target. For more power, use your body weight. Keep your eyes on your opponent at all times. Because of the sensitive nature of the brain, which can be damaged by repeated impact, practicing headbutting is not recommended.

Major Targets: Sauce Receptacle (CV24), White Bone-Orifice (GV25), Great Bone-Orifice (ST03), Eyeball (AD-H1), Temple (EX-HN5), Turtledove Tail (CV15), Jade Hall (CV18), Seal Hall (EX-HN3), Leading Valley (GB08), Auditory Palace (SI19)

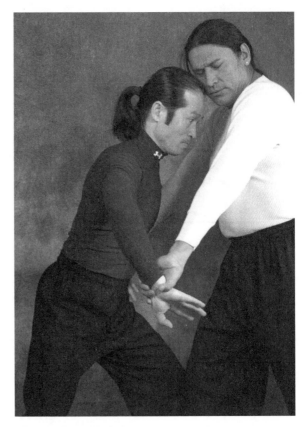

Straight headbutt to the Great Bone-Orifice (ST03).

Use your head to push on the Seal Hall (EX-HN3) and force the opponent to move away from you.

Steady the opponent's head and deliver a forward headbutt to the Upper Star (GV23).

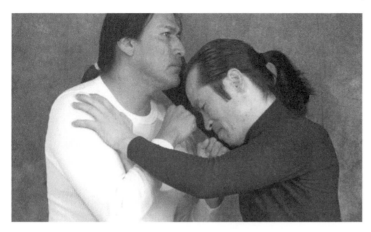

A headbutt to the Sauce Receptacle (CV24) can damage the opponent's nose and mouth.

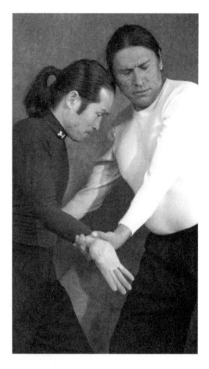

Step in and deliver a straight head-butt to the Auditory Palace (SI19) against a wrist grab.

Against a larger opponent drive a headbutt to the Turtledove Tail (CV15) against his wrist grab.

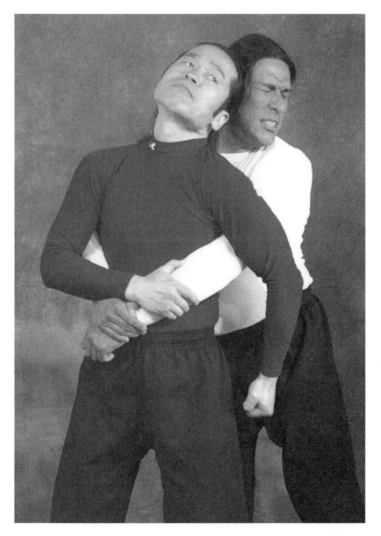

While pressing the Pool at the Bend (LI11) with your thumb and striking the groin with your left hammer fist, deliver a headbutt to the Leading Valley (GB08) to shock the opponent into releasing his grip.

129

BOOK 2

VITAL POINTS AND TECHNIQUES

OVERVIEW

Book 2 details 202 vital points that can be struck or pressed to cause pain or physical damage to an opponent during a physical confrontation. In addition to the traditionally recognized acupoints and extra points, there are 16 additional points like the groin, temple, gallbladder and eyeball that are included for their importance as targets in the fighting arts and combat sports. These points are coded AD- and are indicated on the charts with light gray circles.

The description for each point details where to strike, neighboring anatomy, how to strike, and the potential effects on an opponent. The descriptions are short and succinct to allow you to easily review and scan the points for reference. For accuracy, the location of each point is described using anatomically specific terms that may not be familiar to the layperson. To supplement the descriptions, anatomical and scientific words are defined in lay terms in the glossary at the back of the book and each point location is identified on a human model. Of course, there is no substitute for learning the point locations from a knowledgeable teacher, however this section can serve as a definitive reference. Additionally, the involved major nerves and blood vessels are identified for those readers interested in connecting the Western scientific aspect of vital point theory with the traditional Chinese medicine approach. Finally, each point description lists suggested techniques and potential effects. While the effects are possible outcomes, actual outcomes and your choice of techniques is entirely dependent on your skill level, training and ability to apply the techniques in a chaotic and stressful self-defense, combat or competitive situation.

Book 2 begins with a brief overview of the plexus concept. A plexus is a complex system of nerve networks, creating a highly vulnerable spot on the human body. It is a worthwhile subject of study for martial artists and sport fighters because of its potential for creating knockout blows and complex physical reactions in an opponent. The remaining chapters of Book 2 divide the body into sections: Chapter 6 introduces vital points on the head and neck; Chapter 7 vital points on the trunk; Chapter 8 vital points on the arm and hand; Chapter 9 vital points on the leg and foot. After the points for each area of the body are introduced, sample applications are provided to give a practical visual illustration of some of the techniques mentioned in the point descriptions.

It should be noted that many of the applications for vital points on the leg show a pressing or striking technique that is intended to be applied if you have been knocked to the ground, are being dominated by a standing opponent or are struggling on the ground in a deadlock. In such a situation, pressing a point on the opponent's calf, thigh or foot can be a tactical move to distract the opponent or cause him to loosen his grip, allowing you an opening to deliver a stronger technique. From the given examples, it's up to you to experiment with applications in a wide variety of fighting situations.

CHAPTER 5

PLEXUS STRIKES

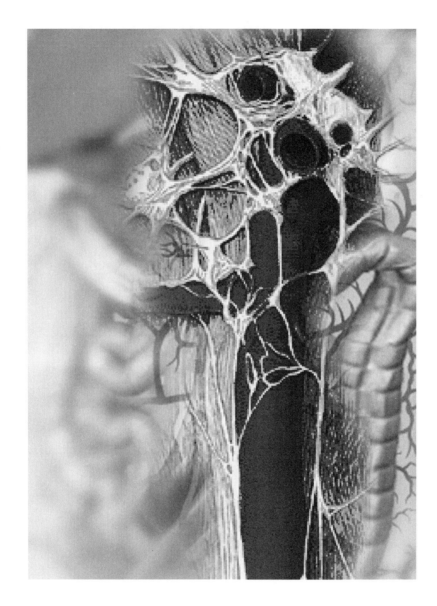

NERVE NETWORKS

What is a Plexus?

A plexus is an area where nerves divide and reunite. It is a complex network of nerves. Two or more of these nerve networks form a concentrated web of nerve fibers running from the brain or spine through the neck, heart, stomach, arms or legs, creating a highly vulnerable spot on the human body.

What are Ganglia?

A ganglion (pl. ganglia) is a mass of nerve tissue containing nerve cells located outside of the brain or spinal cord. Ganglia are often interconnected with other ganglia, forming a plexus. They function as nerve hubs relaying impulses between body parts and the Peripheral and Central Nervous Systems.

What are Nerve Junctions?

While a plexus is a cluster of nerve networks, a nerve junction is where a major nerve branches out into two or more nerves. When a nerve junction is struck, the impact spreads simultaneously to multiple parts of the body. Even when you miss the precise center of the junction, as long as you hit the branches of the nerve, you can achieve a similar degree of impact.

Why Strike a Nerve Network?

It's hard to strike a small target, such as a single vital point, accurately. It's even more difficult if the target is in constant irregular motion. A nerve network strike has a high degree of success because the target is large, which allows for a greater margin of error in combat. A plexus or nerve junction is like an enlarged vital target, consisting of many vital points in a concentrated area. These are vulnerable, complicated, and easy-to-strike targets. You can generate double or triple the impact of an average strike by attacking multiple nerves at once.

12 MAJOR PLEXUS

Anterior Region

TEMPORAL PLEXUS

The Temporal Plexus, also known as the Superficial Temporal Plexus, is an autonomic network of nerves on the temporal region. The major nerves in this region are the trigeminal nerve, the facial nerve, the oculomotor nerve and trochlear nerve. Striking this area can instantly shock the brain leading to blurred vision, severe headache, and a knockout.

CERVICAL PLEXUS

The Cervical Plexus, located in the neck, is a plexus of the first four cervical spinal nerves. The nerves originate from the back of the head and neck. They are located lateral to the transverse processes. Nerve branches from the Cervical Plexus are the lesser occipital nerve, great auricular nerve, transverse cervical nerve, and supraclavicular nerves. Striking or choking this region can shock the brain and deplete the brain's blood and oxygen supply, causing an instant knockout or death.

BRACHIAL PLEXUS

The Brachial Plexus is a network of nerves on the neck and shoulder that control the muscles and sensations in the shoulders, arms and hands. The nerves found here originate from the neck and branch out into the arms and hands via the shoulder. Striking this region can damage the neck, shoulder, or upper arm, and can cause paralysis of the trunk.

CARDIAC PLEXUS

The Cardiac Plexus is a plexus of nerves located at the base of the heart. It is connected to the Coronary Plexus, the Pulmonary Plexus, the cervical ganglia of the sympathetic trunk, and the cardiac branches of the vagus and recurrent laryngeal nerves. Striking this region can cause damage to the heart, unconsciousness and potentially death.

CELIAC PLEXUS

The Celiac Plexus, commonly known as the Solar Plexus, is located on the level of the first lumbar vertebra in the abdomen, behind the stomach. It is a large complex network of sympathetic nerves, ganglia and interconnecting fibers. The branches of the plexus are connected to the nerves in the abdominal viscera. Striking this region can cause stoppage of the heart and breathing, severe pain in the stomach, spasm in the diaphragm, and a knockout.

SUPERIOR HYPOGASTRIC PLEXUS

The Superior Hypogastric Plexus, also known as the Hypogastric Plexus, is a network of nerves situated in front of the 5th lumbar vertebra below the umbilicus, above the sacrum and between the two common iliac arteries. It is composed of many filaments branched off from the aortic plexus and the lumbar plexus. Kicking this region can cause severe pain or spasm in the lower stomach, damage to the organs, and a knockout.

PELVIC PLEXUS

The Pelvic Plexus, also known as the Inferior Hypogastric Plexus, is a network of nerves in the viscera of the pelvic cavity. Many branches of nerves that innervate the viscera of the pelvis such as the Rectal Plexus, the Vesical Plexus, and the Prostatic Plexus stem from the Pelvic Plexus. Kicking this area can cause paralysis of the lower limbs, severe pain in the lower abdomen, and loss of consciousness.

PATELLA PLEXUS

The Patella Plexus, also known as the Peripatellar Plexus, is located on the knee. It consists of the lateral femoral cutaneous nerve, the anterior cutaneous branches of the femoral nerve, and the infrapatellar branch of the saphenous nerve. Kicking this region with a side kick or pushing kick causes intense pain and can disable the leg instantly.

Figure 5.1 Major plexus on the anterior body.

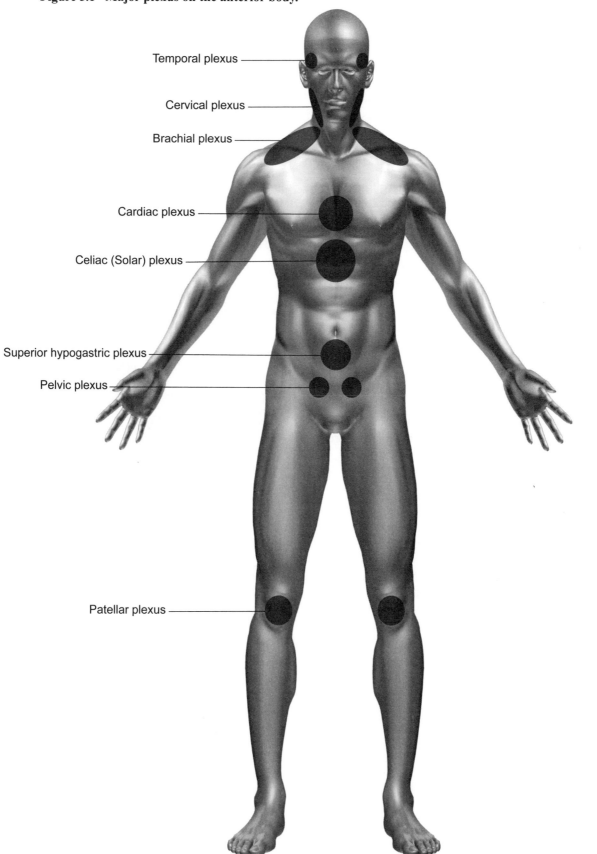

Temporal plexus

Cervical plexus

Brachial plexus

Cardiac plexus

Celiac (Solar) plexus

Superior hypogastric plexus

Pelvic plexus

Patellar plexus

Posterior Region

PULMONARY PLEXUS

The Pulmonary Plexus, an autonomic plexus that includes the pulmonary branches of the vagus nerve, is located below the Cardiac Plexus. Striking this region can shock the lungs and cause stoppage of breath. Tormenting pain in the back can be transmitted along the spinal cord and paralyze the torso.

SUBTRAPEZIAL PLEXUS

The Subtrapezial Plexus is located vertically along the scapula. It is a combined nerve network of the spinal accessory nerve from the 3rd and 4th cervical vertebrae. Striking this region causes excruciating pain in the scapula and can cause paralysis of the upper back.

LUMBAR PLEXUS

The Lumbar Plexus is a network of nerves in the lumbar region of the body. It is located in the posterior part of the psoas major muscle between the 1st and 4th lumbar vertebrae. Several nerves originate from the spinal nerves here and split into branches to the pubis, genitals, hips and thighs. Kicking this region can cause paralysis of the lower limbs, severe pain and fractures in the lower back, and loss of consciousness.

SACRAL PLEXUS

The Sacral Plexus is a network of nerves originating from the sacral vertebrae. It is located between the 4th lumbar vertebra and the 4th sacral vertebra and involves the nerves of the pelvis and lower limbs. Impact on this region can cause unconsciousness, paralysis of the lower back and limbs, and unbearable pain in the lower hip and genitals.

Figure 5.2   Major plexus on the posterior body.

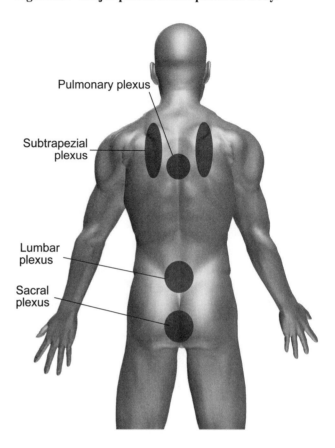

Pulmonary plexus

Subtrapezial plexus

Lumbar plexus

Sacral plexus

APPLICATIONS

TEMPORAL PLEXUS

You can strike the Temporal Plexus from many directions: front, side, and rear. A wide variety of weapons are effective: punch, hammer fist, knifehand strike, palm heel strike, fingertip jab, elbow strike, roundhouse kick, knee kick (on the ground), and headbutt. The key factors for success are precise distance and timing of the strike. A good tactic is to feint with a straight attack to the head, then strike the Temporal Plexus.

CERVICAL PLEXUS

The Cervical Plexus is located in the neck, connecting the head and the trunk. Damage to this region can result in death in a matter of seconds. A good tactic is to attack the face or trunk first and then strike the Cervical Plexus region. Knifehand strike, elbow strike, forearm strike, choke, roundhouse kick, and hammer fist are all effective techniques for attacking the Cervical Plexus.

BRACHIAL PLEXUS

The Brachial Plexus starts from the neck (the 5th and 8th cervical vertebrae and the 1st thoracic vertebra) and branches out to the arm (the radial, median and ulnar nerves) and the armpit (the axillary nerve). Striking this area can incapacitate the neck, shoulder, and arm. Due to the position of the plexus (under the clavicle), you should strike just the below or above the clavicle, unless you intend to chop the clavicle bone with your elbow. The key to success is the angle of striking. If you strike downward on the clavicle with a hammer fist, it will not only shock the Brachial Plexus, but may also break the bone. To attack below the bone, use a hammer fist, thumb or fingertip press, or elbow strike. For striking above the clavicle, use a downward elbow strike or fingertip press.

CARDIAC PLEXUS

The heart is protected by the 3rd, 4th, 5th and 6th ribs and the sternum in the middle of the chest. The sternum is composed of porous vascular tissue covered by a thin flattened layer of compact bone. The bottom of the sternum, called the xiphoid process, is the weakest spot. Striking the Cardiac Plexus can generate severe pain in the heart, and potentially break the bone of the sternum into pieces, leading to death.

CELIAC PLEXUS

The Celiac Plexus, also known as the Solar Plexus, is located right behind the stomach. Kicking or punching this region shocks the nerves of the abdominal organs, causing the stoppage of breath, spasm of the diaphragm, and unconsciousness. The key to success is striking when the opponent is inhaling.

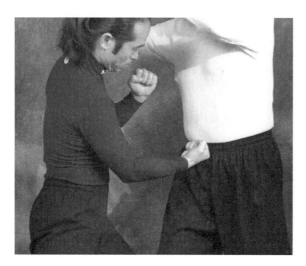

SUPERIOR HYPOGASTRIC PLEXUS

The Superior Hypogastric Plexus is located right below the umbilicus. This is a good spot to strike when your opponent is attacking your face or trying to choke you. Repetitive knee kicks or uppercuts to the Superior Hypogastric Plexus damage your opponent's stamina and cause numbness in the lower abdomen and legs.

PELVIC PLEXUS

The Pelvic Plexus is located right above the pubic bone. Many other plexus are located in this region including the Rectal Plexus, the Vesical Plexus, and the Prostatic Plexus. Pull your opponent toward you and raise your knee with a short snapping strike to the Pelvic Plexus. The key is the angle of the strike: pull his body slightly toward you and kick upward and perpendicularly into the center of the body.

PATELLA PLEXUS

The Patella Plexus is located on the knee. A kick to this region is useful for stopping an opponent who is charging toward you. For offensive purposes, a front kick or front pushing kick is effective. For defense, the side kick is most effective. The key is distance: use footwork to adjust the distance between you and your opponent and kick the target without losing your balance.

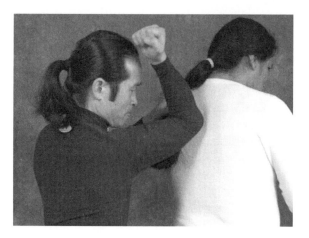

PULMONARY PLEXUS

The Pulmonary Plexus is located below the Cardiac Plexus. It is easiest to strike the Pulmonary Plexus from the rear. An elbow strike, punch, or palm heel strike on the back can shock the lungs and cause the stoppage of breath. The pain can be unbearable. A stealthy strike to the Pulmonary Plexus can knock out an assailant instantly.

SUBTRAPEZIAL PLEXUS

The origin of the Subtrapezial Plexus begins in the Central Nervous System and travels backwards and downwards into the trapezius muscle. It contributes to the motor function of the upper body, so striking this region diminishes or incapacitates the function of the sternocleidomastoid muscle and the upper portion of the trapezius muscle. The key is the striking angle. Strike the upper inner side of the scapula at a 45 to 60 degree angle with a knifehand or elbow strike. A hammer fist can be used at any angle.

LUMBAR PLEXUS

The Lumbar Plexus is in the lower back. This region consists of a complex interconnecting network of nerves, joints, muscles, tendons and ligaments. Striking anywhere in the area of the Lumbar Plexus causes pain. Forceful techniques such as a side kick, roundhouse kick or knee kick can damage the spine and cause temporary or permanent paralysis of the legs and arms.

SACRAL PLEXUS

The Sacral Plexus is where the tailbone is located. If you participate in a combat sport, you may have experienced being kicked in this region. The pain is excruciating and the damage from a kick to this region can cause pain that lasts for months. Effective techniques for attacking the Sacral Plexus are the knee kick and back kick. To be successful, you should move to a position that allows you to control the opponent's body (example: grabbing the shoulders while executing a knee kick). A back kick can be used in long range fighting when the opponent turns his hip to attack. The key is to strike at the right angle at the right time. Because of the difficulty of striking this region most injuries to the Sacral Plexus occur by accident.

CHAPTER 6

VITAL POINTS ON THE
HEAD & NECK

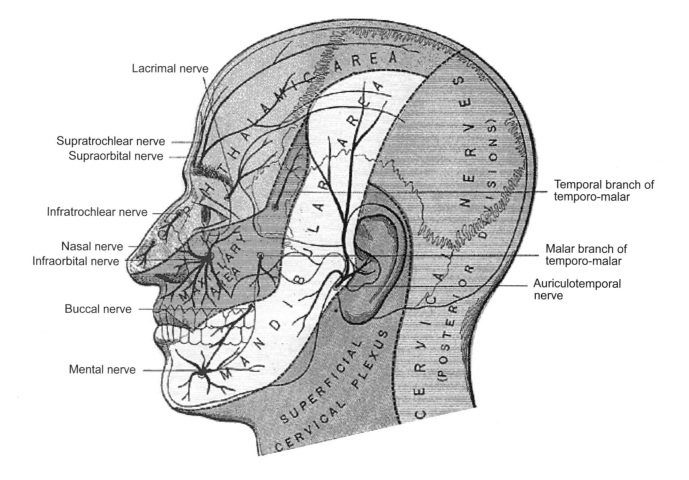

Lacrimal nerve

Supratrochlear nerve
Supraorbital nerve

Infratrochlear nerve

Nasal nerve
Infraorbital nerve

Buccal nerve

Mental nerve

Temporal branch of
temporo-malar

Malar branch of
temporo-malar

Auriculotemporal
nerve

OPHTHALMIC AREA

MAXILLARY AREA

MANDIBULAR AREA

CERVICAL NERVES (POSTERIOR DIVISIONS)

SUPERFICIAL CERVICAL PLEXUS

CERVICAL (POSTERIOR DIVISIONS)

The head is the command center of the nervous system. Information of sight, sound, smell, taste, and thinking is processed in the brain. It is vulnerable to injury and sensitive to pain.

Significance of the Head & Neck

The Head

The head is the command center of the nervous system. Sensations of sight, sound, smell, taste, and touch are processed in the brain, which is vulnerable to injury. A thumb thrust in the eye can cause blurred vision and even blindness. A slap to the ear can cause deafness, loss of balance and loss of consciousness.

As a tactical target, the nose is one of the most vulnerable spots on the head due to its protrusion and lack of a hard bone structure. Blows from any direction can damage the nose: the septal cartilage can be fractured by a downward strike, severe bleeding can be caused by a straight strike, and pain on the base of the nose can be used to manipulate an opponent by pressing upward. Injury to the nose hinders breathing and often vision and damage to the nose, if broken, can be permanent.

When the head is struck by a powerful blow, the brain shifts in the skull, which causes loss of consciousness or disorientation. The resulting brain damage or excessive hemorrhaging can easily result in death. Repeated blows to the head complicate the conditions of brain injury and the danger can become fatal if you are exhausted and hit defenselessly on major vital points. Strikes on the temple, the back of the skull, or the side of the jaw are among the most dangerous.

The Neck

The neck is the bridge between the head and the trunk and limbs, channeling blood and oxygen to the brain via arteries and transmitting sensory impulses through nerves. Attacking the neck is like cutting off a bridge between two strategic locations. Choking the carotid artery or the windpipe stops the flow of blood and air to the brain. In six seconds, you can choke out an opponent. Striking the windpipe with a knifehand or a punch causes sensory overload to the brain, severe pain in the neck or death.

Caution

When facing an unexpected assailant, it is difficult to selectively strike specific targets. Initially your instinct may take over your thought process: run away or fight back, then utilize whatever means are available to cover, strike, pull, push, etc. Any action you take to save your life in a life-threatening situation can be justifiable. However, striking the head and neck can cause unintended permanent damage to an opponent, assailant or suspect. Therefore, you should make every effort to use the proper amount of force and justifiable techniques in response to the type and seriousness of the threat.

VITAL POINTS ON THE HEAD

ANTERIOR HEAD

Spirit Court (GV24)

Location: On the midsagittal line of the head.
Nerve: The branch of the frontal nerve.
Blood Vessels: The branches of the frontal artery and vein.
Techniques: Palm strike, hammer fist strike.
Effects: Headache, pain on the forehead, knockout by shock to the brain.

Seal Hall (EX-HN3)

Location: Between the supraorbital notches.
Nerve: The medial branch of the frontal nerve.
Blood Vessels: The frontal artery and vein.
Techniques: Palm strike, elbow strike.
Effects: Headache, blurred vision, knockout by shock to the brain.

White Bone-Orifice (GV25)

Location: On the tip of the nose.
Nerve: Anterior ethmoidal nerve.
Blood Vessels: The facial artery and veins.
Techniques: Punch, palm strike, elbow strike.
Effects: Damage to the septal cartilage and the angular artery, bleeding, knockout by shock to the brain.

Philtrum (GV26)

Location: One-third of the way down between the nose and the upper lip.
Nerve: The anterior alveolar nerve.

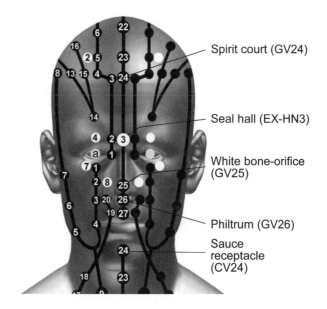

Blood Vessel: The superior labial artery.
Techniques: Punch, elbow strike.
Effects: Dizziness, damage to the teeth, bleeding.

Sauce Receptacle (CV24)

Location: On the tip of the chin.
Nerve: The branch of the facial nerve.
Blood Vessels: The branches of the inferior labial artery and vein.
Techniques: Punch, palm strike, elbow strike.
Effects: Dizziness, knockout by shock to the brain.

Figure 6.1   Facial nerves and partial trigeminal nerves.

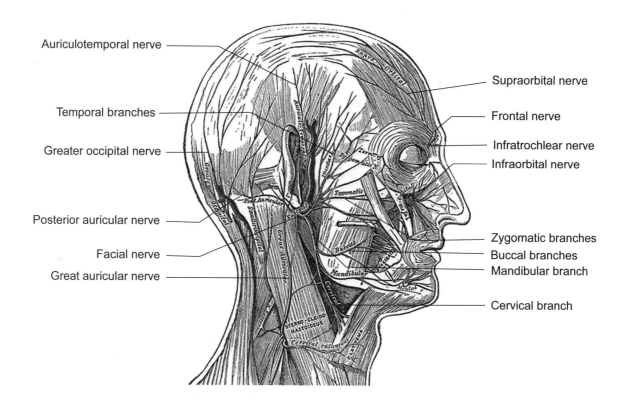

Bamboo Gathering (BL02)

Location: On the medial end of the eyebrow.
Nerve: The supratrochlear nerve.
Blood Vessels: The frontal artery and vein.
Techniques: Palm strike, punch, elbow strike.
Effects: Headache, blurred vision, knockout by shock to the brain.

Four Whites (ST02)

Location: At the center of the infraorbital foramen.
Nerve: The infraorbital nerve.
Blood Vessels: The branches of facial artery and veins, the infraorbital artery and vein.
Techniques: Punch, palm strike, elbow strike.
Effects: Facial paralysis, cheekbone fracture, dizziness, blurred vision.

Great Bone-Orifice (ST03)

Location: In the depression of the lower border of the cheekbone.
Nerves: The facial and infraorbital nerves.
Blood Vessels: The branches of the transverse facial artery and vein.
Techniques: Punch, palm strike, elbow strike.
Effects: Knockout by shock to the brain.

Figure 6.2 Trigeminal nerves.

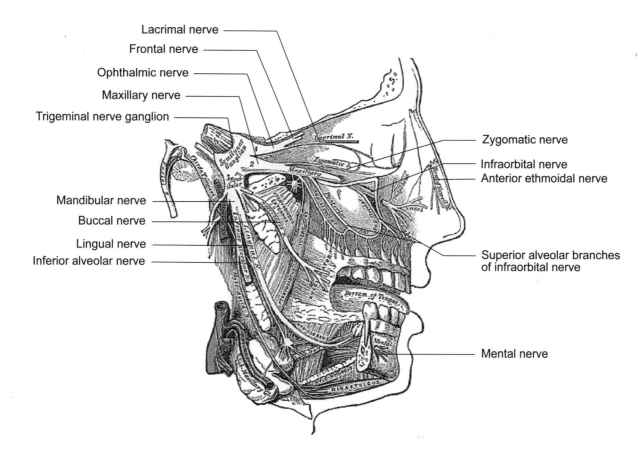

Lacrimal nerve
Frontal nerve
Ophthalmic nerve
Maxillary nerve
Trigeminal nerve ganglion

Zygomatic nerve
Infraorbital nerve
Anterior ethmoidal nerve

Mandibular nerve
Buccal nerve
Lingual nerve
Inferior alveolar nerve

Superior alveolar branches
of infraorbital nerve

Mental nerve

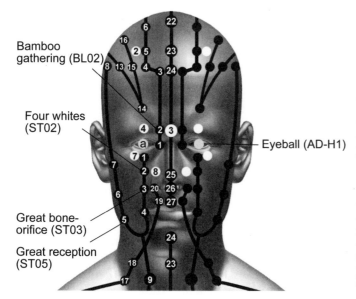

Bamboo
gathering (BL02)

Four whites
(ST02)

Eyeball (AD-H1)

Great bone-
orifice (ST03)

Great reception
(ST05)

Great Reception (ST05)

Location: Anterior to the angle of the mandible.
Nerves: The facial and the buccal nerves.
Blood Vessels: The facial artery and vein.
Techniques: Punch, hammer fist, elbow strike.
Effect: Mandible dislocation, knockout by shock to the brain.

Eyeball (AD-H1)

Location: The orbital socket.
Nerves: The ophthalmic nerve, the trochlear nerve, the ciliary nerves, the oculomotor nerve.
Blood Vessels: The internal carotid artery.
Techniques: Thumb thrust, knuckle punch, elbow strike.
Effects: Loss of sight, permanent blindness, unconsciousness.

151

APPLICATIONS

Hammer Fist to the Spirit Court

With the bottom of your clenched fist, strike at the median point located a half inch above the hairline. As a surprise attack, this is useful to initiate a takedown. This strike can cause momentary disorientation, dizziness, or a severe headache.

Elbow Strike to the Seal Hall

Strike the point between the eyebrows with a downward elbow strike. It must be done quickly and deceptively. This strike can cause a knockout, dizziness, severe headache, double or blurred vision.

Knee Kick to the White Bone-Orifice

Grab the opponent's head and lower it toward your rising knee. Kick in a sharp vertical motion to the tip of the opponent's nose. You may use either knee according to situation. This technique can cause damage to the septal cartilage, nose bleeding, swelling, or knockout by shock to the brain.

* A knee kick to the nose is also effective when the opponent tries to tackle you straight on. Press his head with your hands while retracting one of your legs. As he moves in closer, kick his nose.

Knuckle Punch to the Philtrum

Nail the knuckle of the middle finger on the philtrum right above the upper lip. You don't need to use maximum force but you do need to be precise. This technique can cause dizziness, the loosening or loss of teeth, bleeding, or facial paralysis.

Punch to the Sauce Receptacle

Throw a straight or downward punch to the tip of the chin. Transfer your body weight into the punch to deliver your power all the way to the brain. Done right, this technique can cause an instant knockout or a broken jaw.

Elbow Strike to the Bamboo Gathering

In a close quarter fight, throw your elbow in a sharp circular motion at the ridge of the eye. Strike quickly and deceptively at a 45 to 60 degree angle. This technique can cause facial cuts, headache, blurred vision, or knockout.

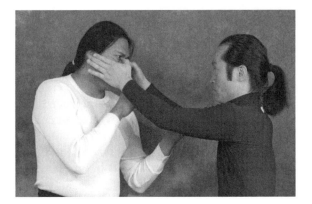

Thumb Press to the Eyeballs

In a close quarter fight, thrust into the eyeballs with the tips of your thumbs. This technique can cause blurred vision, severe pain in the eyes, loss of sight, permanent blindness or unconsciousness.

Elbow Strike to the Four Whites

Strike the center of the cheekbone right below the eye with a straight elbow strike or reverse elbow strike. This technique can cause facial paralysis, cheekbone fracture, dizziness, or blurred vision.

Knifehand Strike to the Philtrum

Strike or press with your knifehand below the nose, one-third of the way down between the nose and the upper lip. A strike can cause facial paralysis, damage to the teeth, and severe pain in the nose. A knifehand press can be used to move or manipulate the opponent into a more advantageous position.

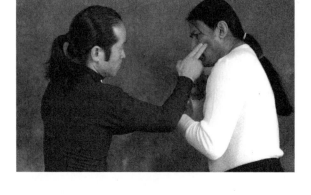

Fingertip Thrust to the Great Bone-Orifice

Strike or thrust to the depression of the lower border of the cheekbone with your knuckles, fingertips, thumb tip or elbow. A strike can cause facial paralysis. A pressing technique can be used to keep the opponent's head away from you in a clinch.

Strike the Great Reception

The anterior region of the jaw is a popular target for knockouts in boxing due to the branches of the cranial nerves and the complex impact on the brain when this point is struck. You can strike the jaw with a punch, palm or elbow strike, or even the knuckles and fingertips. Striking the jaw can cause dislocation of the mandible or a knockout by shock to the brain.

LATERAL HEAD

Forehead Fullness (GB04)

Location: Within the hairline of the temporal region.
Nerve: The temporal branch of the auriculotemporal nerve.
Blood Vessels: The superficial temporal artery and vein.
Techniques: Palm, hammer fist, elbow strike.
Effects: Headache, blurring vision, damage to the Central Nervous System, knockout.

Temporal Hairline (GB07)

Location: Within the hairline anterior and superior to the auricle.
Nerve: The branch of the auriculotemporal nerve.
Blood Vessels: The branches of the superficial temporal artery and vein.
Techniques: Punch, palm, hammer fist, elbow strike.
Effects: Concussion, blurring vision, knockout by shock to the brain.

Temple (EX-HN05)

Location: In a depression about 1 cun posterior to the lateral end of the eye.
Nerves: The branches of the ophthalmic nerve, the temporal branches of the facial nerve.
Blood Vessels: The frontal branches of the superficial temporal artery and vein.
Techniques: Palm, hammer fist, backfist, elbow strike, roundhouse kick.
Effects: Headache, blurring vision, knockout by shock to the brain.

Auditory Convergence (GB02)

Location: Anterior to the intertragic notch at the posterior edge of the condyloid process of the mandible.
Nerves: The great auricular nerve, the facial nerve.
Blood Vessel: The superficial temporal artery.
Techniques: Palm, back fist, hammer fist, elbow strike, thumb tip thrust, roundhouse kick.
Effects: Severe headache, knockout by shock to the brain.

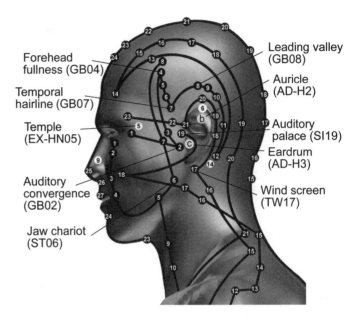

Forehead fullness (GB04)
Temporal hairline (GB07)
Temple (EX-HN05)
Auditory convergence (GB02)
Jaw chariot (ST06)
Leading valley (GB08)
Auricle (AD-H2)
Auditory palace (SI19)
Eardrum (AD-H3)
Wind screen (TW17)

Jaw Chariot (ST06)

Location: At the lower mandible.
Nerves: The branches of the mandibular and facial nerves.
Blood Vessels: The facial artery and vein.
Techniques: Punch, palm strike, elbow strike, roundhouse kick.
Effects: Dislocation of the mandible, knockout by shock to the brain.

Leading Valley (GB08)

Location: 1.5 cun within the hairline above the ear.
Nerves: The branches of the auriculotemporal nerve and the greater occipital nerve.
Blood Vessels: The branches of the superficial temporal artery and vein.
Techniques: Palm, hammer fist, elbow strike, roundhouse kick.
Effects: Severe headache, dizziness, knockout by shock to the brain.

Auricle (AD-H2)

Location: The outer projecting portion of the ear.
Nerves: The great auricular nerve, the facial nerve.
Blood Vessels: The branches of the auricular artery.
Techniques: Grabbing, pulling.
Effects: Unbearable pain in the region of the ear, damage to the auricular tissue.

Auditory Palace (SI19)

Location: On the depression between the tragus and the mandibular joint.
Nerves: The branch of the facial nerve, the auriculo-temporal nerve.
Blood Vessels: The branches of the superficial temporal artery and veins.
Techniques: Palm, backfist, elbow strike.
Effects: Deafness, severe headache.

Eardrum (AD-H3)

Location: Inside of the ear, a thin membrane called the Tympanic membrane.
Nerves: The facial nerve, the vestibular nerve.
Blood Vessel: The internal carotid artery.
Techniques: Palm strike.
Effects: Deafness, loss of balance.

Wind Screen (TW17)

Location: Posterior to the earlobe in the depression between the mandible and mastoid process.
Nerves: The great auricular nerve, the facial nerve.
Blood Vessels: The external jugular vein, the posterior auricular artery and vein.
Techniques: Thumb, knuckle press.
Effects: Unbearable pain in the region of the ear.

APPLICATIONS

Hammer Fist to the Forehead Fullness

The Forehead Fullness point is located inside the hairline at the temple. Striking this point with a hammer fist, elbow strike or palm strike is a good entry technique from the lateral direction. This technique can cause a severe headache, blurred vision or a knockout.

Punch to the Temporal Hairline

The Temporal Hairline is located inside the hairline near the temple. Strike it with a straight punch, hammer fist, elbow strike or palm strike. A forceful strike can lead to a knockout or disorient your opponent.

Strike the Temple

The temple is one of the most vulnerable areas of the human body due to its location near the trigeminal and facial nerves. Strike the temple with your palm, hammer fist, back fist, elbow, or roundhouse kick. A thumb tip press or fingertip tap can cause the opponent to flinch and close his eyes, creating a momentary distraction.

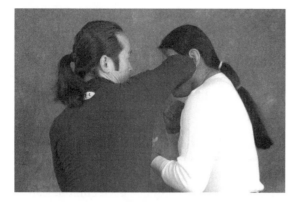

Elbow Strike to the Auditory Convergence

With your elbow or fist, strike the depression on the lower cheekbone. This region is rich with the branches of the trigeminal nerves and a strike can cause severe headache, loss of hearing, or a knockout.

Press the Jaw Chariot

Press the lower mandible (jaw) with your middle fingertip or thumb to cause electric pain in the jaw and face. Striking the Jaw Chariot with a punch or elbow strike can cause dislocation of the mandible or loss of consciousness.

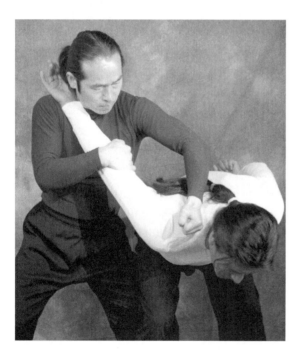

Backfist to the Leading Valley

With your backfist or palm heel, strike the Leading Valley located within the hairline above the ear. Striking this target can cause severe headache, dizziness, and unconsciousness.

A Leading Valley strike is a good transitional technique when you are to the side of your opponent. When used at an unexpected time and position, it causes disorientation.

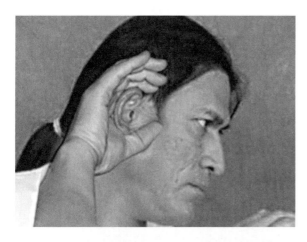

Pinch the Auricle

The auricle is the outer projecting portion of the ear. This skin-covered cartilage can be easily damaged by pinching, pulling, or rubbing. In self-defense, use this technique to quickly repel an opponent. Since it's easy to escape from pinching, attack major vital points such as the eyes, neck and groin as soon as you get an opening.

*CAUTION: Repeated damage to the cartilage causes nutrient starvation of the tissue which forms a lumpy distorted shape called Cauliflower Ear or Wrestler's Ear.

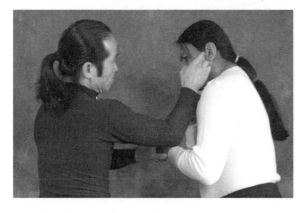

Strike the Auditory Palace

Located on the depression in front of the ear, the Auditory Palace is vulnerable due to the location of several nerves. Striking this spot with an elbow strike can cause deafness and severe headache. Press with your fingertips or a knuckle to manipulate or control the position of your opponent.

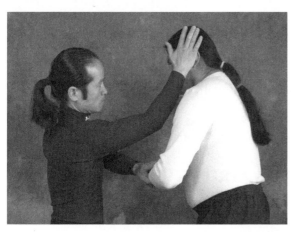

Palm Strike to the Eardrum

The eardrum is a thin membrane called the Tympanic Membrane located inside of the ear. It separates the external ear from the middle ear. Its function is to transmit sound from the air to the ossicles inside the middle ear. Striking the eardrum can cause severe pain and permanent hearing loss.

*CAUTION: For safety, never strike the eardrum in practice and use this technique only in justified self-defense situations. Damage to the ear can be permanent.

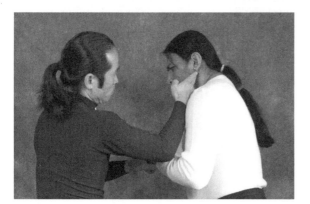

Press the Wind Screen

The Wind Screen is a painful spot that is widely used to subdue an opponent on the ground. The Wind Screen is in the depression behind the earlobe. Pressing this spot causes unbearable pain in the region of the ear, which can allow you to gain compliance from an opponent or suspect.

POSTERIOR HEAD

Jade Pillow (BL09)

Location: On the lateral side of the superior border of the external occipital protuberance.
Nerve: The branch of the greater occipital nerve.
Blood Vessels: The occipital artery and vein.
Techniques: Hammer fist, palm, elbow strike.
Effects: Knockout by shock to the brain.

Wind Pool (GB20)

Location: On the neck, below the occipital bone, in the depression between the sternocleidomastoid and trapezius muscles.
Nerve: The branch of the lesser occipital nerve.
Blood Vessels: The branches of the occipital artery and vein.
Techniques: Thumb press, knifehand, elbow strike.
Effects: Sharp pain in the neck and head regions, knockout by shock to the brain.

Celestial Pillar (BL10)

Location: In the posterior hairline, lateral to the trapezius muscle.
Nerve: The greater occipital nerve.
Blood Vessels: The occipital artery and vein.
Techniques: Thumb press, knifehand, elbow strike.
Effects: Headache, knockout by shock to the brain.

Unyielding Space (GV18)

Location: Three inches below the top of the skull where the occipital bone and the parietal bone meet.
Nerve: The branch of the greater occipital nerve.
Blood Vessels: The branches of the occipital artery and vein.
Techniques: Hammer fist, knifehand, palm strike.
Effects: Dizziness, knockout by shock to the brain.

Brain Door (GV17)

Location: 1 cun above Wind Mansion (GV16), superior to the external occipital protuberance.
Nerve: The branch of the greater occipital nerve.
Blood Vessels: The branches of the occipital artery and vein.
Techniques: Hammer fist, palm strike.
Effects: Knockout by shock to the brain.

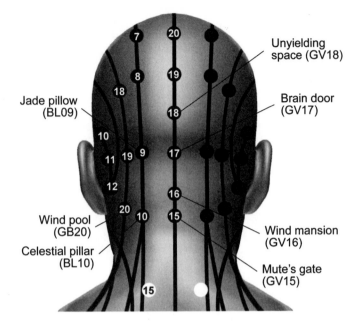

Wind Mansion (GV16)

Location: At the midpoint of the back of the neck where the base of the skull meets the spine.
Nerve: The occipital nerve.
Blood Vessels: The occipital artery and vein.
Techniques: Knifehand, elbow, forearm strike.
Effects: Knockout, fracture of the cervical vertebrae.

Mute's Gate (GV15)

Location: At the midpoint of the nape, .5 cun below Wind Mansion (GV16)
Nerve: The occipital nerve.
Blood Vessels: The branches of the occipital artery and vein.
Techniques: Knifehand, elbow, forearm strike.
Effects: Knockout, fracture of the cervical vertebrae.

APPLICATIONS

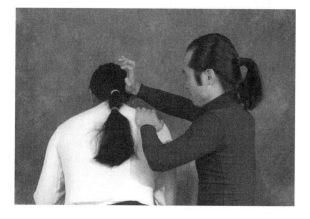

Palm Strike to the Jade Pillow

Striking the Jade Pillow can cause a shifting of the brain in the skull leading to a concussion or brain damage. The hammer fist, palm, and elbow strikes are effective techniques for striking the Jade Pillow.

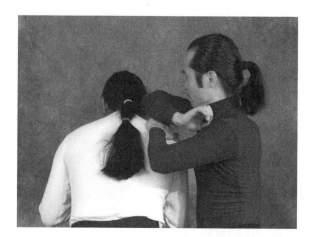

Elbow Strike to the Wind Pool

The Wind Pool is located at the back of the neck, lateral to the Celestial Pillar point. Striking this point results in instant shock to the brain causing disorientation, dizziness, and unbearable pain in the neck and head. Effective techniques are thumb tip press, knifehand or elbow strike.

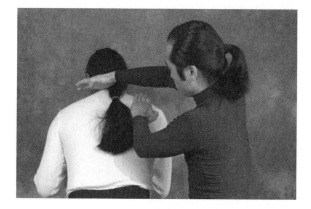

Knifehand Strike to the Celestial Pillar

The Celestial Pillar is located lateral to the Wind Mansion point. Due to its proximity to the Wind Mansion, striking this point generates a similar effect on the brain. Effective techniques are the thumb press, knifehand or elbow strike. This technique can cause intense headache or loss of consciousness.

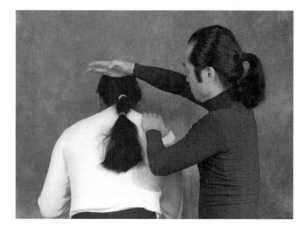

Knifehand Strike to the Unyielding Space

Strike the middle of the upper region of the posterior skull with a hammer fist, knifehand, or palm strike. This technique can cause severe dizziness, blackout, or unconsciousness.

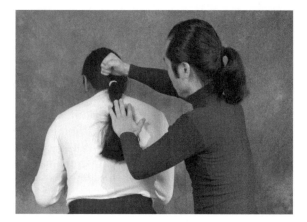

Hammer Fist Strike to the Brain Door

Striking the Brain Door on the rear of the skull can cause unbearable headache, dizziness or knockout. Hammer fist strike and palm strike are effective techniques for attacking this point.

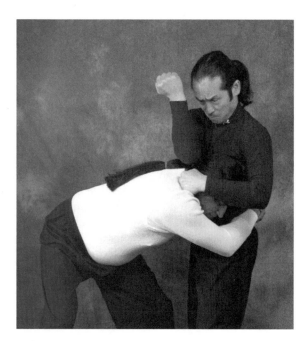

Elbow Strike to the Wind Mansion

The Wind Mansion is located on the midpoint of the nape of the neck in the depression above the hairline where the base of the skull meets the spine. This spot is one of the most vulnerable points on the human body. An elbow strike to this point can cause an immediate loss of consciousness. A forceful blow can cause an instant knockout or a fracture of the cervical vertebrae. A knifehand, elbow or forearm strike is recommended.

* CAUTION: This is a deadly spot and you should be extremely cautious when practicing this technique. For safety, never practice striking this point on another person. Use it only in a justified case of self-defense.

TOP OF THE HEAD

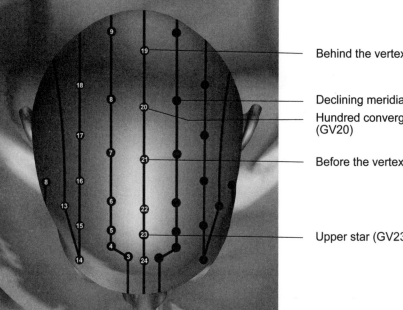

Behind the vertex (GV19)

Declining meridian (BL08)

Hundred convergences (GV20)

Before the vertex (GV21)

Upper star (GV23)

Behind the Vertex (GV19)

Location: 1.5 cun posterior to Hundred Convergences (GV20).
Nerve: The branch of the greater occipital nerve.
Blood Vessels: The branches of the occipital arteries and veins.
Techniques: Hammer fist, palm strike.
Effects: Knockout by shock to the brain.

Hundred Convergences (GV20)

Location: The midpoint of the line connecting the two apexes of the ears.
Nerve: The branch of the greater occipital nerve.
Blood Vessels: The superficial temporal arteries and veins, the occipital artery and vein.
Techniques: Hammer fist, palm strike.
Effects: Knockout by shock to the brain.

Declining Meridian (BL08)

Location: 1.5 cun posterior to Temporal Hairline Curve (BL07), lateral to the midline.
Nerve: The branch of the greater occipital nerve.
Blood Vessels: The branches of the occipital arteries and veins.
Techniques: Hammer fist, palm strike.
Effects: Intense headache, disorientation.

Before the Vertex (GV21)

Location: 1.5 cun anterior to Hundred Convergences (GV20).
Nerves: The branch of the frontal nerve, the greater occipital nerve.
Blood Vessels: The superficial temporal arteries and veins.
Techniques: Hammer fist, palm strike.
Effects: Disorientation, loss of consciousness.

Upper Star (GV23)

Location: 1 cun within the anterior hairline.
Nerve: The branch of the frontal nerve.
Blood Vessels: The branches of the frontal artery and vein, the branches of the superficial temporal artery and vein.
Techniques: Hammer fist, palm strike.
Effects: Dizziness, disorientation.

APPLICATIONS

Hammer Fist to Behind the Vertex

It is easier to strike this point from the rear. A powerful hammer fist on this spot can cause a concussion or severe headache. Repeated forceful blows on this region can result in a knockout or brain damage. Effective techniques are hammer fist and palm strike.

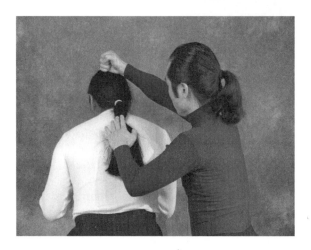

Striking the Hundred Convergences

The Hundred Convergences point is at the top of the skull, at the midpoint of the line connecting the apexes of the ears. For a shorter person, it is impossible to strike this point from a standing position. In groundfighting, you can strike this point with a palm heel, hammer fist, or knee kick. This technique can cause a knockout, severe headache, brain damage, or cause the opponent to bite his tongue, resulting in pain and bleeding.

Hammer Fist to the Declining Meridian

The Declining Meridian is located next to the Hundred Convergences point. The effects of striking this point are less severe than the Hundred Convergences point, however, striking with sufficient force can result in a concussion, dizziness, or loss of consciousness. Effective techniques are hammer fist and palm strike.

Palm Strike to the Before the Vertex

Before the Vertex is located before the Hundred Convergences point. This spot is tactically advantageous for intimidating the opponent. Effective techniques for striking this point are hammer fist and palm strike.

Headbutt to the Upper Star

The Upper Star point is located within the anterior hairline. Striking this region can numb the facial muscles and cause disorientation. You should have a good amount of experience in headbutting for this technique to be safe and effective. Safer and still effective techniques are hammer fist and palm strike.

VITAL POINTS ON THE NECK

ANTERIOR NECK

Protuberance Assistance (LI18)

Location: Adjacent to the Adam's Apple (AD-N1), on the common carotid artery.
Nerves: The branches of the cervical nerve, the vagus nerve, the cutaneous cervical nerve.
Blood Vessels: The branches of the jugular vein, carotid artery, thyroid artery.
Techniques: Knifehand strike, thumb push, punch, hammer fist, elbow strike, choking.
Effects: Pain in the upper neck, damage to the circulatory system, damage to the thyroid cartilage, unconsciousness, death.

Energy Abode (ST11)

Location: At the upper inner corner of the clavicle, between the sternal head and the clavicle head of the sternocleidomastoid muscle.
Nerves: The branches of the supraclavicular nerve and the ansa hypoglossi.
Blood Vessels: The jugular vein, the common carotid artery.
Techniques: Fingertip, knuckle thrust.
Effects: Unbearable pain in the lower neck, damage to the circulatory system, loss of consciousness.

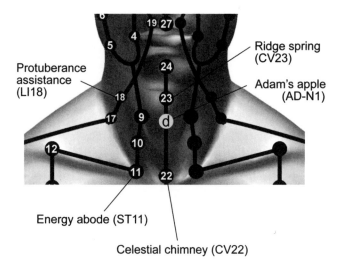

Protuberance assistance (LI18)

Ridge spring (CV23)

Adam's apple (AD-N1)

Energy abode (ST11)

Celestial chimney (CV22)

Ridge Spring (CV23)

Location: Approximately 1 cun above the Adam's Apple (AD-N1), in the depression above the hyoid bone.
Nerves: The branches of the cutaneous cervical nerve and the glossopharyngeal nerve, the hypoglossal nerve.
Blood Vessel: The anterior jugular vein.
Techniques: Arc hand strike, palm push or strike, knifehand strike, forearm push.
Effects: Pain in the upper neck, constriction of the airway, damage to the thyroid cartilage.

Adam's Apple (AD-N1)

Location: On the thyroid cartilage.
Nerves: The branches of the laryngeal nerve.
Blood Vessels: The branches of the anterior jugular vein and thyroid artery.
Techniques: Arc hand, knifehand, forearm strike, elbow strike, choking.
Effects: Damage to the thyroid cartilage, immobility of the neck, difficulty swallowing and breathing.

Celestial Chimney (CV22)

Location: In the center of the suprasternal fossa, also called the vertebrate trachea or windpipe.
Nerves: The medial supraclavicular nerve and the branches of the laryngeal nerve.
Blood Vessels: The branches of the jugular vein, the thyroid artery, aortic arch.
Techniques: Fingertip, knuckle thrust, hammer fist.
Effects: Damage to the circulatory system and the trachea, death.

APPLICATIONS

Strike the Protuberance Assistance

The Protuberance Assistance is on the sternocledo-mastoid muscle. This region is rich with networks of nerves and blood vessels such as the cervical nerves, Brachial Plexus and carotid artery and jugular vein. A fingertip press, knifehand strike, or hammer fist can contract the vessels and halt the blood passage. Choking this area can lead to unconsciousness or death.

Fingertip Press to the Energy Abode

The Energy Abode, also known as the suprasternal notch, is on the Brachial Plexus. A fingertip thrust into the point can cause electrifying pain in the arm and paralyze the body under the shoulder. Hammer fist strikes or downward elbow strikes can dislocate the clavicle from the sternum, which can cause hemor-rhaging, unconsciousness, and death.

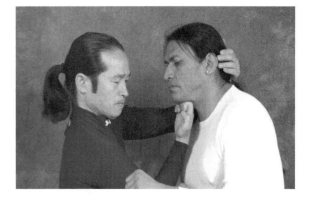

Knuckle Thrust to the Ridge Spring

The Ridge Spring is located approximately one inch above the Adam's Apple. There are multiple branches of nerves in this region, which makes the spot pain sensitive. Striking or thrusting the Ridge Spring causes pain in the upper neck, damage to the thyroid cartilage, or a knockout.

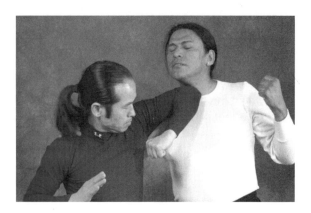

Elbow Strike to the Adam's Apple

The Adam's Apple is on the thyroid cartilage. Striking or pressing this spot causes pain, damage to the cartilage, immobility of the neck, difficulty swallowing and breathing, loss of consciousness or possibly death. Effective techniques are arc hand, knifehand, forearm strike, elbow strike, and choking. Never practice striking this point on a training partner because even a less than full power strike can cause permanent damage.

Press the Celestial Chimney

The Celestial Chimney is located on the windpipe, one of the most vulnerable parts of human body, covered only with tubular cartilage and a layer of skin. Pressing the region with a thumb tip or middle fingertip can damage the cartilage causing unbearable pain and stoppage of air and blood circulation. This technique is useful for subduing a larger aggressive assailant.

CHAPTER 7

VITAL POINTS ON THE
TRUNK

SIGNIFICANCE OF THE TRUNK

If the head is the command center of the body, the trunk is the hub of supply and disposal. The heart pumps blood out through the blood vessels, retrieves, and purifies the blood. The lungs take oxygen from the air into the bloodstream, and expel carbon dioxide from the bloodstream. The kidneys maintain the homeostatic balance of bodily fluids. The liver produces bile for digestion, detoxifies the body, and controls the biochemical reactions in the tissues. The stomach produces gastric acid and digestive enzymes, and holds food for digestion. The small intestine digests and absorbs food. The large intestine stores and excretes waste from the body. The vertebrae support the structure of the body along with the muscles. The nerves and blood vessels are highways for the supply and cleansing of the organs and muscles.

If anything goes wrong in these essential and interconnected parts of the anatomy, the body is in trouble. Vital point strikes to the trunk aim at doing just that. A strike, kick, thrust or press to the trunk can result in damage to one or several of the organs, resulting in anything from mild pain to death, depending on the force, accuracy and placement of the technique. Because the nerves in the trunk are linked to vital organs, it is sometimes not even necessary to deliver a direct blow to an organ to cause damage. Striking the Solar Plexus (Turtledove Tail: CV15) can paralyze neighboring muscles and cause the stoppage of breathing. A blow to the liver can shock the liver causing tormenting pain or a knockout. As shocks to the trunk multiply, the pain adds up resulting in catastrophic consequences. This is why boxers spend several rounds punching an opponent's body. Body blows weaken the organs, slow the body's responses, and drain the stamina of an opponent. The goal of attacking the opponent's trunk is to weaken him, mentally and physically. The damage can be lasting and complex.

The trunk is the largest and the clumsiest part of the body and thus an easy target. In training, you should toughen the trunk muscles, especially the abdominals, to withstand unavoidable blows to your body. You can also protect your trunk by using skillful slipping, weaving, and parrying techniques and speedy footwork.

Figure 7.1 Meridian charts for conception vessel and governing vessel.

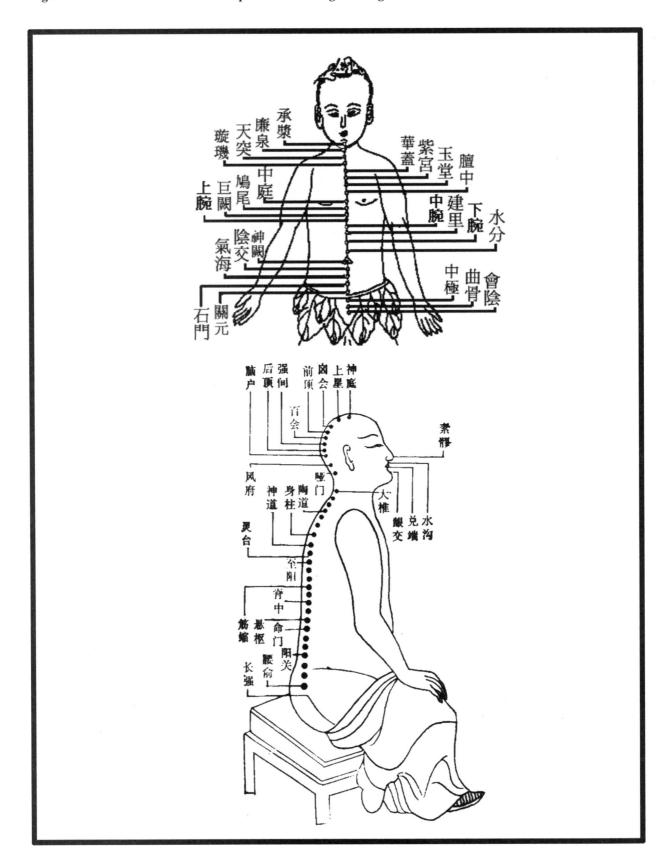

VITAL POINTS ON THE TRUNK

ANTERIOR TRUNK

Empty Basin (ST12)

Location: In the midpoint of the supraclavicular fossa.
Nerves: The intermediate supraclavicular nerve, the brachial plexus.
Blood Vessel: The transverse cervical artery.
Techniques: Fingertip, hammer fist, axe kick.
Effects: Pain and damage to the clavicle.

Energy Door (ST13)

Location: On the lower border of the clavicle, on the mammillary line.
Nerves: The branches of the supraclavicular nerve and the anterior thoracic nerve.
Blood Vessels: The branches of the thoracoacromial artery and vein.
Techniques: Fingertip, hammer fist, elbow strike, straight punch.
Effects: Sharp pain in the upper chest region.

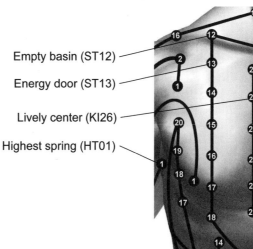

Lively Center (KI26)

Location: In the 1st intercostal space, 2 cun lateral from the anterior midline.
Nerves: The branch of the 1st intercostal nerve, the medial supraclavicular nerve.
Blood Vessels: The 1st intercostal artery and vein.
Techniques: Punch, hammer fist, elbow strike, fingertip strike or press.
Effects: Pain in the chest, loss of breath, damage to the heart.

Highest Spring (HT01)

Location: In the center of the axilla (armpit), on the medial side of the axillary artery.
Nerves: The ulnar nerve, the median nerve, the medial brachial cutaneous nerve.
Blood Vessel: The axillary artery.
Techniques: Knifehand strike, thumb push, punch, hammer fist, elbow strike, choking.
Effects: Pain in the shoulder and arm.

Breast Center (ST17)

Location: In the center of the nipple.
Nerves: The branches of the intercostal nerve.
Blood Vessels: The lateral mammary branches of posterior intercostal arteries.
Techniques: Palm, elbow strike, roundhouse kick.
Effects: Pain in the chest.

Cycle Gate (LV14)

Location: 2 ribs below the nipple in the 6th intercostal space.
Nerve: The 6th intercostal nerve.
Blood Vessels: The 6th intercostal artery and vein.
Techniques: Punch, hammer fist, elbow strike, knee kick, roundhouse kick.
Effects: Pain in the ribs, damage to the liver can cause a knockout.

Sun and Moon (GB24)

Location: Below the nipple between the 7th and 8th ribs.
Nerve: The 7th intercostal nerve.
Blood Vessels: The 7th intercostal artery and vein.
Techniques: Hook punch, uppercut, elbow strike, knee kick, roundhouse kick.
Effects: Pain in the ribs, damage to the liver can cause a knockout.

Not Contained (ST19)

Location: 6 cun above the umbilicus, 2 cun lateral to Great Tower Gate (CV14).
Nerve: The branch of the 7th intercostal nerve.
Blood Vessels: The branches of the 7th intercostal and superior epigastric arteries and veins.
Techniques: Punch, hammer fist, elbow strike, knee kick, roundhouse kick.
Effects: Pain in the ribs and diaphragm, damage to the liver can cause a knockout.

Gallbladder (AD-T2)

Location: 2 cun below the Solar Plexus, 3 cun lateral to Upper Venter (CV13).
Nerve: The branch of the 8th intercostal nerve.
Blood Vessels: The 8th intercostal artery and vein.
Techniques: Elbow strike, hook punch, uppercut, knee kick, roundhouse kick.
Effects: Knockout.

Abdominal Lament (SP16)

Location: 3 cun above Great Horizontal (SP15).
Nerve: The 8th intercostal nerve.
Blood Vessels: The 8th intercostal artery and vein.
Techniques: Hammer fist, knifehand, elbow strike, hook punch, knee kick, roundhouse kick.
Effects: Pain in the trunk, unconsciousness.

Camphorwood Gate (LV13)

Location: Below the free end of the 11th floating rib.
Nerve: The 10th intercostal nerve.
Blood Vessel: The branch of the 10th intercostal artery.
Techniques: Hammer fist, knifehand, elbow strike, hook punch, knee kick, roundhouse kick.
Effects: Severe pain in the trunk can cause loss of consciousness.

Outer Mound (ST26)

Location: 1 cun below, 2 cun lateral to the umbilicus.
Nerve: The branch of the 10th intercostal nerve.
Blood Vessels: The branches of the 10th intercostal and inferior epigastric arteries and veins.
Techniques: Hammer fist, knee kick, front kick, roundhouse kick.
Effects: Pain in the trunk, knockout.

Linking Path (GB28)

Location: Anterior and inferior to the anterior superior iliac spine.
Nerve: The ilioinguinal nerve.
Blood Vessels: The superficial iliac artery and vein.
Techniques: Thumb press, knuckle strike.
Effects: Sharp pain in the upper iliac spine region, paralysis of the leg.

Waterway (ST28)

Location: 3 cun below the umbilicus, 2 cun lateral to Passage of Origin (CV04).
Nerve: The branch of the subcostal nerve.
Blood Vessels: The branches of the subcostal artery and vein.
Techniques: Knee kick, hammer fist strike, front kick.
Effects: Excruciating pain in the lower abdomen.

Surging Gate (SP12)

Location: In the upper inguinal groove, on the level of the upper border of the pubic symphysis.

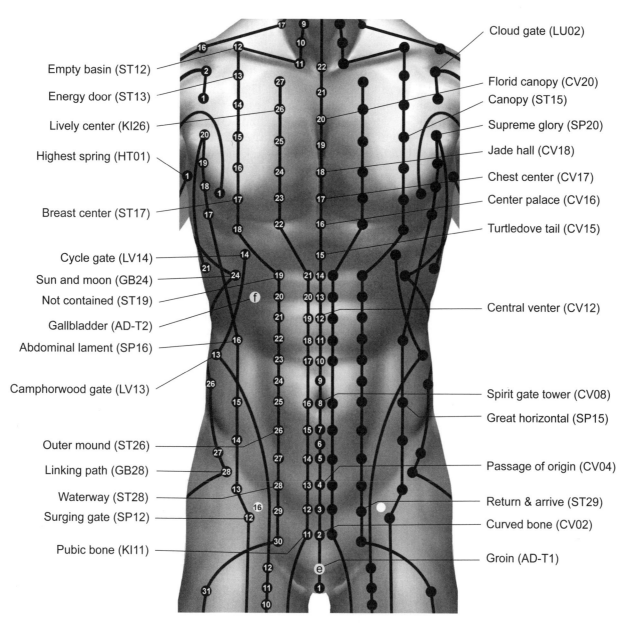

Empty basin (ST12)
Energy door (ST13)
Lively center (KI26)
Highest spring (HT01)
Breast center (ST17)
Cycle gate (LV14)
Sun and moon (GB24)
Not contained (ST19)
Gallbladder (AD-T2)
Abdominal lament (SP16)
Camphorwood gate (LV13)
Outer mound (ST26)
Linking path (GB28)
Waterway (ST28)
Surging gate (SP12)
Pubic bone (KI11)

Cloud gate (LU02)
Florid canopy (CV20)
Canopy (ST15)
Supreme glory (SP20)
Jade hall (CV18)
Chest center (CV17)
Center palace (CV16)
Turtledove tail (CV15)
Central venter (CV12)
Spirit gate tower (CV08)
Great horizontal (SP15)
Passage of origin (CV04)
Return & arrive (ST29)
Curved bone (CV02)
Groin (AD-T1)

Nerve: The traversal of the femoral nerve.
Blood Vessel: The femoral artery.
Techniques: Front pushing kick, stomping kick on the ground, elbow strike, knuckle punch.
Effects: Pain in the legs, possible temporary paralysis of the pelvic region.

Pubic Bone (KI11)

Location: 5 cun below the umbilicus, on the superior border of the pubic symphysis.
Nerve: The branch of the iliohypogastric nerve.
Blood Vessels: The inferior epigastric artery, the external pudendal artery.

Techniques: Knee kick, side kick, front kick.
Effects: Excruciating pain in the pelvic region.

Cloud Gate (LU02)

Location: In the depression below the acromial extremity of the clavicle.
Nerves: The intermediate and lateral supraclavicular nerve, the branches of the anterior thoracic nerve, the lateral cord of the Brachial Plexus.
Blood Vessels: The cephalic vein, the thoracoacromial artery and vein, the axillary artery.
Techniques: Punch, hammer fist, palm heel strike, forearm strike, elbow strike.
Effects: Pain in the chest, dislocation of the shoulder.

175

Florid Canopy (CV20)

Location: On the midline of the sternum, level with the 1st intercostal space.
Nerve: The branch of the 1st intercostal nerve.
Blood Vessels: The branches of the internal mammary arteries and veins.
Techniques: Punch, hammer fist, elbow strike.
Effects: Pain in the chest, damage to the heart.

Canopy (ST15)

Location: In the 2nd intercostal space, on the mammillary line.
Nerve: The branch of the anterior thoracic nerve.
Blood Vessels: The thoracoacromial artery and vein.
Techniques: Punch, hammer fist, elbow strike.
Effects: Shock to the lung, stoppage of breath, chest pain.

Supreme Glory (SP20)

Location: In the 2nd intercostal space, 6 cun lateral to the median line.
Nerves: The branches of the anterior thoracic nerve, the lateral cutaneous branch of the 2nd intercostal nerve.
Blood Vessels: The lateral thoracic artery and vein, the 2nd intercostal artery and vein.
Techniques: Punch, hammer fist, elbow strike.
Effects: Pain in the chest, damage to the heart.

Jade Hall (CV18)

Location: On the midline of the sternum, level with the 3rd intercostal space.
Nerve: The branch of the 3rd intercostal nerve.
Blood Vessels: The branches of the internal mammary arteries and veins.
Techniques: Straight punch, hammer fist, elbow strike, front kick, headbutt.
Effects: Pain in the Solar Plexus, damage to the heart, stoppage of breath, unconsciousness.

Chest Center (CV17)

Location: Between the nipples, level with the 4th intercostal space.
Nerve: The branch of the 4th intercostal nerve.
Blood Vessels: The branches of the internal mammary arteries and veins.
Techniques: Straight punch, elbow strike, front kick.
Effects: Damage to the sternum and heart, stoppage of breath, unconsciousness.

Center Palace (CV16)

Location: On the xiphoid process, level with the 5th intercostal space.
Nerve: The branch of the 6th intercostal nerve.
Blood Vessels: The branches of the internal mammary arteries and veins.
Techniques: Punch, hammer fist, elbow strike, finger-tip thrust, knuckle punch, front kick, back kick.
Effects: Pain in the Solar Plexus region, damage to the xiphoid process, instant death.

Turtledove Tail (CV15)

Location: On the Solar Plexus, 7 cun above the center of the umbilicus.
Nerve: The branch of the 7th intercostal nerve.
Blood Vessels: The superior epigastric artery and vein.
Techniques: Straight punch, uppercut, hammer fist, elbow strike, knee kick, front kick, back kick.
Effects: Pain in the Solar Plexus, stoppage of organ function, stoppage of breath, unconsciousness.

Central Venter (CV12)

Location: 4 cun above the umbilicus.
Nerve: The branch of the 7th intercostal nerve.
Blood Vessels: The superior epigastric artery and vein.
Techniques: Uppercut, hook, knee kick, front kick, side kick, back kick.
Effects: Pain in the abdominal region, stoppage of breath.

Spirit Gate Tower (CV08)

Location: In the center of the umbilicus.
Nerve: The branch of the 10th intercostal nerve.
Blood Vessels: The inferior epigastric artery and vein.
Techniques: Uppercut, hook, knee kick, front kick, side kick, back kick.
Effects: Sharp pain in the organs in the abdominal region.

Great Horizontal (SP15)

Location: 4 cun lateral to the umbilicus, on the mammillary line.
Nerve: The 10th intercostal nerve.
Blood Vessels: The 10th intercostal artery and vein.
Techniques: Knee kick, roundhouse kick.
Effects: Damage to the intestines.

Passage of Origin (CV04) (Danjun, Dantien)

Location: 3 cun below the umbilicus.
Nerve: The branch of the subcostal nerve.
Blood Vessels: The branches epigastric arteries and veins.
Techniques: Uppercut, hook punch, hammer fist, knee kick, front kick, side kick, back kick.
Effects: Sharp, sustained pain in the lower abdomen.

Return & Arrive (ST29)

Location: 4 cun below the umbilicus, 2 cun lateral to Central Pole (CV03).
Nerve: The iliohypogastric nerve.
Blood Vessels: The inferior epigastric artery and vein.
Techniques: Front pushing kick, side kick, back kick.
Effects: Sharp pain in the pelvic region, loss of balance, knockout.

Curved Bone (CV02)

Location: On the midline of the abdomen just above the pubic symphysis.
Nerve: The branch of the iliohypogastric nerve.
Blood Vessels: The branches of the inferior epigastric artery and the obturator artery.
Techniques: Front kick, hammer fist, downward punch, elbow strike.
Effects: Pain in the pubic region, possible paralysis.

Groin (AD-T1)

Location: Under the pubic symphysis in the genital region.
Nerves: The branches of the perineal nerve.
Blood Vessels: The branches of perineal artery and vein.
Techniques: Knee kick, front kick, stomp kick, back kick, palm strike, back fist.
Effects: Damage to the groin, severe pain, loss of consciousness.

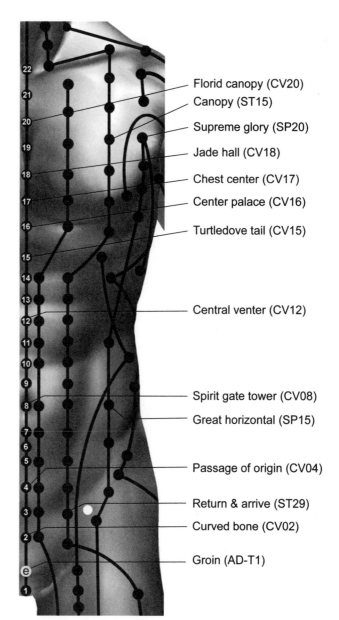

Florid canopy (CV20)
Canopy (ST15)
Supreme glory (SP20)
Jade hall (CV18)
Chest center (CV17)
Center palace (CV16)
Turtledove tail (CV15)
Central venter (CV12)
Spirit gate tower (CV08)
Great horizontal (SP15)
Passage of origin (CV04)
Return & arrive (ST29)
Curved bone (CV02)
Groin (AD-T1)

177

APPLICATIONS

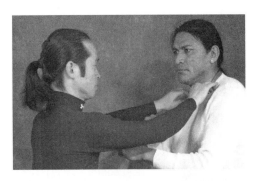

Fingertip Thrust to the Empty Basin

The Empty Basin is located at the lateral end of the clavicle under which the Brachial Plexus passes. With the tip of the middle finger, press the point deeply and quickly to intensify the pain. Alternatively, striking this spot with a snapping downward elbow strike can cause dislocation of the shoulder.

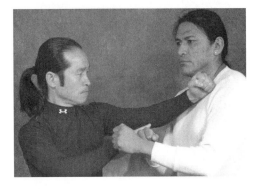

Hammer Fist to the Energy Door

Striking this spot causes a startling pain that can stop the opponent's breathing momentarily. Pressing the spot causes deep pain in the chest. Lock your arm and use your body weight to add more force when pressing.

Strike the Lively Center

The Lively Center is located on top of the lung. An elbow strike or downward punch to this region can stop the function of the lung causing difficulty in breathing. Bend your elbow tightly and snap the edge of the elbow into the target. A forceful strike can damage the heart due to a sudden increase in the internal pressure of the chest cavity.

Kick the Highest Spring

The armpit is a hidden spot that has shock value in fighting. When your opponent punches or grabs you, deflect his arm and kick quickly to the armpit. The pain is excruciating. This is a good spot to attack to slow the opponent's punching speed and impair his grappling ability.

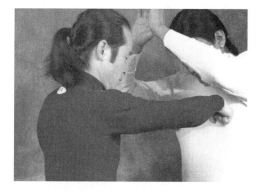

Punch the Breast Center

The Breast Center is the nipple. We don't normally attack this region, thus it can be a surprise. Punch quickly and precisely at the nipple. A well aimed punch will result in a shooting stinging pain spreading throughout the opponent's chest, which can delay his reaction time. This is a tactically advantageous spot to attack.

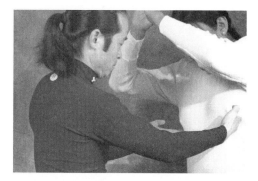

Knuckle Punch to the Cycle Gate

Behind the Cycle Gate is the liver. The impact of a well aimed knuckle punch can penetrate deeply into the liver. It can stop or impair the function of the internal organs, causing a knockout. While punching, keep your elbow bent and load your body weight into the target to deliver extra power.

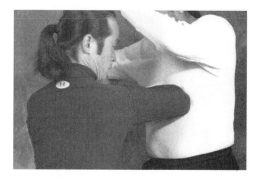

Elbow Strike to the Sun and Moon

This is one of the most popular regions for knocking out an opponent. An elbow strike to the right side of the body can cause unbearable pain in the liver and stoppage of breath. Pivot your body inward while striking to deliver more focused power to the Solar Plexus. Aim your force into the spinal cord.

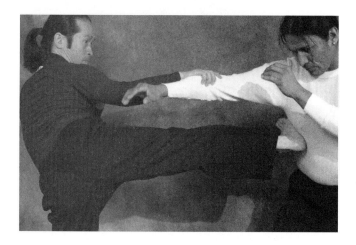

Side Kick the Not Contained

The Not Contained spot is the location of the liver and the gallbladder which are covered by the diaphragm. This spot is connected to the Solar Plexus, therefore a forceful kick can damage all of these organs and generate severe pain in the region, causing a knockout. Bend your knee and snap your kick quickly at the target when the opponent inhales. A well timed side kick can cause an instant stoppage of breath and fracture the ribs.

Knee Kick to the Gallbladder

The Gallbladder is located under the liver between the 8th and 9th vertebrae on the right side of the body. Striking this spot can rupture the gallbladder and injure the liver. Kicking or punching upward toward the spine from the 9th vertebra can shock the liver causing the opponent to lose his fighting energy and will.

Elbow Strike the Abdominal Lament

The Abdominal Lament is at the bottom of the floating ribs. Step in stealthily and snap a tightly bent elbow into the target. This technique can damage the large intestine and the liver, causing piercing pain in the upper abdomen.

Knee Kick to the Camphorwood Gate

A knee kick to this target causes severe pain in the kidney, making this a good technique to use against a clinching opponent. The impact of a knee kick can penetrate deep into the Celiac Plexus. To increase the chance of a knockout, combine the knee kick with an inward elbow strike to the chin or an uppercut to the Solar Plexus.

Roundhouse Ball Kick to the Outer Mound

The Outer Mound is on the surface of the ureter. Below it is the appendix. A kick to this spot causes an excruciating pain that can make the opponent kneel down suddenly and involuntarily. This vital point is good for stopping an opponent who rushes in recklessly.

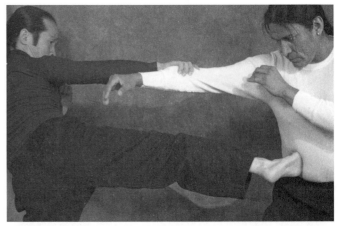

Snap Kick to the Linking Path

The Linking Path bridges between the leg and the trunk. This is a pain sensitive spot due to the nerves from the Lumbar Plexus that run down to the leg. Parry the opponent's attack while moving slightly outward, and throw a snappy roundhouse kick. Kicking, jabbing, or poking this region gives you a tactical advantage by reducing the mobility of the opponent's legs.

Push Kick to the Waterway

This spot is a good target for knocking down an incoming opponent. Since this spot is located approximately 2 inches lateral to the center of the body (Danjeon or Dantien), kicking the Waterway makes the opponent's body rotate and drop to the ground, instantly taking away his equilibrium.

Snapping Punch to the Surging Gate

The Surging Gate is located in the upper inguinal groove, on the level of the upper border of the pubic symphysis. Block the opponent's attack then throw a quick penetrating punch at the target. Punching the Surging Gate causes acute pain on the femoral nerve. Kicking this spot can paralyze the pelvic region.

Kick the Pubic Bone

The Pubic Bone is on the superior border of the pubic symphysis. Most martial artists, at one point or another, have been kicked in this region. The intense pain lasts for several minutes. The pain is often unbearable and can stop the function of the organs in the pelvic region. A knee kick to this point is effective in close combat. Pull the opponent toward you and drive your knee into the target while keeping your standing knee slightly bent for balance.

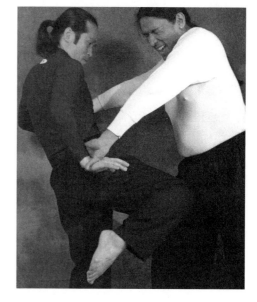

Elbow Strike the Cloud Gate

The Cloud Gate is in the depression below the end of the clavicle. Striking this spot produces severe pain in the chest and can cause dislocation of the shoulder. When the opponent attempts to grab you from behind, turn and lift your elbow in front of his face then drop it onto the target immediately. You may throw multiple strikes on the same spot or in combination to the face.

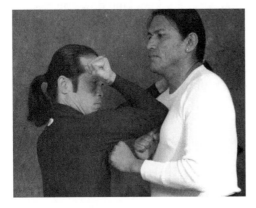

Elbow Strike the Florid Canopy

The Florid Canopy is in the midline of the sternum which is a long, flat fragile bone connected to the collarbone and ribs. Behind the sternum is the heart and Cardiac Plexus. A forceful downward elbow strike to this region can fracture the bone and damage the heart.

Hammer Fist to the Canopy

The Canopy is between the nipple and the clavicle. Beneath it is the lung. When the opponent attempts to grab you from behind, side step and strike the Canopy with a hammer fist. Hammering this spot can shock the lung causing a loss of breath and stabbing pain.

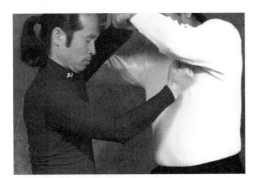

Hammer Fist to the Supreme Glory

The Supreme Glory is located lateral to the Canopy. Striking this point causes a tearing pain in the chest and can cause damage to the heart. It also impairs the opponent's use of his hand and arm.

Elbow Strike to the Jade Hall

The Jade Hall is on the midline of the sternum. Behind it is the Cardiac Plexus. When the opponent attempts to lift you, pull his neck toward you and slam the Jade Hall point with an elbow strike. This strike can damage the heart, cause loss of breath or a knockout. At the very least, you'll make him change his mind about lifting you up.

Elbow Strike to the Chest Center

The Chest Center is between the nipples on the sternum. Beneath it is the Cardiac Plexus. When your opponent lifts his arms, stab the tip of your elbow into the Chest Center. This penetrating strike will cause damage to the sternum, loss of breath and possibly a knockout.

Punch to the Center Palace

The Center Palace is on the xiphoid process, which is the smallest of the three divisions of the sternum and serves as a fragile protective device for the heart. As soon as your opponent raises his hands to grab you, punch the Center Palace. This strike can easily damage the xiphoid process and can cause a stoppage of breathing, and even instant death.

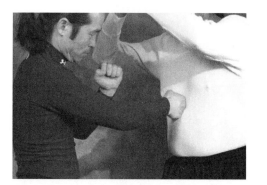

Punch to the Turtledove Tail

This spot is the Solar Plexus, which is rich with vital nerves and blood vessels. You do not need to hit hard but time your strike to impact when your opponent inhales. Striking this spot produces intense pain and can cause a stoppage of functioning in nearby organs, loss of breath, and loss of consciousness. Because of the network of nerves in this area, even an imprecise strike can cause pain and debilitation.

Knee Kick to the Central Venter

The Central Venter is above the umbilicus. When the opponent attempts to reach for you, lean slightly to the side and throw your tightly bent knee at the target. A kick to this point can cause a loss of breath.

Punch the Spirit Gate Tower

This point is the center of the umbilicus. Punching the Spirit Gate Tower is a good defensive tactic in close combat. Against a knee kick, block and punch deeply into the target. This can cause sharp pain in the organs in the abdominal region. (below)

Elbow Strike to the Great Horizontal

The Great Horizontal is a pain-sensitive area on the Lumbar Plexus. Duck your opponent's lunge or strike and throw a short elbow strike. Attacking the Great Horizontal can damage the intestines. (above)

Knuckle Punch to the Passage of Origin

The Passage of the Origin is also called the Danjeon or Dantien. Strike it as you would thrust a needle into a balloon to pop it. Punching here causes sharp sustained pain in the lower abdomen, and reduces the opponent's stamina. (right)

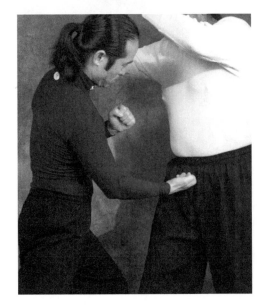

Kick the Return & Arrive

The Return & Arrive is located below the umbilicus. As the opponent moves in, move to the side slightly, bend your knee and snap your foot at the target. Impact to this spot disturbs the balance of the opponent's inner energy. It causes acute pain in the pelvic crest region and can knock out the opponent.

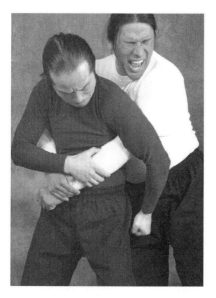

Hammer Fist to the Curved Bone

The Curved Bone is on the midline of the abdomen just above the pubic symphysis. As you deflect the opponent's attack, snap your hammer fist on a lateral angle. To follow up, you can immediately take the opponent down to his rear. The pain from this strike is excruciating and can cause paralysis.

Hammer Fist to the Groin

The groin is under the pubic symphysis in the genital region. When the opponent grabs you from behind, move your hip to the side and slam the target with your rear hammer fist. This strike causes instant pain and can damage the groin permanently. (It is illegal to hit the groin in most tournament fighting.) In practice, you should use extreme caution for safety and wear protective gear. In a self-defense situation, you can also apply pinching, pressing or thrusting techniques to the soft tissue of the groin to distract or manipulate the position of your opponent.

Posterior Trunk

Great Hammer (GV14)

Location: Between the 7th cervical vertebra and 1st thoracic vertebra.
Nerves: The branches of the 1st thoracic nerve and 8th cervical nerve.
Blood Vessels: The branch of transverse cervical artery.
Techniques: Hammer fist, palm strike, elbow strike.
Effects: Knockout.

Body Pillar (GV12)

Location: Below the 3rd thoracic vertebra.
Nerve: The branch of the 3rd thoracic nerve.
Blood Vessels: The branch of the 3rd intercostal artery.
Techniques: Hammer fist, palm strike, elbow strike.
Effects: Knockout by shock to the brain and heart.

Spirit Path (GV11)

Location: Below the 5th thoracic vertebra.
Nerve: The branch of the 5th thoracic nerve.
Blood Vessel: The branch of the 5th intercostal artery.
Techniques: Hammer fist, punch, elbow strike.
Effects: Shock to the heart.

Spirit Tower (GV10)

Location: Below the 6th thoracic vertebra, on the opposite side of the Solar Plexus.
Nerve: The branch of the 6th thoracic nerve.
Blood Vessel: The branch of the 6th intercostal artery.
Techniques: Hammer fist, punch, elbow strike.
Effects: Shock to the heart, stoppage of breath.

Extremity of Yang (GV09)

Location: Below the 7th thoracic vertebra.
Nerve: The branch of the 7th thoracic nerve.
Blood Vessel: The branch of the 7th intercostal artery.
Techniques: Hammer fist, punch, elbow strike.
Effects: Shock to the heart, stoppage of breath.

Suspended Pivot (GV05)

Location: Below the 1st lumbar vertebra.
Nerves: The branches of the lumbar nerve.
Blood Vessel: The branch of the lumbar artery.
Techniques: Hammer fist, punch, elbow strike.
Effects: Shock to viscera (preaortic nodes) anterior to the lumbar vertebrae.

Life Gate (GV04)

Location: Below the 2nd lumbar vertebra.
Nerves: The branches of the lumbar nerve.
Blood Vessel: The branch of the lumbar artery.
Techniques: Knee kick, side kick, elbow strike.
Effects: Shock to viscera (preaortic nodes) anterior to the lumbar vertebrae, fracture of lumbar vertebrae.

Lumbar Yang Joint (GV03)

Location: Below the 4th lumbar vertebra.
Nerves: The branches of the lumbar nerve.
Blood Vessel: The branch of the lumbar artery.
Techniques: Knee kick, side kick, elbow strike.
Effects: Fracture of the lower back, paralysis of the lower body, knockout by shock to the spinal cord.

Lumbar Transport (GV02)

Location: In the hiatus of the sacrum.
Nerve: The branch of the coccygeal nerve.
Blood Vessels: The branches of the median sacral artery and vein.
Techniques: Knee kick, front kick, back kick.
Effects: Paralysis of the entire body, fracture of the tailbone, knockout by shock to the spinal cord.

Lasting Strong (GV01)

Location: Midway between the tip of the coccyx and the anus.
Nerves: The branches of the coccygeal nerve, the hemorrhoid nerve.
Blood Vessels: The branches of the inferior hemorrhoid artery and vein.
Techniques: Knee kick, front kick.
Effects: Paralysis of the entire body, knockout by shock to the spinal cord.

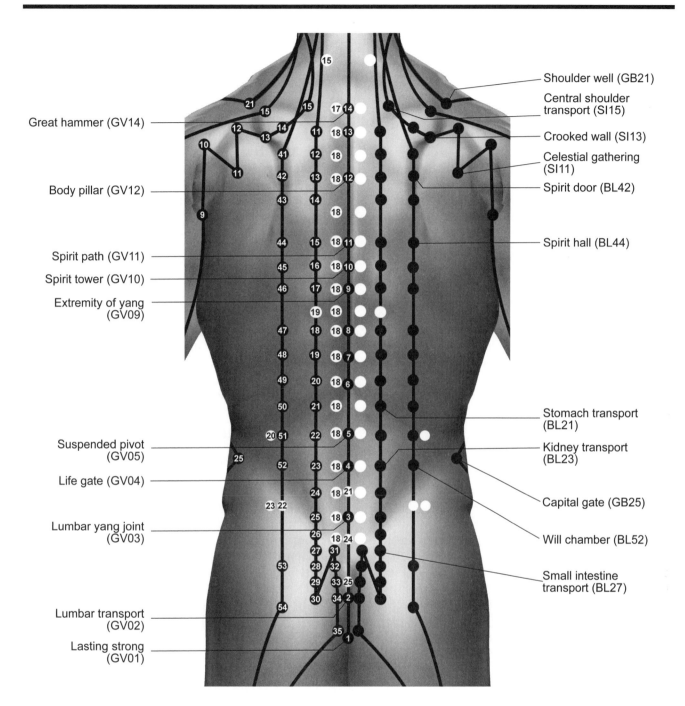

Shoulder well (GB21)
Central shoulder transport (SI15)
Crooked wall (SI13)
Celestial gathering (SI11)
Spirit door (BL42)
Spirit hall (BL44)
Stomach transport (BL21)
Kidney transport (BL23)
Capital gate (GB25)
Will chamber (BL52)
Small intestine transport (BL27)

Great hammer (GV14)
Body pillar (GV12)
Spirit path (GV11)
Spirit tower (GV10)
Extremity of yang (GV09)
Suspended pivot (GV05)
Life gate (GV04)
Lumbar yang joint (GV03)
Lumbar transport (GV02)
Lasting strong (GV01)

Shoulder Well (GB21)

Location: Midway between Great Hammer (GV14) and the acromion of the shoulder.
Nerves: The branch of the supraclavicular nerve, the accessory nerve.
Blood Vessels: The transverse cervical artery and vein.
Techniques: Knifehand strike, hammer fist, thumb press, fingertip press, elbow strike.
Effects: Paralysis of the shoulder and arm, shock to the Brachial Plexus.

Central Shoulder Transport (SI15)

Location: 2 cun lateral to the lower edge of the 7th cervical vertebra.
Nerves: The branches of the 1st and 2nd thoracic nerves, the accessory nerve.
Blood Vessels: The transverse cervical artery and vein.
Techniques: Knifehand, hammer fist, elbow strike.
Effects: Severe pain on the upper shoulder.

187

Crooked Wall (SI13)

Location: On the medial extremity of the suprascapula fossa.
Nerves: The lateral branch of the 2nd thoracic nerve, the accessory nerve.
Blood Vessels: The branches of the transverse cervical artery and vein.
Techniques: Knifehand strike, hammer fist, elbow strike.
Effects: Severe pain on the upper back, paralysis of the shoulder and arm.

Celestial Gathering (SI11)

Location: On the scapula in a depression in the center of the infrascapula fossa at the junction of the upper and middle third between the lower border of the scapula spine and the inferior angle of the scapula.
Nerve: The suprascapula nerve.
Blood Vessels: The branches of the circumflex scapula artery and vein.
Techniques: Hammer fist, elbow strike, palm heel strike.
Effects: Paralysis of the shoulder and arm, damage to the scapula.

Spirit Door (BL42)

Location: 3 cun lateral to the lower border of the 3rd thoracic vertebra.
Nerves: The branches of the 2nd and 3rd thoracic nerves.
Blood Vessels: The branches of the intercostal artery and vein, the branch of the transverse cervical artery.
Techniques: Hammer fist, elbow strike, palm heel strike.
Effects: Paralysis of the shoulder and arm, damage to the scapula and the lung, stoppage of breath.

Spirit Hall (BL44)

Location: 3 cun lateral to the lower border of the 5th thoracic vertebra.
Nerves: The branches of the 4th and 5th thoracic nerves.
Blood Vessels: The branches of the intercostal artery and vein, the branch of the transverse cervical artery.
Techniques: Hammer fist, back fist, elbow strike, thumb press.
Effects: Acute pain in the back.

Stomach Transport (BL21)

Location: 1.5 cun lateral to the lower border of the 12th thoracic vertebra.
Nerve: The branch of the 12th thoracic nerve.
Blood Vessels: The branches of the subcostal artery and vein.
Techniques: Hammer fist, uppercut, elbow strike, thumb press, knee kick, roundhouse kick, side kick.
Effects: Pain in the kidney region, loss of consciousness due to pain in the stomach and kidney.

Kidney Transport (BL23)

Location: 1.5 cun lateral to the lower border of the 2nd lumbar vertebra.
Nerve: The branch of the 1st lumbar nerve.
Blood Vessels: The branches of the 2nd lumbar artery and vein.
Techniques: Hammer fist, uppercut, elbow strike, thumb press, knee kick, roundhouse kick, side kick.
Effects: Pain throughout the trunk, loss of consciousness due to pain in the kidney, loss of stamina.

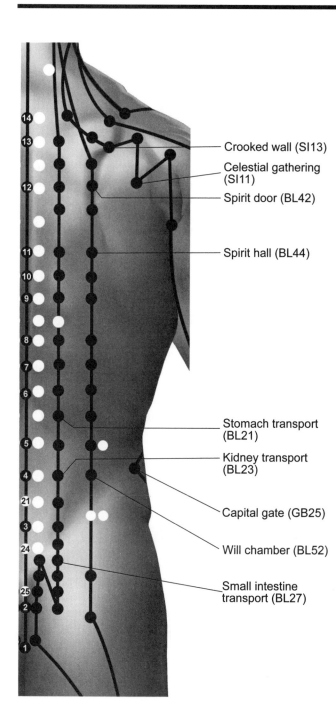

Crooked wall (SI13)

Celestial gathering (SI11)

Spirit door (BL42)

Spirit hall (BL44)

Stomach transport (BL21)

Kidney transport (BL23)

Capital gate (GB25)

Will chamber (BL52)

Small intestine transport (BL27)

Capital Gate (GB25)

Location: On the lower edge of the free end of the 12th rib.
Nerve: The 11th intercostal nerve.
Blood Vessels: The 11th intercostal artery and vein.
Techniques: Hammer fist, uppercut, elbow strike, thumb press, knee kick, roundhouse kick.
Effects: Paralysis of the entire body.

Will Chamber (BL52)

Location: 3 cun lateral to the lower border of the 2nd lumbar vertebra.
Nerves: The branches of the 12th thoracic nerve and 1st lumbar nerve.
Blood Vessels: The branches of the 2nd lumbar artery and vein.
Techniques: Hammer fist, uppercut, elbow strike, thumb press, knee kick, side kick.
Effects: Pain throughout the trunk.

Small Intestine Transport (BL27)

Location: At the level of the 1st posterior sacral foramen
Nerve: The branch of the 1st sacral nerve.
Blood Vessels: The branches of the lateral sacral artery and vein.
Techniques: Thumb press, hammer fist, elbow strike, knee kick, roundhouse kick.
Effects: Sharp pain in the hip and leg, numbness in the leg

APPLICATIONS

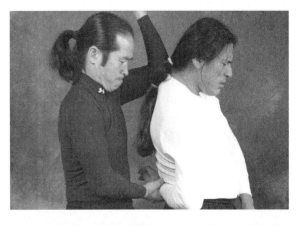

Elbow Strike to the Great Hammer

The Great Hammer is on the shoulder above the Brachial Plexus. This is one of the most vulnerable spots on the back. When the opponent refuses to cooperate during a restraint or immobilization technique, drop your elbow downward on the shoulder. This strike can instantly drop the opponent to the ground and possibly result in a knockout.

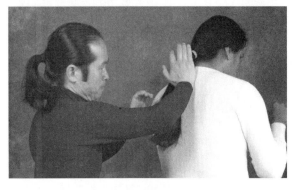

Palm Heel Strike to the Body Pillar

The Body Pillar is located on the upper back. With the bony edge of the palm heel, strike the target with snapping force. This strike can cause punishing pain in the heart, stoppage of breath, and loss of consciousness.

Elbow Strike to the Spirit Path

The Spirit Path is located at the center of the posterior heart. When the opponent attempts to tackle you, lower your center of gravity and drop an elbow strike on the target. This strike can cause punishing pain in the heart, stoppage of breath, and loss of consciousness.

Elbow Strike to the Spirit Tower

The Spirit Tower is located opposite the Solar Plexus on the back of the body. When you have successfully positioned yourself behind an opponent, grab one of his shoulders for control and leverage, and strike the Spirit Tower with a downward elbow. Twist your body into the target to add more power. This technique can cause an instant stoppage of breath.

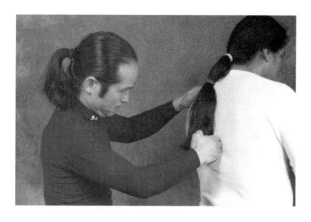

Knuckle Punch to the Extremity of Yang

The Extremity of Yang is located behind the Celiac Plexus. With your knuckles, strike forcefully into the target. For beginners, a conventional punch is a safer technique. Hitting this spot can cause unbearable pain in the back and stoppage of breath.

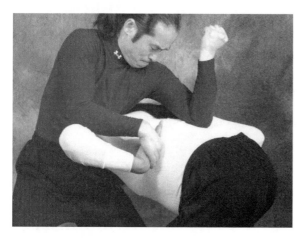

Elbow Strike to the Suspended Pivot

The Suspended Pivot region is loaded with nerves and ganglia. When your opponent attempts to escape from your control, strike this point with a downward elbow strike. Striking the Suspended Pivot can damage the lumbar vertebrae.

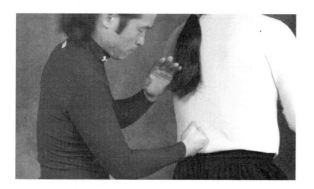

Punch to the Life Gate

The Life Gate region is rich with nerves, ganglia and major blood vessels. When you have an opportunity to attack from the rear, lower your body and punch slightly upward into the target. You may combine this attack with a knee kick and takedown to gain control over the opponent. Striking this spot can cause shock to the lower back.

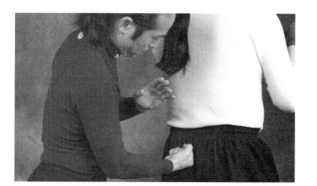

Punch to the Lumbar Yang Joint

The Lumbar Yang Joint is just below the belt line on the back, a region that is also the site of the abdominal aorta and small intestine. Keep your elbow bent and snap the punch into the target using your body weight to increase the force of your punch. This causes sudden shock to the inner organs and lower back pain.

191

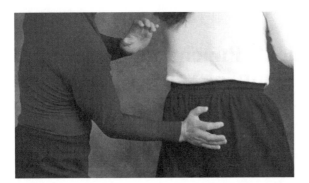

Palm Heel Strike to the Lumbar Transport

The Lumbar Transport is located on the tailbone, where the branch of the coccygeal nerve passes. With your elbow bent, snap a palm heel at the target using your body weight to increase the force of the strike. A knee kick to this spot can cause paralysis of the entire body, fracture of the tailbone, and a knockout by shock to the spinal cord.

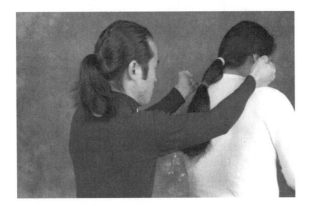

Knee Kick to the Lasting Strong

The Lasting Strong is hidden midway between the tip of the coccyx and the anus. When you are faced with a tough opponent, kicking this spot can cause paralysis of the whole body. This technique is dangerous and you should refrain from using it except in justified self-defense situations.

Hammer Fists to the Shoulder Well

The Shoulder Well is located between the median line and the acromion on the shoulder on top of the Brachial Plexus. Snap your hammer fists quickly into the target like hammering nails. Striking this spot can cause paralysis of the shoulders and arms and potentially loss of consciousness.

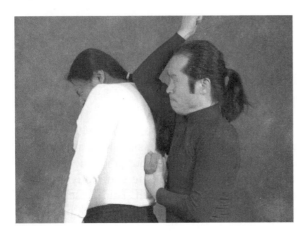

Elbow Strike to the Central Shoulder Transport

The Central Shoulder Transport is located below the shoulder, on the Brachial Plexus. While controlling the opponent from the rear, striking this target with your elbow is a good way to initiate a takedown. Pounding this spot can cause paralysis of the shoulder and arm.

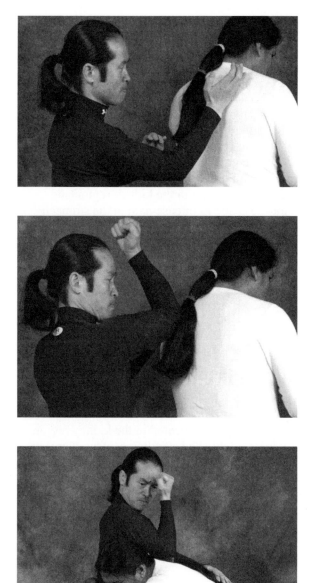

Knifehand Strike to the Crooked Wall

The Crooked Wall is located below the spine of the scapula. This spot is pain sensitive due to the location of the accessory nerve and the trapezius muscle. For effectiveness, strike quickly at an angle with your knifehand. This technique can cause severe pain on the upper back and paralysis of the shoulder and arm.

Elbow Strike to the Celestial Gathering

The Celestial Gathering is located on the scapula in a depression in the middle of the scapula. Raise your arm and snap your elbow quickly down into the Celestial Gathering. Striking this spot can cause paralysis of the shoulder and arm, and damage to the scapula.

Elbow Strike to the Spirit Door

The Spirit Door is located at the inner edge of the scapula. Branches of the Cardiac Plexus spread into the region. Raise your elbow and drop it deeply into the target. This technique can shock the heart and cause a stoppage of breath, paralysis of the shoulder and arm, and damage to the scapula and the lung.

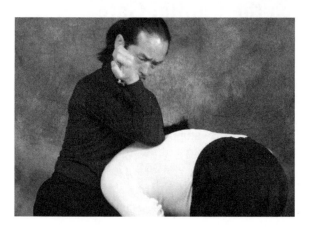

Elbow Strike to the Spirit Hall

The Spirit Hall is located at the inner bottom of the scapula. This region is the location of the branches of the Cardiac Plexus, the heart and lungs. When your opponent tries to tackle you, hold his body for balance, raise your other arm and nail your elbow into the target. Striking this spot can cause acute pain in the muscles on the back, stoppage of breath and sustained pain along the border of the scapula.

Knee Kick to the Stomach Transport

The Stomach Transport is located next to the upper edge of the kidney, where the lumbar vertebra joins with the thoracic vertebra. When you've pinned the opponent on the ground and want to finish the fight, raise your leg and drop your knee on the target. This technique can cause pain in the kidney region and unconsciousness due to intense pain in the stomach and kidney.

Elbow Strike to the Kidney Transport

The Kidney Transport is located in the kidney region. Once you have established standing control over your opponent, raise your arm quickly and snap it into the target with a forceful twist to drop your opponent to the ground. This strike can cause acute pain in the kidney region, potentially leading to unconsciousness.

Punch the Capital Gate

The Capital Gate is on the lower edge of the free end of the 12th rib. Also in this region are the kidneys on both sides of the body, the liver on the right side of the body, and branches of the Celiac Plexus. When your opponent attempts to tackle you, apply a guillotine choke, then strike the Capital Gate repetitively. Striking this spot can cause stoppage of breath, paralysis, and intense pain in the area of the kidney and liver.

Elbow Strike to the Will Chamber

The Will Chamber is located at the lower center of the kidney next to the Kidney Transport. When you escape from your opponent's choke and move to his back, repeatedly strike the Will Chamber with quick elbow strikes. Striking this spot can cause excruciating pain in the kidney region and loss of consciousness due to damage to the kidney.

Elbow Strike to the Small Intestine Transport

The Small Intestine Transport is next to the sacral foramen. When your opponent attempts to escape from your armbar, sharply drive your elbow into this spot. This technique causes acute pain in the lower back and the leg, making it easier for you to take the opponent down to the ground.

Figure 7.2 Meridian charts for the body.

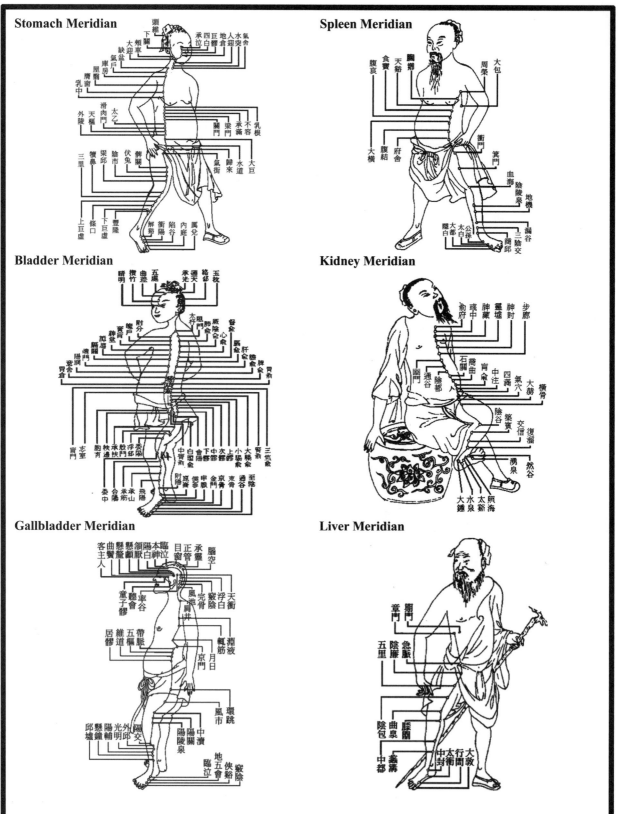

CHAPTER 8

VITAL POINTS ON THE
ARM & HAND

SIGNIFICANCE OF THE ARM & HAND

When you control the opponent's hand, you can manipulate his arm. With the opponent's arm under your control, you can dominate over his body. When his body is under your control, you can access his neck and head, which is essential to victory. Thus the hand and arm are a valuable entrance to the center of the opponent's body. A skillful martial artist can manipulate the opponent by applying pressure to a single finger.

In grappling, pressing or striking points on the wrist, hand or forearm can make an opponent involuntarily release his grip on you, allowing you to escape from a grab, choke or lock. When your opponent has you in a hold or grab, meeting force with force is a draining strategy and one that is nearly impossible to win with if you are the smaller fighter. But by strategically pressing or striking pain sensitive points on the opponent's gripping hand or arm, you can induce a surprise reaction in the opponent, giving you a brief opening to free yourself and follow up with a more powerful technique.

Attacking the arms and hands is also a way to disable an opponent's fastest and most dexterous weapons. By striking the Lesser Sea (HT03), you can cause numbness in the arm, making it temporarily impossible for the opponent to use his arm to attack or control you. By striking the Lower Biceps (AD-UE1), you can slow the opponent's punching speed and disrupt his striking strategy.

Vital Points on the Arm

Anterior Arm

Celestial Storehouse (LU03)

Location: On the radial side of the upper biceps.
Nerve: The lateral brachial cutaneous nerve.
Blood Vessels: The cephalic vein, branches of the brachial artery and vein.
Techniques: Knifehand strike, hammer fist strike, thumb press.
Effects: Excruciating pain on the biceps, paralysis of the arm.

Guarding White (LU04)

Location: On the medial aspect of the upper arm, 1 cun below the Celestial Storehouse (LU03).
Nerve: The lateral brachial cutaneous nerve.
Blood Vessels: The cephalic vein, branches of the brachial artery and vein.
Techniques: Knifehand strike, hammer fist strike, thumb press.
Effects: Unbearable pain on the biceps, acute muscle spasm, paralysis of the arm.

Lower Biceps (AD-UE1)

Location: On the lower biceps muscle.
Nerve: The lateral antebrachial cutaneous nerve.
Blood Vessel: The branch of the brachial artery.
Techniques: Knifehand strike, hammer fist strike, thumb press.
Effects: Extreme pain on the biceps, muscle swelling and injury, paralysis of the arm.

Celestial storehouse (LU03)
Guarding white (LU04)
Lower biceps (AD-UE1)
Cubit marsh (LU05)
Marsh at the bend (PC03)

Cubit Marsh (LU05)

Location: On the radial side of the tendon of the biceps, when the elbow is slightly flexed.
Nerves: The lateral antebrachial cutaneous nerve, the radial nerve.
Blood Vessels: The branches of the radial recurrent artery and vein, the cephalic vein.
Techniques: Thumb press, knifehand strike.
Effects: Excruciating pain in the arm.

Marsh at the Bend (PC03)

Location: On the transverse cubital crease, at the ulnar side of the biceps tendon.
Nerve: The median nerve.
Blood Vessels: The brachial artery and vein.
Techniques: Thumb press.
Effects: Tormenting pain in the arm.

Collection Orifice (LU06)

Location: On the palmar aspect of the forearm.
Nerves: The lateral antebrachial cutaneous nerve, the radial nerve.
Blood Vessels: The radial artery and vein, the cephalic vein.
Techniques: Thumb press, knifehand strike, forearm strike.
Effects: Tormenting pain in the arm.

Two Whites (EX-UE2)

Location: Two points on the anterior forearm, 4 cun from the crease of the wrist.
Nerve: The radial nerve.
Blood Vessel: The radial artery.
Techniques: Thumb press, knifehand strike, hammer fist, forearm strike.
Effects: Excruciating pain in the arm, paralysis of the forearm.

Inner Passage (PC06)

Location: 2 cun above the transverse crease of the wrist, between the palmaris longus and flexor carpi radialis.
Nerves: The branches of the antebrachial cutaneous nerves, the median nerve.
Blood Vessels: The median artery and vein.
Techniques: Thumb press.
Effects: Pain in the arm.

Broken Sequence (LU07)

Location: Superior to the styloid process of the radius.
Nerves: The lateral antebrachial cutaneous nerve, the radial nerve.
Blood Vessel: Branches of the radial artery and vein, the cephalic vein.
Techniques: Knifehand strike, thumb press.
Effects: Sharp pain in the arm.

Supreme Abyss (LU09)

Location: At the transverse crease of the wrist.
Nerves: The lateral antebrachial cutaneous nerve, the radial nerve.
Blood Vessel: The radial artery and vein.
Techniques: Thumb press.
Effects: Acute pain in the hand.

Celestial Spring (PC02)

Location: 2 cun below the end of the anterior axillary fold, between the heads of the biceps muscle.
Nerves: The medial brachial cutaneous nerve, the musculocutaneous nerve.
Blood Vessels: The branches of the brachial artery and vein.
Techniques: Thumb press.
Effects: Excruciating pain in the arm.

Blue Spirit (HT02)

Location: 3 cun above the medial end of the transverse cubital crease, when the elbow is flexed.
Nerves: The medial brachial cutaneous nerve, the medial antebrachial cutaneous nerve, the ulnar nerve.
Blood Vessels: The basilic vein, the superior ulnar collateral artery.
Techniques: Thumb press, pinching.
Effects: Tormenting pain in the arm.

Lesser Sea (HT03)

Location: At the medial end of the transverse cubital crease.
Nerve: The medial antebrachial cutaneous nerve.
Blood Vessels: The basilic vein, the inferior ulnar collateral artery, the ulnar recurrent artery and vein.
Techniques: Thumb press, knifehand strike.
Effects: Agonizing pain in the arm.

Inner Upper Forearm (AD-UE2)

Location: 2 cun below the ulna head, between the palmaris longus and flexor carpi radialis.
Nerve: The median nerve.
Blood Vessel: The branch of the ulnar artery.
Techniques: Thumb press, knifehand strike, hammer fist strike.
Effects: Sharp pain and numbness in the arm.

Cleft Gate (PC04)

Location: 5 cun above the crease of the wrist.
Nerve: The median nerve.
Blood Vessels: The median artery and vein.
Techniques: Thumb press.
Effects: Acute pain and numbness in the arm.

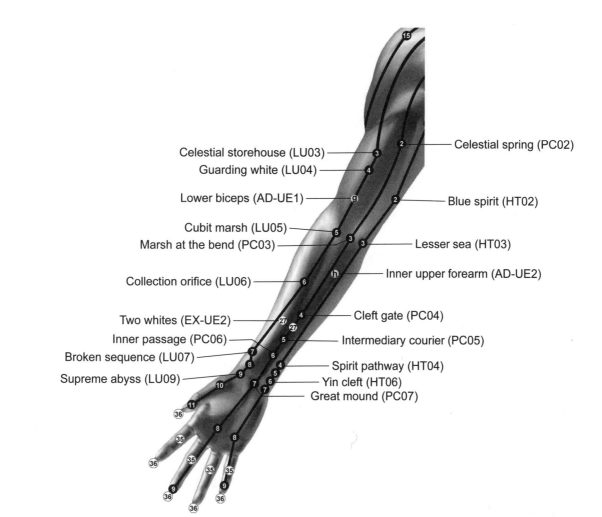

Celestial storehouse (LU03)
Guarding white (LU04)
Lower biceps (AD-UE1)
Cubit marsh (LU05)
Marsh at the bend (PC03)
Collection orifice (LU06)
Two whites (EX-UE2)
Inner passage (PC06)
Broken sequence (LU07)
Supreme abyss (LU09)

Celestial spring (PC02)
Blue spirit (HT02)
Lesser sea (HT03)
Inner upper forearm (AD-UE2)
Cleft gate (PC04)
Intermediary courier (PC05)
Spirit pathway (HT04)
Yin cleft (HT06)
Great mound (PC07)

Intermediary Courier (PC05)

Location: 3 cun above the transverse crease of the wrist.
Nerves: The medial and lateral antebrachial cutaneous nerves.
Blood Vessels: The median artery and vein.
Techniques: Thumb press, hammer fist strike.
Effects: Intense pain in the arm, numbness in the forearm.

Spirit Pathway (HT04)

Location: On the radial side of the wrist, 1.5 cun above the transverse crease of the wrist.
Nerve: The medial antebrachial cutaneous nerve.
Blood Vessel: The ulnar artery.
Techniques: Thumb press, knifehand strike.
Effects: Severe pain in the arm.

Yin Cleft (HT06)

Location: On the radial side of the wrist, 0.5 cun above the crease of the wrist.
Nerve: The medial antebrachial cutaneous nerve.
Blood Vessel: The ulnar artery.
Techniques: Thumb press.
Effects: Acute pain in the wrist and arm.

Great Mound (PC07)

Location: In the depression in the middle of the transverse crease of the wrist.
Nerve: The median nerve.
Blood Vessels: The palmar branches of the radial and ulnar arteries.
Techniques: Thumb press.
Effects: Severe pain in the arm, numbness of the wrist.

APPLICATIONS

Knifehand to the Celestial Storehouse

The Celestial Storehouse is on the upper biceps. When your opponent grabs your wrist, lift your wrist abruptly pulling his body toward you, then strike the Celestial Storehouse with your knifehand or hammer fist. When his arm is paralyzed by a muscle spasm from this strike, strike his face with a palm heel.

Knuckle Punch to the Guarding White

The Guarding White is 1 cun below the Celestial Storehouse. Strike the spot with a horizontal knuckle punch, punch, knifehand strike, or hammer fist. Hit quickly and keep moving so that your opponent cannot strike your face.

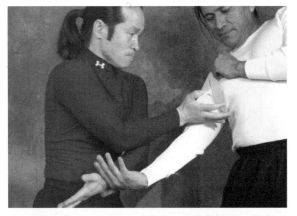

Knifehand to the Lower Biceps

The Lower Biceps is at the lower lateral area of the biceps. Striking or pressing this point causes electrifying pain along the entire arm. When you press it with your thumb, the deeper you insert the tip of the thumb, the more excruciating the pain will be.

Fingertip Thrust to the Cubit Marsh

The Cubit Marsh is on the radial side of the tendon of the biceps, on the inside of the elbow joint. Thrusting into the Cubit Marsh with the tips of the fingers or knifehand, causes an electrifying sensation along the arm.

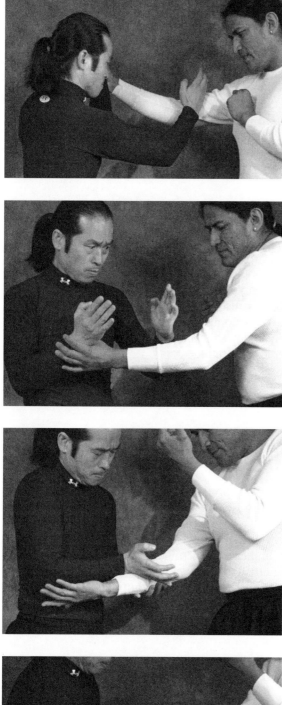

Knifehand to the Marsh at the Bend

The Marsh at the Bend is in the transverse cubital crease, on the ulnar side of the biceps muscle tendon. This is one of the most pain sensitive spots on the arm. Striking this point with a knifehand or hammer fist should cause a muscle spasm or paralysis of the arm.

Knifehand to the Collection Orifice

The Collection Orifice is on the palm side of the forearm. This is a good spot to strike to escape from a wrist grab. Pivot your body abruptly toward your opponent's center and strike the point with a knifehand, hammer fist, or elbow strike forcefully.

Knifehand to the Two Whites

The Two Whites is located above the crease of the wrist. Striking or pressing this point causes a startling sensation of pain in the arm. As soon as your opponent exposes his inner forearm, don't miss the opportunity and strike with a quick snapping movement. Follow up with strikes to the face or a choke.

Thumb Press on the Inner Passage

The Inner Passage is located in the middle of the inner wrist. This is a great spot to press with the thumb tip due to the location of the median nerve, artery and vein beneath the point. Press the Inner Passage quickly and forcefully to shock the opponent. This technique works well when the opponent's inner forearm is facing upward such as when he is grabbing your clothing or belt to pull you toward him.

Knuckle Punch to the Broken Sequence

The Broken Sequence is on the styloid process of the radius. This is a good spot to strike or press to break your opponent's grip. If your opponent grabs your belt or wrist, hold his wrist with your other hand and strike downward with a knifehand or knuckle punch. Pressing the Broken Sequence with your middle knuckle is effective too. Pressing this spot causes acute pain that is enough to make an opponent release his grip.

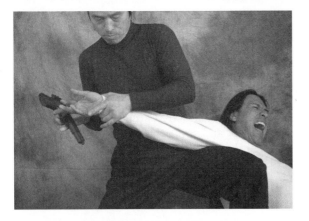

Thumb Press on the Supreme Abyss

The Supreme Abyss is at the transverse crease of the wrist. When you press this point with your thumb or fingertip, it causes excruciating pain, making this a good spot for controlling an opponent during a restraint technique. This technique also adds more power to wrist lock techniques.

Thumb Press on the Celestial Spring

The Celestial Spring is located below the armpit on the inner arm. There are branches of the brachial nerve and the branches of the brachial artery and vein running through this area. Pressing this spot with your thumb causes excruciating pain in the arm. Keep moving circularly or backward while controlling the opponent to prevent him from hitting you.

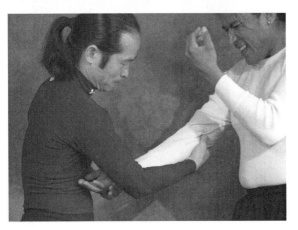

Pinching the Blue Spirit

The Blue Spirit is located above the elbow. This point is rich with nerves and pinching the Blue Spirit causes tormenting pain in the arm. You may combine pinching with a thumb press into the spot to magnify the effect.

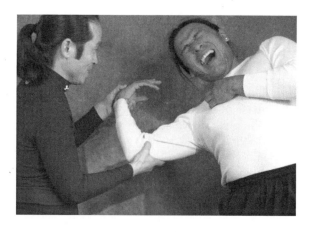

Thumb Press on the Lesser Sea

The Lesser Sea is located at the inner elbow, on the medial end of the transverse cubital crease. When you strike this spot with a punch or knifehand, it causes an electrifying sensation along the arm. Pressing the point causes unbearable pain in the arm. Combining a thumb press with a wrist lock is an effective way to subdue the opponent in a standing confrontation.

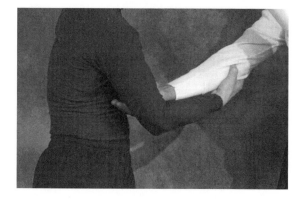

Thumb Press on the Inner Upper Forearm

The Inner Upper Arm is located below the ulnar head, between the muscles of the forearm. When you press this spot, it causes a sharp pain in the forearm. When you strike it with a hammer fist, shocking pain makes the forearm numb.

Knifehand to the Cleft Gate

The Cleft Gate is in the middle of the inner forearm. This is a good spot to press with your thumb due to the passage of the median nerve and the median artery and vein beneath it. A knifehand strike to the Cleft Gate point can cause numbness of the arm and fingers.

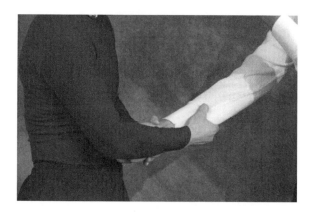

Thumb Press on the Intermediary Courier

The Intermediary Courier is above the crease of the wrist, on the inner arm. Press it with your thumb while holding the opponent's wrist, causing intense pain in the arm that can numb the fingers.

Knifehand Strike to the Spirit Pathway

The Spirit Pathway is on the radial side of the wrist, above the crease of the wrist. Pressing or striking this spot affects the ulnar nerve causing numbness of the 3rd, 4th, and 5th fingers.

Thumb Press on the Yin Cleft

The Yin Cleft is just above the crease of the wrist. Pressing this spot with the thumb tip suppresses the function of the hand. This technique is useful to break your opponent's grip.

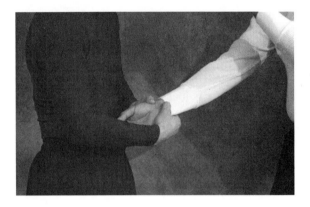

Thumb Press on the Great Mound

The Great Mound is located on the depression in the middle of the transverse crease of the wrist. Pressing this spot does not cause as much pain as other points, however, when you press it long enough, it affects the function of the arm causing diminished power. It is most effective when used with other combination techniques such as a biceps strike or the Lesser Sea press.

Figure 9.1 Meridian charts for the arm and hand.

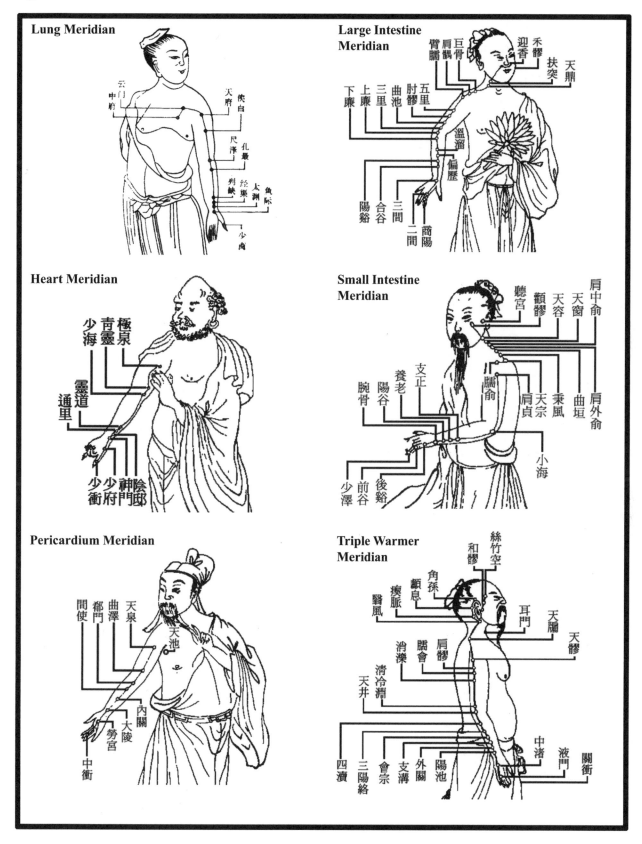

POSTERIOR ARM

Upper Arm (LI14)

Location: On the upper radial side of the humerus.
Nerves: The branches of the brachial cutaneous nerve.
Blood Vessels: The branches of the humeral artery and vein.
Techniques: Hammer fist strike, elbow strike, roundhouse kick.
Effects: Acute pain in the arm, numbness of the shoulder.

Arm Five Li (LI13)

Location: 3 cun above the Pool at the Bend (LI11).
Nerves: The branches of the brachial cutaneous nerve.
Blood Vessels: The radial collateral artery and vein.
Techniques: Hammer fist strike, elbow strike, roundhouse kick, thumb press.
Effects: Extreme pain in the arm, paralysis of the arm.

Elbow Bone-Orifice (LI12)

Location: 1 cun above the Pool at the Bend (LI11).
Nerves: The branches of the brachial cutaneous nerve.
Blood Vessels: The radial collateral artery and vein.
Techniques: Hammer fist strike, knifehand strike, roundhouse kick, thumb press.
Effects: Sharp pain in the arm, paralysis of the arm.

Pool at the Bend (LI11)

Location: In the depression at the lateral end of the transverse cubital crease.
Nerves: The posterior antebrachial cutaneous nerve, the radial nerve.
Blood Vessels: The branches of the radial recurrent artery and vein.
Techniques: Knifehand strike, thumb press.
Effects: Acute pain in the arm.

Arm Three Li (LI10)

Location: 2 cun below Pool at the Bend (LI11).
Nerves: The posterior antebrachial cutaneous nerve, the radial nerve.
Blood Vessels: The radial artery, the cephalic vein.
Techniques: Knifehand strike, thumb press.
Effects: Excruciating pain in the arm.

Veering Passageway (LI06)

Location: 3 cun above Yang Ravine (LI05).
Nerves: The branches of the radial nerve.
Blood Vessel: The cephalic vein.
Techniques: Knifehand strike, hammer fist strike.
Effects: Acute pain in the arm.

Yang Ravine (LI05)

Location: On the radial side of the wrist.
Nerve: The radial nerve.
Blood Vessels: The radial artery and its branches, the cephalic vein.
Techniques: Thumb press, knifehand strike.
Effects: Excruciating pain in the arm.

Shoulder Bone-Orifice (TW14)

Location: At the tip of the shoulder.
Nerve: The branch of the axillary nerve.
Blood Vessel: The branch of the humeral artery.
Techniques: Hammer fist, knifehand strike.
Effects: Excruciating pain in the arm and shoulder.

Dispersing Riverbed (TW12)

Location: On the lower end of the bulge of the lateral head of the triceps.
Nerve: The branch of the radial nerve.
Blood Vessels: The median collateral artery and vein.
Techniques: Hammer fist, knifehand strike, elbow strike, roundhouse kick.
Effects: Shooting pain in the arm, numbness of the upper arm.

Clear Cold Abyss (TW11)

Location: 1 cun above Celestial Well (TW10).
Nerve: The branch of the radial nerve.
Blood Vessels: The branches of the median collateral artery and vein.
Techniques: Hammer fist, knifehand strike, elbow strike, roundhouse kick, pinching.
Effects: Stabbing pain in the arm, paralysis of the upper arm.

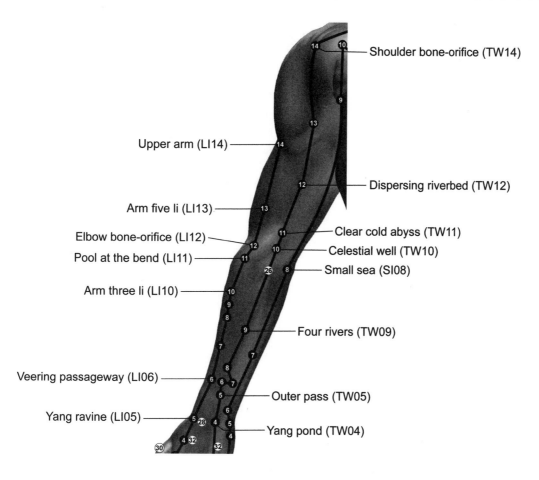

Shoulder bone-orifice (TW14)

Upper arm (LI14)

Dispersing riverbed (TW12)

Arm five li (LI13)

Elbow bone-orifice (LI12)
Clear cold abyss (TW11)
Pool at the bend (LI11)
Celestial well (TW10)
Small sea (SI08)

Arm three li (LI10)

Four rivers (TW09)

Veering passageway (LI06)

Outer pass (TW05)

Yang ravine (LI05)
Yang pond (TW04)

Celestial Well (TW10)

Location: In the depression 1 cun superior to the olecranon with the elbow flexed.
Nerve: The branch of the radial nerve.
Blood Vessels: The arterial and venous network of the elbow.
Techniques: Knifehand strike, thumb press.
Effects: Tormenting pain in the arm.

Small Sea (SI08)

Location: Between the olecranon and the medial epicondyle of the humerus.
Nerve: The branch of the ulnar nerve.
Blood Vessels: The branches of the ulnar artery and vein.
Techniques: Knifehand strike, thumb press.
Effects: Unbearable pain in the arm.

Four Rivers (TW09)

Location: 5 cun below the olecranon, between the radius and the ulna.
Nerves: The antebrachial cutaneous nerves.
Blood Vessel: The branch of the brachial artery.
Techniques: Thumb press.
Effects: Acute pain in the arm.

Outer Pass (TW05)

Location: 2 cun above Yang Pond (TW04), between the ulna and radius.
Nerve: The posterior antebrachial cutaneous nerve.
Blood Vessels: The interosseous arteries and veins.
Techniques: Thumb press, arc hand press.
Effects: Acute pain on the wrist.

Yang Pond (TW04)

Location: At the junction of the ulna and carpal bones.
Nerve: The branch of the ulnar nerve.
Blood Vessel: The posterior carpal artery.
Techniques: Thumb press, knuckle strike, knifehand.
Effects: Sharp pain in the wrist.

APPLICATIONS

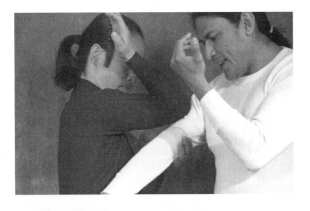

Strike the Upper Arm

The Upper Arm is located on the upper radial side of the humerus. Striking this area can not only cause pain in the shoulder and arm but also dislocate the shoulder. First grab the opponent's arm to expose the spot for an easy strike, then quickly snap downward with an elbow, forearm or hammer fist.

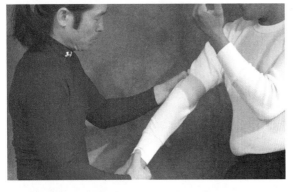

Press the Arm Five Li

The Arm Five Li is located on the lower part of the triceps. Once you grab the wrist of the opponent, immediately press this spot with the tip of your thumb. This technique generates extreme pain in the region and can paralyze the arm. Other effective techniques for striking the Arm Five Li are the hammer fist, elbow, and roundhouse kick.

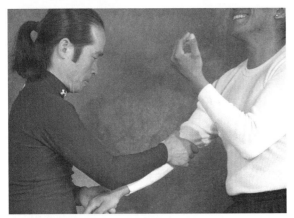

Press the Elbow Bone-Orifice

The Elbow Bone-Orifice is located right above the elbow. Pressing this point causes excruciating pain. Striking the spot can dislocate the elbow joint. Effective techniques for attacking the Elbow Bone-Orifice are hammer fist strike, knifehand strike and thumb press.

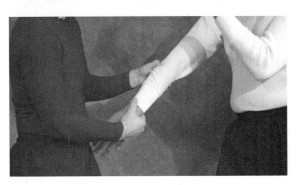

Thumb Press on the Pool at the Bend

The Pool at the Bend is located in the depression at the outside of the elbow. Pressing this spot causes instant sharp pain that goes all the way down to the hand. Striking the Pool at the Bend can cause muscle spasms that incapacitate the forearm and hand.

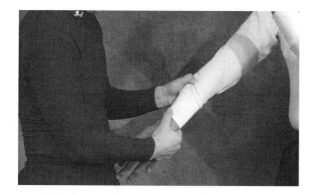

Press the Arm Three Li

The Arm Three Li is located in the large muscles on the upper forearm. Due to the many layers of muscles in this region, it is easy to find the point making it practical in application. Even though you may miss the exact spot, pressing in the vicinity of the Arm Three Li can cause severe pain. A knifehand or hammer fist strike can cause a muscle spasm and numbness in the entire forearm.

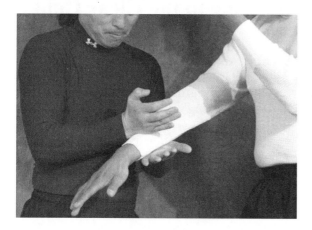

Strike the Veering Passageway

The Veering Passageway is a good target to strike when the opponent attacks with a knife. Using a knifehand or hammer fist, strike the spot and your opponent will instantly drop his weapon because he will involuntarily open his hand. Acute pain from striking the Veering Passageway can numb the forearm momentarily.

Knuckle Strike to the Yang Ravine

The Yang Ravine is in the radial side of the wrist, where the radial nerve branches off to the thumb and index finger. This is a useful spot for controlling the wrist by pressing it with the proximal phalange of the thumb. Striking this point causes excruciating pain in the hand. Effective techniques are knuckle press, knuckle strike, and knifehand strike

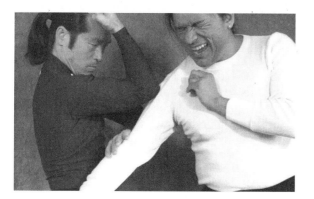

Elbow Strike to the Shoulder Bone-Orifice

The Shoulder Bone-Orifice is located at the tip of the shoulder. When you have control of the opponent's arm, pull it toward you and strike this spot with a hammer fist, forearm, or elbow strike. The pain in the shoulder is unbearable. A forceful strike may dislocate the shoulder.

Strike the Dispersing Riverbed

The Dispersing Riverbed is located on the upper triceps. Striking this point causes a shooting pain in the arm and can cause paralysis of the upper arm. Repetitive strikes on the Dispersing Riverbed can incapacitate the arm. Effective techniques are hammer fist, knifehand strike, elbow strike, and roundhouse kick.

Palm Strike to the Clear Cold Abyss

The Clear Cold Abyss is located above the elbow. Striking this spot causes a shocking pain when the nerves and blood vessels are compressed between the humerus and the striking weapon. The opponent will likely drop and shake or grab his arm so be prepared to follow up with a combination technique while he is distracted. Effective techniques are hammer fist, knifehand strike, elbow strike, palm strike, roundhouse kick, and pinching.

Knifehand Strike to the Celestial Well

The Celestial Well is in the depression above the elbow. Striking this point causes an electrifying shock in the upper arm. Effective techniques are knifehand strike, palm strike, forearm strike, and thumb press.

Forearm Press on the Small Sea

The Small Sea is located at the medial elbow. Striking or pressing this spot causes an electrifying sensation throughout the arm. This technique is good for an arm bar. As soon as you grab his wrist, twist it and press the Small Sea with your knifehand or forearm.

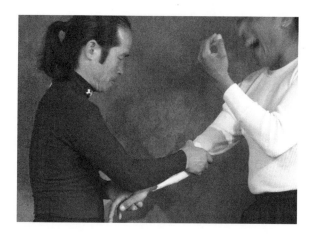

Press the Four Rivers

The Four Rivers is located in the middle of the posterior forearm. Under layers of the extensor carpi ulnaris muscle and the extensor digitorum muscle, lie the branches of the ulnar nerve and artery. Pressing this spot causes acute pain in the arm that is powerful enough to cause the opponent to release his grip on you immediately.

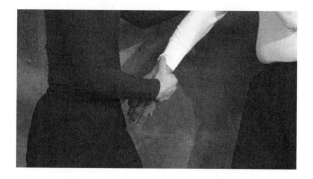

Thumb Press at the Outer Pass

The Outer Pass is located above the crease of the wrist, between the ulna and radius bones. This is a good place to strike or press when the assailant grabs your wrist or handbag. Strike the spot just like hammering a nail. Effective techniques are thumb press, arc hand press, hammer fist, and forearm strike.

Control the Yang Pond

The Yang Pond is located in the middle of the wrist at the junction of the ulna and carpal bones. This point is easy to grab and press with the thumb tip or the middle knuckle. When you grab the wrist, press quickly down toward your foot. This technique generates a sharp pain that penetrates into the wrist and is good for breaking your opponent's grip without using excessive force.

VITAL POINTS ON THE HAND

ANTERIOR HAND

Fish Border (LU10)

Location: In the middle of the thenar muscle.
Nerves: The branches of the lateral antebrachial cutaneous, radial and median nerves.
Blood Vessels: The branches of the palmar digital proprial artery and veins.
Techniques: Thumb press.
Effects: Acute pain on the hand.

Thumb Joint (AD-UE3)

Location: On the thumb.
Nerves: The branches of the radial nerve.
Blood Vessel: The branch of the radial artery.
Techniques: Hyper-extension, squeezing.
Effects: Tormenting pain on the hand, damage to the thumb joint.

Work Palace (PC08)

Location: Between the 2nd and 3rd metacarpal bones, on the radial side of the 3rd metacarpal bone.
Nerve: The branch of the median nerve.
Blood Vessels: The brachial artery and vein.
Techniques: Thumb press.
Effects: Numbing pain in the palm and arm.

Lesser Mansion (HT08)

Location: On the palmar point between the 4th and 5th metacarpal bones.
Nerve: The branch of the median nerve.
Blood Vessel: The common palmar digital artery.

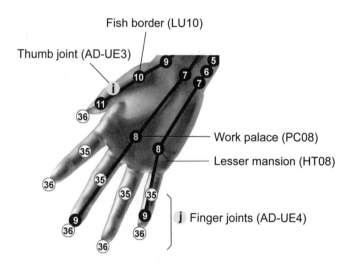

Techniques: Thumb press.
Effects: Numbness in the palm.

Finger Joints (AD-UE4)

Location: On the fingers.
Nerves: The branches of the ulnar and radial nerves.
Blood Vessels: The dorsal digital arteries.
Techniques: Hyper-extension.
Effects: Unbearable pain in the finger and arm.

217

APPLICATIONS

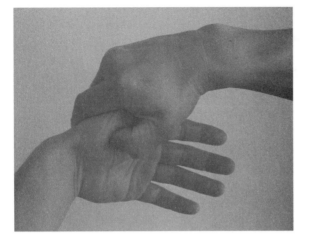

Thumb Press on the Fish Border

The Fish Border is in the middle of the muscle just above the thumb. When the opponent grabs your collar or sleeve, press this point with the tip of your thumb or middle finger. Pressing deeply into the Fish Border will cause the opponent to release his grip.

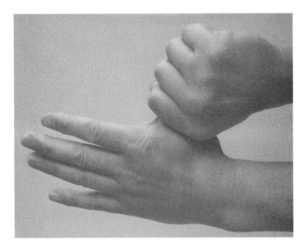

Hyper-extend the Thumb Joint

The thumb is a useful weak point in grappling. You can grab it and hyper-extend it. You can also wrap the bent thumb with your hand and squeeze, pressing the distal phalange as hard as you can. The resulting pain is intense enough to make an opponent release his grip. This can also damage the thumb joint.

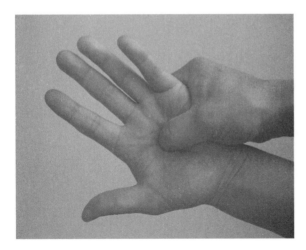

Thumb Press on the Work Palace

The Work Palace is located in the middle of the palm between the 2nd and 3rd metacarpal bones. When you press the Work Palace deeply with the tip of the thumb, an electrifying sensation spreads to the upper arm. Prolonged pressure on this point can numb the entire arm incapacitating the arm and making it useless for grabbing or grappling.

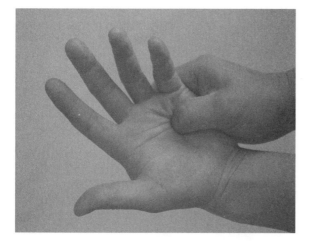

Thumb Press on the Lesser Mansion

The Lesser Mansion is on the palm between the 4th and 5th metacarpal bones. Beneath this point is the branch of the ulnar nerve, so pressing on this point generates acute pain that spreads all the way to the upper arm. Although this technique may not always be practical in fighting, it is useful in studying the power and function of the nerves in the arm.

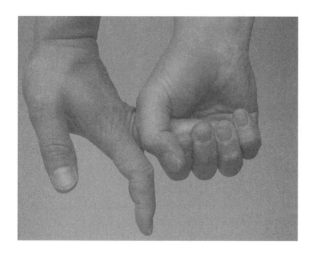

Hyper-extend the Finger Joints

The fingers are useful in controlling a larger opponent. As long as you can sustain the hyper-extended position, you can control an opponent until he submits. Once you secure your grip on his finger, press him downward to the ground where you can apply a more secure lock or immobilization technique. In a standing confrontation, unbearable pain in the finger and arm can also give you time to apply a choke or a lock. Until you have the opponent under control, constantly adjust your position according to how he moves to stay in the most advantageous position.

POSTERIOR HAND

Union Valley (LI04)

Location: Between the 1st and 2nd metacarpal bones on the radial side of the hand, in the middle of the 2nd metacarpal bone.
Nerve: The radial nerve.
Blood Vessels: The dorsal venous network of the hand.
Techniques: Thumb press, knuckle strike.
Effects: Excruciating pain in the arm, numbness in the hand.

Third Space (LI03)

Location: On the radial side of the index finger, in the depression near the head of the 2nd metacarpal bone.
Nerve: The radial nerve.
Blood Vessels: The dorsal venous network of the hand, branch of the 1st dorsal metacarpal artery.
Techniques: Thumb press, squeezing.
Effects: Acute pain in the metacarpal region.

Exterior Pericardium (EX-UE8)

Location: On the dorsum of the hand, between the 2nd and 3rd metacarpal bones.
Nerve: The common palmar digital nerve.
Blood Vessel: The common palmar digital artery.
Techniques: Thumb press.
Effects: Sharp pain on the back of the hand.

Lumbar Pain Point (EX-UE7)

Location: Two points on the dorsum of the hand between the 2nd and 3rd and between the 4th and 5th metacarpal bones.
Nerves: The branches of the radial and ulnar nerves.
Blood Vessels: The dorsal metacarpal arteries.
Techniques: Thumb press, knuckle punch.
Effects: Agonizing pain on the back of the hand.

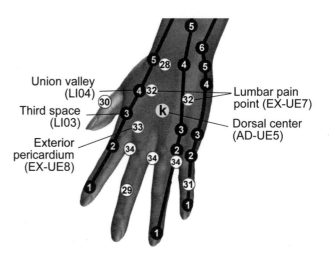

Dorsal Center (AD-UE5)

Location: 2 cun below the transverse crease of the wrist between the 3rd and 4th metacarpal bones.
Nerves: The superficial branch of the radial nerve and the dorsal branch of the ulnar nerve.
Blood Vessels: The dorsal nervous network.
Techniques: Thumb press, knuckle punch.
Effects: Acute pain on the back of the hand.

APPLICATIONS

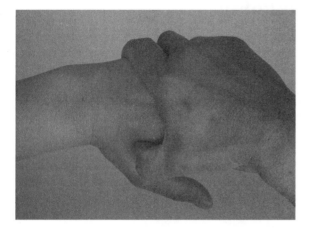

Thumb Press on the Union Valley

The Union Valley is located between the 1st and 2nd metacarpal bones on the radial side of the hand. Due to the branches of the radial nerve and the dorsal venous network found here, this point is extremely pain sensitive, and thus popular in grappling arts such as Hapkido and Aikido. You may press the point with the thumb tip from any direction. Make sure to hold the opponent's hand firmly with your fingers. This is a good spot to press during a wrist lock.

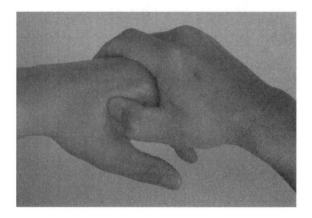

Thumb Press on the Third Space

The Third Space is on the radial side of the index finger. Secure your grip with your fingers, then press the spot with the tip of your thumb. When pressing the Third Space, acute pain spreads to the upper arm and the hand. Grab the opponent's forearm with the other hand to prevent his hand from escaping your grip.

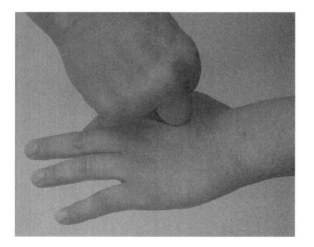

Knuckle Punch to the Exterior Pericardium

The Exterior Pericardium is located on the back of the hand, between the 2nd and 3rd metacarpal bones. When the opponent grabs your sleeve or belt, strike or press this spot with the knuckle of the middle finger. The excruciating pain in his hand will cause him to release his grip.

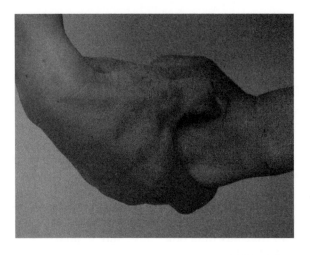

Thumb Press on the Lumbar Pain Points

The Lumbar Pain Points are located in two places: on the back of the hand between the 2nd and 3rd and between the 4th and 5th metacarpal bones. Striking or pressing this point with your knuckle causes agonizing pain on the back of the hand. This is a great spot to anchor your thumb tip in wrist manipulation techniques.

Thumb Press on the Dorsal Center

The Dorsal Center is located below the crease of the wrist between the 3rd and 4th metacarpal bones. Beneath this point is the superficial branch of the radial nerve and the dorsal branch of the ulnar nerve. Pressing with the thumb tip or striking with the middle finger knuckle causes acute pain on the back of the hand and is a good way to augment a locking technique or soften the opponent's grip.

CHAPTER 9

VITAL POINTS ON THE
LEG & FOOT

SIGNIFICANCE OF THE
LEG & FOOT

The feet and legs are primarily used for mobility and kicking. Your prime objectives in attacking them, therefore, are to incapacitate the opponent's kicking ability and to disable his mobility.

To reduce his kicking ability, at medium and close range attack the following vital points with your knees - Anterior side of the leg: Crouching Rabbit (ST32), Yin Market (ST33), Sea of Blood (SP10), Winnower Gate (SP11); Inner lateral side: Spring at the Bend (LV08), Yin Bladder (LV09); Posterior side: Support & Assist (BL36), Gate of Abundance (BL37), Posterior Lower Thigh (AD-LE2).

To incapacitate his mobility, attack the following points with roundhouse kick, side kick, inside heel kick or stomp kick- Anterior side: Bountiful Bulge (ST40), Anterior Tibia (AD-LE1), Divided Ravine (ST41), Supreme Surge (LV03); Inner lateral side: Inner Calf (AD-LE6), Guest House (KI09), Recover Flow (KI07); Posterior side: Outer Calf (AD-LE3), Supporting Sinews (BL56), Supporting Mountain (BL57), Lower Calf (AD-LE5), Achilles Tendon (AD-LE5).

There may also be times when the legs are the only targets available to you. For example, the opponent has you bent over in a side headlock. Because the opponent is standing and you are bent over, you cannot strike his head or trunk, but his legs are close. By pressing with your thumb tip into the Supporting Sinews (BL56) on his calf or sticking the knuckle of your middle finger into the Supreme Surge (LV03) on his foot, you can shock him into moving and create an opening for a follow up strike or takedown.

Similarly, in groundfighting, you may not be able to gain access to the opponent's upper body, but have easy access to his feet or legs (example: heel lock). Delivering a tactical strike to lower body targets is a good way to break a stalemate on the ground or turn the momentum of a fight in your favor.

VITAL POINTS ON THE LEG

ANTERIOR LEG

Thigh Joint (ST31)

Location: Directly below the anterior superior iliac spine, in the depression on the lateral side of the sartorius muscle.
Nerve: The lateral femoral cutaneous nerve.
Blood Vessels: The branches of the lateral circumflex femoral artery and vein.
Techniques: Side kick, elbow strike, knifehand strike.
Effects: Acute pain in the thigh, paralysis of the leg.

Winnower Gate (SP11)

Location: 6 cun above Sea of Blood (SP10).
Nerve: The anterior femoral cutaneous nerve.
Blood Vessel: The great saphenous vein.
Techniques: Side kick, front kick, elbow strike, knifehand strike.
Effects: Agonizing pain in the thigh, paralysis of the leg, loss of mobility.

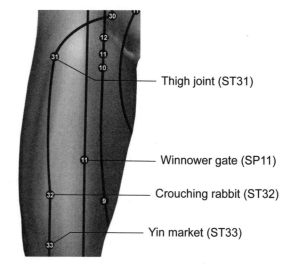

Crouching Rabbit (ST32)

Location: 6 cun above the laterosuperior border of the patella.
Nerves: The lateral and anterior femoral cutaneous nerves.
Blood Vessels: The branches of the lateral circumflex femoral artery and vein.
Techniques: Roundhouse kick, side kick, front kick, elbow strike, hammer fist, knifehand strike, thumb press, punch.
Effects: Agonizing pain in the thigh, paralysis of the leg, loss of mobility.

Yin Market (ST33)

Location: 3 cun above the laterosuperior border of the patella.
Nerves: The lateral and anterior femoral cutaneous nerves.
Blood Vessel: The branch of the lateral circumflex femoral artery.
Techniques: Roundhouse kick, side kick, front kick.
Effects: Acute pain in the lateral thigh, paralysis of the leg, loss of mobility.

Pelvic Bone (EX-L31)

Location: In the lower anterior part of the thigh.
Nerve: The lateral femoral cutaneous nerve.
Blood Vessels: The branches of the femoral artery and vein.
Techniques: Side kick, elbow strike, knifehand strike.
Effects: Acute pain in the lateral thigh.

Sea of Blood (SP10)

Location: 2 cun above the mediosuperior border of the patella, on the bulge of the medial quadriceps muscle when the knee is flexed.
Nerves: The anterior femoral cutaneous nerve, branch of the femoral nerve.
Blood Vessels: The branches of the femoral artery and vein.
Techniques: Roundhouse kick, side kick.
Effects: Punishing pain in the inner thigh, paralysis of the leg.

Crane's Summit (EX-LE2)

Location: In the depression above the knee.
Nerves: The branches of the saphenous nerve.
Blood Vessel: The articular branch of the genicular artery.
Techniques: Side kick, pushing kick.
Effects: Damage to the knee joint, loss of mobility.

Medial Eyes of the Knee (EX-LE4)

Location: In the depression on the inner patellar ligament.
Nerve: The infrapatellar branch of the saphenous nerve.
Blood Vessels: The medial genicular artery, the great saphenous vein.
Techniques: Side kick, pushing kick, elbow strike, knifehand strike.
Effects: Extreme pain in the knee, fracture or dislocation of the knee, loss of mobility.

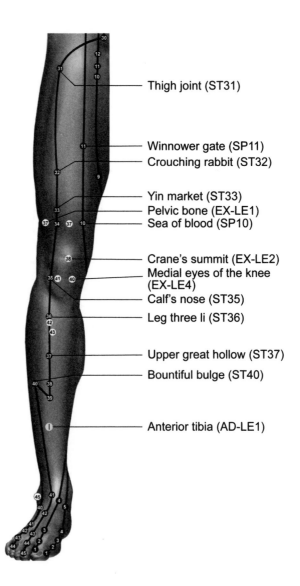

Thigh joint (ST31)

Winnower gate (SP11)
Crouching rabbit (ST32)

Yin market (ST33)
Pelvic bone (EX-LE1)
Sea of blood (SP10)

Crane's summit (EX-LE2)
Medial eyes of the knee (EX-LE4)
Calf's nose (ST35)
Leg three li (ST36)

Upper great hollow (ST37)
Bountiful bulge (ST40)

Anterior tibia (AD-LE1)

Calf's Nose (ST35)

Location: The depression below the patella, next to the patellar ligament when the knee is flexed.
Nerves: The lateral sural cutaneous nerve, the branch of the common peroneal nerve.
Blood Vessels: The arteries and veins around the knee joint.
Techniques: Side kick.
Effects: Grueling pain in the knee, fracture of the knee bone, loss of mobility.

Leg Three Li (ST36)

Location: 3 cun below Calf's Nose (ST35), one finger width from the anterior crest of the tibia.
Nerves: The lateral sural cutaneous nerve, the cutaneous branch of the saphenous nerve.
Blood Vessels: The anterior tibial artery and vein.
Techniques: Side kick.
Effects: Sharp pain on the shin, damage to the knee joint.

Upper Great Hollow (ST37)

Location: 6 cun below Calf's Nose (ST35), one finger width from the anterior crest of the tibia.
Nerves: The lateral sural cutaneous nerve, the cutaneous branch of the saphenous nerve.
Blood Vessels: The anterior tibial artery and vein.
Techniques: Side kick.
Effects: Excruciating pain on the shin.

Bountiful Bulge (ST40)

Location: 8 cun superior and anterior to the external malleolus.
Nerves: The superficial peroneal nerves.
Blood Vessels: The branches of the anterior tibial artery and vein.
Techniques: Side kick, front kick.
Effects: Excruciating pain on the shin.

Anterior Tibia (AD-LE1)

Location: On the surface of the tibia.
Nerve: The medial branch of the peroneal nerve.
Blood Vessel: The anterior tibial artery.
Techniques: Side kick, front kick, downward sliding stomp kick.
Effects: Excruciating pain on the shin.

APPLICATIONS

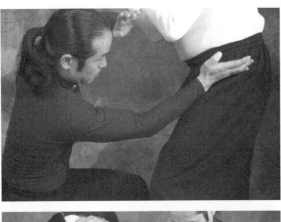

Strike the Thigh Joint

The Thigh Joint is a point that you should strike to slow down the mobility of the opponent. Striking this spot shocks the femoral nerve and makes the opponent limp. Effective techniques are side kick, elbow strike, knifehand strike and forearm strike.

Knee Kick to the Winnower Gate

The Winnower Gate is on the inner median side of the front of the thigh. This is a great point to attack in head-on close range fighting. Bring your knee up and snap it into the target. If the opponent bends his body forward in pain, attack his neck. If he moves backward, throw another knee kick to his stomach. This technique can paralyze the leg.

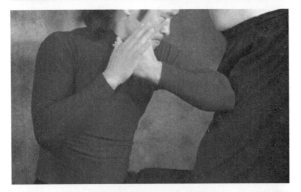

Elbow to the Crouching Rabbit

The Crouching Rabbit is in the outer side of the front of the thigh. This is a great point to attack from outside with a knee kick in close range fighting. If you are in a lower position than your opponent, attack with your elbow, then take him down by tackling him. Other effective techniques are roundhouse kick, side kick, front kick, elbow strike, hammer fist, knifehand strike, thumb press, and punch.

Strike the Yin Market

The Yin Market is one of the most commonly used points in clinching. Striking this spot causes severe pain in the thigh muscles and generates muscle spasms in the vastus medialis muscle. Effective techniques are roundhouse kick, side kick, front kick and elbow strike.

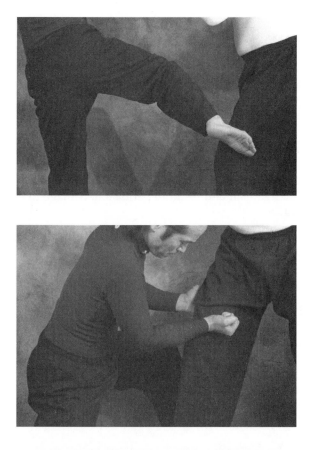

Kick the Pelvic Bone

The Pelvic Bone is on the lateral side of the thigh above the knee. Attacking this point can destroy the opponent's balance. Kick at a slightly downward angle toward the upper region of the knee. This causes sharp pain in the knee joint and the lower thigh, and if done right, the opponent's leg can collapse.

Hammerfist to the Sea of Blood

The Sea of Blood is on the bulge of the medial quadriceps muscle. This spot is quite often injured in martial arts tournament fighting and a severe spasm from being kicked here can disable a fighter. Nail a hammer fist on the Sea of Blood and the opponent will have punishing pain in the thigh. This is good way to reduce his mobility and then attack the torso or groin afterward.

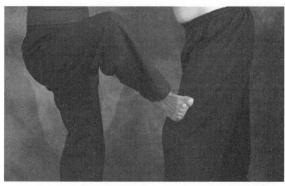

Stomp Kick on the Crane's Summit

The Crane's Summit is on top of the knee. Kick the point at a 45 degree downward angle for maximum effect. This causes pain in the knee, damage to the ligament, and breaks the equilibrium. This kick will earn you time for an escape or follow-up attacks.

Strike on the Medial Eyes of the Knee

The Medial Eyes of the Knee is in the depression on the inner patellar ligament. Striking this spot causes a toothache type of pain on the infrapatellar branch of the saphenous nerve. Hit at a horizontal angle with a side kick, pushing kick, elbow strike, or knifehand strike.

Elbow Strike the Calf's Nose

The Calf's Nose is in the depression below the patella, next to the patellar ligament when the knee is flexed. Deliver your elbow strike on an inward angle toward the center of the knee. Alternatively a side kick is effective if you are in a standing position. Intense pain in the knee as a result of attacking the Calf's Nose can make the opponent's leg collapse immediately, causing him to kneel or fall down. This technique can damage the knee ligament and result in permanent damage to the joint.

Side Kick the Leg Three Li

The Leg Three Li is located just below the knee. This is a perfect spot to throw a side kick to stop an incoming opponent. Bend your standing leg to maintain balance and add more the power of your body weight to the kick. After kicking, immediately throw straight and hook punch combinations at the face.

Side Kick the Upper Great Hollow

The Upper Great Hollow is in the middle of the shin. Kicking this spot causes excruciating and sustained pain in the shin. Lift your foot, kick and slide the blade of your foot or shoe down the shin bone to increase the effect of this kick.

Heel Kick to the Bountiful Bulge

The Bountiful Bulge is in the middle of the lateral shin. In a clinching situation, kick this spot with your heel to distract your opponent. Kick very quickly while holding onto the opponent for balance, then follow up with a sweep or a headbutt to his face.

Instep Kick to the Anterior Tibia

The Anterior Tibia is on the surface of the lower shin. Hitting this point with a hard bony weapon causes unbearable pain. Against an incoming opponent, move slightly to the side and kick the point with your instep. From a longer range, use the blade of your foot to strike with a side kick.

POSTERIOR LEG

Support & Assist (BL36)

Location: In the middle of the transverse gluteal fold.
Nerve: The posterior femoral cutaneous nerve.
Blood Vessels: The artery and vein beside the sciatic nerve.
Techniques: Front kick, pushing kick, side kick, knee kick.
Effects: Sharp pain in the whole body, paralysis of the leg, loss of mobility.

Gate of Abundance (BL37)

Location: 6 cun below Support & Assist (BL36).
Nerve: The posterior femoral cutaneous nerve.
Blood Vessels: The branches of the deep femoral artery and vein.
Techniques: Front kick, side kick, knee kick.
Effects: Acute pain in the rear thigh, paralysis of the leg, loss of mobility.

Posterior Lower Thigh (AD-LE2)

Location: 6 cun above Bend Center (BL40).
Nerve: The tibial nerve.
Blood Vessels: The popliteal artery and vein.
Techniques: Front kick, side kick, knee kick, pushing kick.
Effects: Tormenting pain in the lower hamstring muscle, paralysis of the leg, loss of mobility.

Bend Center (BL40)

Location: Midpoint of the transverse crease of the popliteal fossa.
Nerves: The posterior femoral cutaneous nerve, the tibial nerve.
Blood Vessel: The femoropopliteal vein.
Techniques: Front kick, pushing kick, side kick, thumb press, inside sweep kick.
Effects: Sharp pain in the whole body, paralysis of the leg, loss of mobility.

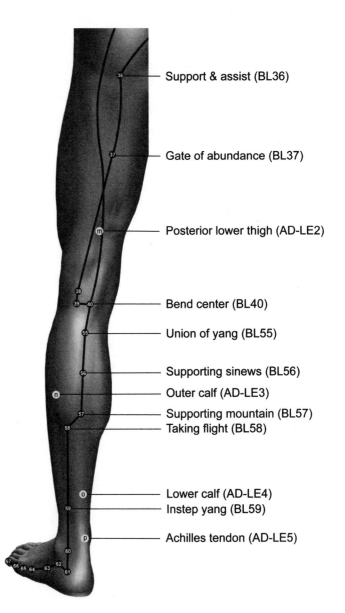

Support & assist (BL36)

Gate of abundance (BL37)

Posterior lower thigh (AD-LE2)

Bend center (BL40)

Union of yang (BL55)

Supporting sinews (BL56)

Outer calf (AD-LE3)

Supporting mountain (BL57)
Taking flight (BL58)

Lower calf (AD-LE4)

Instep yang (BL59)

Achilles tendon (AD-LE5)

Union of Yang (BL55)

Location: 2 cun below Bend Center (BL40), between the medial and lateral heads of the gastrocnemius muscle.
Nerve: The medial sural cutaenous nerve.
Blood Vessel: The small saphenous vein.
Techniques: Front kick, pushing kick, side kick, thumb press.
Effects: Shooting pain in the upper calf, paralysis of the leg, loss of mobility.

Supporting Sinews (BL56)

Location: Midway between Union of Yang (BL55) and Supporting Mountain (BL57), in the belly of the gastrocnemius muscle.
Nerve: The medial sural cutaneous nerve.
Blood Vessel: The small saphenous vein.
Techniques: Front kick, pushing kick, side kick, thumb press, knifehand strike.
Effects: Sharp pain in the whole body, paralysis of the leg, loss of mobility.

Outer Calf (AD-LE3)

Location: On the outer lower part of the gastrocnemius muscle.
Nerve: The lateral sural cutaneous nerve.
Blood Vessel: The branch of the small saphenous vein.
Techniques: Roundhouse kick, side kick, thumb press, knifehand strike.
Effects: Unbearable pain in the calf, paralysis of the leg, loss of mobility.

Supporting Mountain (BL57)

Location: Directly below the belly of the gastrocnemius muscle.
Nerve: The medial sural cutaneous nerve.
Blood Vessel: The small saphenous vein.
Techniques: Front kick, side kick, roundhouse kick, thumb press.
Effects: Tearing pain on the calf, paralysis of the leg.

Taking Flight (BL58)

Location: On the posterior edge of the fibula, 7 cun above Kunlun Mountains (BL60).
Nerve: The lateral sural cutaenous nerve.
Blood Vessel: The small saphenous vein.
Techniques: Side kick, roundhouse kick, thumb press.
Effects: Acute pain on the calf, loss of mobility.

Lower Calf (AD-LE4)

Location: 1 cun above Instep Yang (BL 59), in the median of the calf.
Nerve: The sural nerve.
Blood Vessel: The small saphenous vein.
Techniques: Side kick, roundhouse kick, knifehand strike, thumb press.
Effects: Unbearable pain on the calf.

Instep Yang (BL59)

Location: 3 cun directly above Kunlun Mountains (BL60).
Nerve: The sural nerve.
Blood Vessel: The small saphenous vein.
Techniques: Side kick, roundhouse kick, knifehand strike, thumb press.
Effects: Excruciating pain in the lower leg.

Achilles Tendon (AD-LE5)

Location: In the posterior ankle.
Nerves: The branches of the saphenous nerve.
Blood Vessels: The branches of the peroneal artery and vein.
Techniques: Stomp kick, sweeping kick.
Effects: Acute electrifying pain along the leg.

APPLICATIONS

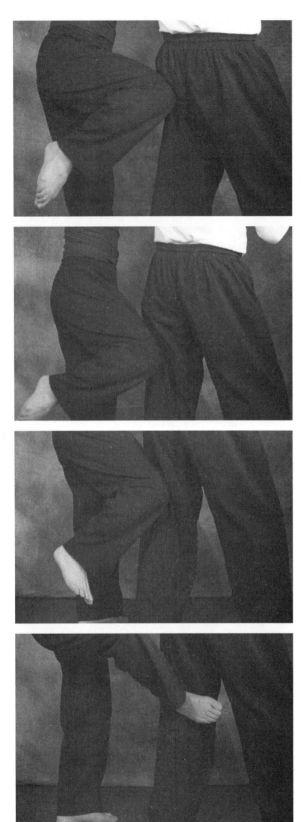

Knee Kick to the Support & Assist

The Support & Assist is in the middle of the transverse gluteal fold right under the buttock. A knee kick from the rear to this spot can cause electrifying pain throughout the entire body. Kick slightly upward to shock the upper side of the sciatic nerve which branches downward from the pelvic cavity.

Knee Kick to the Gate of Abundance

The Gate of Abundance is on the hamstring muscle in the rear of the thigh. Beneath it are the branches of the sciatic nerve which spreads through the thigh. A kick to this spot causes an instant muscle spasm and can cause paralysis of the leg. In addition to the knee kick, you can use a side kick, roundhouse kick, knifehand strike and elbow strike.

Knee Kick to the Posterior Lower Thigh

The Posterior Lower Thigh is above the knee in the rear thigh. A knee kick to this spot causes excruciating pain in the deep layers of the muscle. Pinching this spot causes acute pain on the skin and can be used to free yourself from a standing opponent who is dominating you with a headlock.

Snap Kick to the Bend Center

The Bend Center is on the midpoint of the crease behind the knee. A snap kick to this spot can easily destroy the opponent's balance and cause him to fall. Other effective techniques are front kick, pushing kick, side kick, stomp kick, and thumb press according to where you stand.

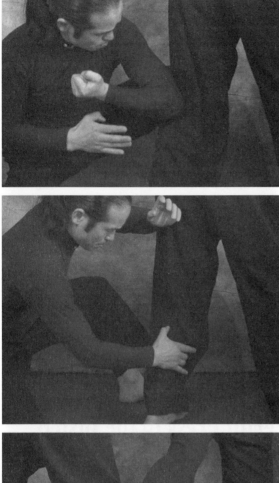

Elbow Strike to the Union of Yang

The Union of Yang is located in the gastrocnemius muscle. An elbow strike to this spot causes shooting pain in the upper calf and a muscle spasm. This is a good technique to distract an opponent who is trying to force you to the ground.

Thumb Press to the Supporting Sinews

The Supporting Sinews point is in the belly of the gastrocnemius muscle. Pressing this point causes unbearable pain and may force an opponent to release his grip on you. If the opponent is wearing tall boots or thick pants, a side kick or rear stomp kick is more effective. Other potential techniques are front kick, pushing kick, and knifehand strike.

Heel Kick to the Outer Calf

The Outer Calf is located on the outer lower part of the gastrocnemius muscle. When your opponent punches at your face, turn your body to slip the punches and throw a low heel kick to this spot. This technique is very powerful and effective in destroying the opponent's mobility and will to fight.

Thumb press on the Supporting Mountain

The Supporting Mountain is directly below the belly of the gastrocnemius muscle on the calf. Pressing this spot when you're caught in a side headlock can force your opponent to loosen his grip. In a clinching situation, strike this spot with an instep or heel kick to cripple the opponent's mobility, by causing intense pain and muscle spasm.

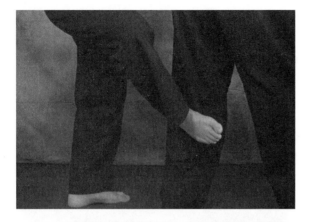

Heel Kick to the Taking Flight

The Taking Flight is on the outer lower part of the gastrocnemius muscle. This point is useful for taking down an opponent who is trying to lift you or tackle you from the front. Hold on to him for balance, and forcefully kick the spot with your instep or heel.

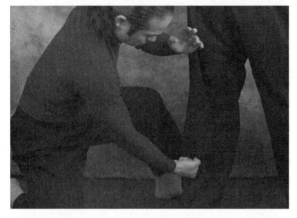

Strike the Lower Calf

Striking the Lower Calf with a knuckle punch can buckle the opponent's leg. In grappling, this point is good for pressing when applying a heel lock, however when applied full force it can tear the muscles or tendons in the region.

Fingertip Press to the Instep Yang

The Instep Yang is on the outer lower side of the calf. Pressing or striking this spot causes sharp pain in the lower leg. Although the pain is momentary, it is enough to distract your opponent so you can follow up with a powerful technique. Kicking this spot with a sweep kick can cause loss of mobility in the leg.

Kick the Achilles Tendon

The Achilles Tendon connects the large muscles in the calf with the bone of the heel. Damage to the Achilles Tendon destroys the opponent's mobility. Kick the Achilles Tendon deeply at a perpendicular angle. The impact can penetrate into the tibial nerve and other neighboring points. Effective techniques are stomp kick, sweeping inside kick, and heel kick.

INTERIOR LEG

Foot Five Li (LV10)

Location: At the upper medial inner thigh.
Nerves: The genitorfemoral nerve, the anterior femoral cutaneous nerve.
Blood Vessels: The branches of the femoral artery and vein.
Techniques: Front kick, pushing kick, punch.
Effects: Sharp pain in the inner thigh, paralysis of the leg, loss of mobility.

Yin Bladder (LV09)

Location: 4 cun above the medial epicondyle of the femur.
Nerve: The branch of the obturator nerve.
Blood Vessels: The femoral artery and vein.
Techniques: Roundhouse kick, side kick.
Effects: Punishing pain in the inner thigh, paralysis of the leg, loss of mobility.

Spring at the Bend (LV08)

Location: Posterior to the medial condyle of the tibia, above the medial end of the transverse popliteal crease.
Nerve: The saphenous nerve.
Blood Vessel: The great saphenous vein.
Techniques: Side kick, roundhouse kick.
Effects: Staggering pain in the region when kicked, loss of mobility.

Knee Joint (LV07)

Location: Posterior and inferior to the medial condyle of the tibia, in the upper portion of the medial head of the gastrocnemius muscle.
Nerves: The branch of the medial sural cutaneous nerve.
Blood Vessel: The posterior tibial artery.
Techniques: Side kick, roundhouse kick.
Effects: Damage to the knee joint.

Yin Mound Spring (SP09)

Location: On the lower border of the medial condyle of the tibia.
Nerve: The medial crural cutaneous nerve.
Blood Vessels: The great saphenous vein, the genu suprema artery.
Techniques: Side kick, roundhouse kick.
Effects: Loss of balance.

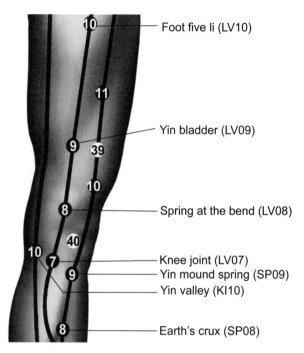

Foot five li (LV10)

Yin bladder (LV09)

Spring at the bend (LV08)

Knee joint (LV07)
Yin mound spring (SP09)
Yin valley (KI10)

Earth's crux (SP08)

Yin Valley (KI10)

Location: On the medial side of the popliteal fossa, between the tendons of the semitendinosus and semimembranosus muscles.
Nerve: The femoral cutaneous nerve.
Blood Vessels: The superior genicular artery and vein.
Techniques: Roundhouse kick, pinching, thumb press.
Effects: Punishing pain in the inner leg.

Earth's Crux (SP08)

Location: 3 cun below the medial condyle of the tibia.
Nerve: The medial crural cutaneous nerve.
Blood Vessels: The great saphenous vein, the branch genu suprema artery.
Techniques: Side kick, roundhouse kick, hammer fist, thumb press, knifehand strike.
Effects: Excruciating pain in the interior shin, paralysis of the leg.

Inner Calf (AD-LE6)

Location: At the inner lower part of the gastrocnemius muscle.
Nerves: The branches of tibial nerve.
Blood Vessels: The branches of the peroneal artery.
Techniques: Roundhouse kick, hammer fist, thumb press, knifehand strike.
Effects: Tormenting pain, paralysis of the leg.

Central Metropolis (LV06)

Location: 7 cun above the tip of the medial malleolus, near the medial border of the tibia.
Nerve: The branch the saphenous nerve.
Blood Vessel: The great saphenous vein.
Techniques: Side kick, pushing kick.
Effects: Excruciating pain in the interior shin.

Leaking Valley (SP07)

Location: 6 cun above the tip of the medial malleolus, 3 cun above Three Yin Intersection (SP06).
Nerve: The medial crural cutaneous nerve.
Blood Vessels: The posterior tibial artery and vein, the great saphenous vein.
Techniques: Side kick, pushing kick, thumb press.
Effects: Acute pain in the interior shin.

Guest House (KI09)

Location: At the lower end of the belly of the gastrocnemius muscle.
Nerves: The medial crural and medial sural cutaenous nerves.
Blood Vessels: The posterior tibial artery and vein.
Techniques: Roundhouse kick, thumb press, forearm press, hammer fist, knifehand strike.
Effects: Sharp pain in the interior shin.

Three Yin Intersection (SP06)

Location: 3 cun above the tip of the medial malleolus, on the posterior border of the tibia.
Nerve: The medial crural cutaneous nerve.
Blood Vessels: The posterior tibial artery and vein, the great saphenous vein.
Techniques: Roundhouse kick, side kick, sweeping kick.
Effects: Excruciating pain in the interior shin.

Intersection Reach (KI08)

Location: 2 cun above Supreme Ravine (KI03), posterior to the medial border of the tibia.
Nerve: The medial crural cutaenous nerve.
Blood Vessels: The posterior tibial artery and vein.
Techniques: Roundhouse kick, sweeping kick, thumb press.
Effects: Extreme pain in the interior shin.

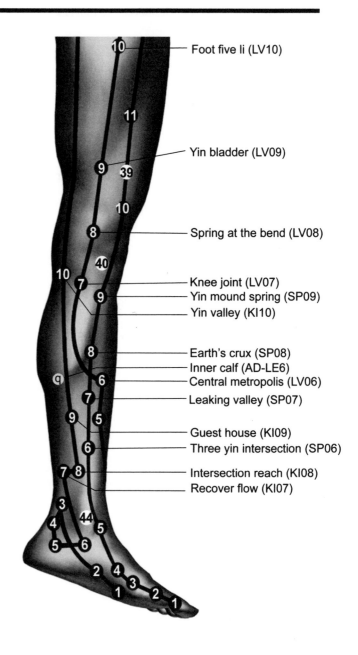

Foot five li (LV10)
Yin bladder (LV09)
Spring at the bend (LV08)
Knee joint (LV07)
Yin mound spring (SP09)
Yin valley (KI10)
Earth's crux (SP08)
Inner calf (AD-LE6)
Central metropolis (LV06)
Leaking valley (SP07)
Guest house (KI09)
Three yin intersection (SP06)
Intersection reach (KI08)
Recover flow (KI07)

Recover Flow (KI07)

Location: 2 cun above Supreme Ravine (KI03), on the anterior border of the Achilles tendon.
Nerves: The medial crural and medial sural cutaenous nerves.
Blood Vessels: The posterior tibial artery and vein.
Techniques: Sweeping kick, roundhouse kick.
Effects: Excruciating pain in the calf, loss of mobility.

APPLICATIONS

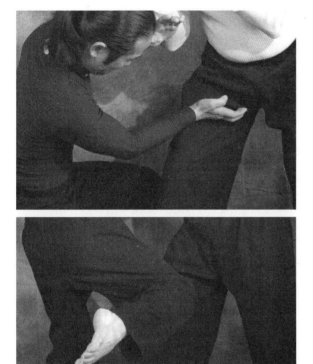

Strike the Foot Five Li

The Foot Five Li is located at the upper medial inner thigh where the branches of the femoral nerves spread down toward leg. Striking this region causes sharp pain in the inner thigh and muscle spasm in the deep layers of the muscles. Effective techniques for attacking the Foot Five Li are front kick, pushing kick, punch, knifehand strike, and elbow strike.

Knee Kick to the Yin Bladder

The Yin Bladder is a useful target for infighting. When the opponent moves his leg forward to launch his attack, kick the Yin Bladder with your front knee. If he loses his balance, immediately attack the head and take him down to the ground.

Kick the Spring at the Bend

The Spring at the Bend is located on the lower part of the inner thigh. This point is good to attack in the initial stage of a fight. Kicking this region causes pain in the inner thigh muscles that are important in lifting the leg for kicking. Repetitive hits on this target can impact the opponent's kicking performance. Kick quickly at an angle perpendicular to the target. The most effective technique is roundhouse kick or knee kick.

Heel Kick to the Knee Joint

The Knee Joint is in the upper portion of the gastrocnemius muscle. Kicking this spot causes sustained pain in the knee and destabilizes the opponent's footwork. Effective techniques for kicking the Knee Joint are side kick, roundhouse kick and inside heel kick.

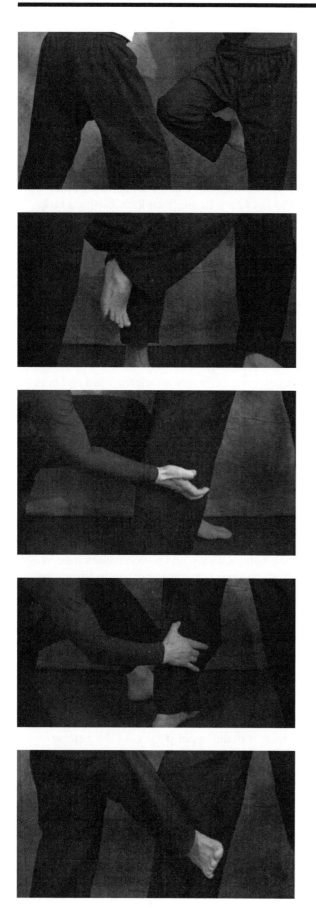

Kick the Yin Mound Spring

The Yin Mound Spring is on the lower edge of the tibia. This spot is where tournament fighters tend to crash into each other when trying to kick at close distance. A side kick, roundhouse kick, or knee kick to this point causes excruciating pain. Kick in a circular motion to avoid a bone-to-bone collision.

Donkey Kick to the Yin Valley

The Yin Valley is located on the side of the rear knee. Due to its location, hidden in the median posterior region of the knee, kicking this spot will shock the opponent, cause punishing pain in the inner leg and possibly collapse the leg. For a donkey kick, snap your foot to the rear as a donkey kicks backward.

Knifehand to the Earth's Crux

The Earth's Crux is between the gastrocnemius muscle and the soleus muscle which run vertically on the inner calf. Deliver your knifehand strike horizontally to the Earth's Crux to generate maximum impact by striking both muscles simultaneously. Other effective techniques are side kick, roundhouse kick, hammer fist, and thumb press.

Thumb Press on the Inner Calf

The Inner Calf is located at the inner posterior lower part of the gastrocnemius muscle. Press this point deeply with your thumb to cause a sharp startling pain in the calf. Additional effective techniques are knifehand strike, hammer fist and sweeping kick.

Kick the Central Metropolis

The Central Metropolis is located on the edge of the tibia. This is a useful spot to attack in infighting. As the opponent steps in, kick it with your heel or the bottom of the foot at a perpendicular angle. Be careful though; your opponent may throw you when you lift your foot, so do it quickly.

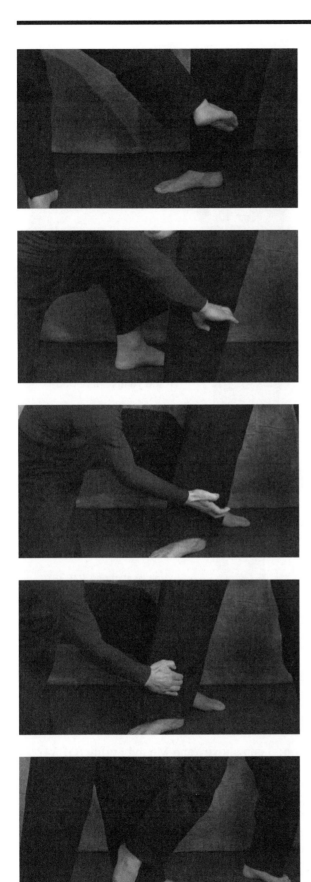

Kick the Leaking Valley

The Leaking Valley is in the center of the inner calf. This spot is a popular target among standing fighters to impair the mobility of an opponent. Kicking here causes sharp pain in the deep layers of the inner calf. Kick in a hooking motion so that you do not lose your balance after kicking and so that you can strike neighboring targets at the same time.

Ridge Knifehand Strike to the Guest House

The Guest House is an area composed of soft tissue located at the lower part of the inner calf. Pinching or a ridge knifehand strike causes acute pain, making this a good spot to attack when trapped in a front head lock. For kicking, use a hooking motion so that you hit the target at a perpendicular angle.

Knifehand to the Three Yin Intersection

The Three Yin Intersection is located above the ankle in the inner calf. Striking this point causes acute pain in the inner tibia. In addition to the knifehand, you can strike it with a palm heel or fingertip thrust then grab the ankle and take the opponent down.

Hitting the Intersection Reach

The Intersection Reach is located on the lower inner calf. This is a great spot for inside sweeping kick for two reasons: it causes pain and takes away the opponent's balance. Striking with a palm heel or knifehand strike is also an effective way to inflict pain prior to executing a takedown by hooking the ankle.

Donkey Kick to the Recover Flow

The Recover Flow is right behind the Intersection Reach point. This spot is hard to hit due to its hidden location. With a donkey kick, kicking back and upward, you can hit the spot on an opponent standing behind you and may be able to unbalance him by hooking the ankle toward you after the kick.

EXTERIOR LEG

Squatting Bone-Orifice (GB29)

Location: Midway between the anterosuperior iliac spine and the great trochanter.
Nerve: The lateral femoral cutaneous nerve.
Blood Vessels: The branches of the superficial circumflex iliac and the lateral circumflex femoral arteries and veins.
Techniques: Side kick, roundhouse kick, punch, elbow strike, knuckle punch, thumb press.
Effects: Sharp pain in the upper thigh, paralysis of the leg, loss of kicking ability.

Ring of Jumping (GB30)

Location: At the junction of the middle and lateral third of the distance between the great trochanter and the hiatus of the sacrum.
Nerves: The inferior cluneal cutaneous nerve, the inferior gluteal nerve.
Blood Vessels: The inferior gluteal artery and vein.
Techniques: Roundhouse kick, knee kick.
Effects: Severe pain in the hip, numbness of the leg.

Wind Market (GB31)

Location: On the midline of the lateral thigh, 7 cun above the transverse popliteal crease.
Nerves: The branches of the femoral nerve.
Blood Vessels: The branches of the lateral circumflex femoral artery and vein.
Techniques: Roundhouse kick, knee kick, side kick, elbow strike, hammer fist.
Effects: Paralysis of the leg.

Central River (GB32)

Location: On the lateral thigh, 5 cun above the transverse popliteal crease.
Nerves: The branches of the femoral nerve.
Blood Vessels: The branches of the lateral circumflex femoral artery and vein.
Techniques: Roundhouse kick, knee kick, elbow strike, hammer fist.
Effects: Paralysis of the leg, muscle spasm.

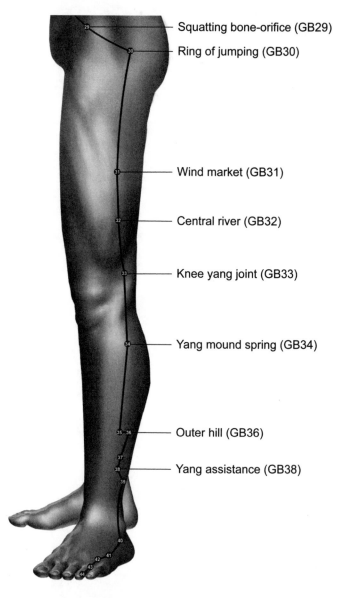

Squatting bone-orifice (GB29)
Ring of jumping (GB30)
Wind market (GB31)
Central river (GB32)
Knee yang joint (GB33)
Yang mound spring (GB34)
Outer hill (GB36)
Yang assistance (GB38)

Knee Yang Joint (GB33)

Location: 3 cun above Yang Mound Spring (GB34) lateral to the knee joint.
Nerve: The branch of the lateral femoral cutaneous nerve.
Blood Vessels: The superior lateral genicular artery and vein.
Techniques: Side kick.
Effects: Damage to the knee joint, loss of mobility.

Yang Mound Spring (GB34)

Location: In the depression anterior and inferior to the head of the fibula.
Nerves: The branches of the common peroneal nerve.
Blood Vessels: The inferior lateral genicular artery and vein.
Techniques: Side kick, roundhouse kick.
Effects: Acute pain on the shin.

Outer Hill (GB36)

Location: 7 cun above the tip of the external malleolus on the anterior border of the fibula.
Nerve: The superficial peroneal nerve.
Blood Vessels: The branches of the anterior tibial artery and vein.
Techniques: Side kick, roundhouse kick.
Effects: Sharp pain on the shin, loss of balance.

Yang Assistance (GB38)

Location: 4 cun above and anterior to the tip of the external malleolus on the anterior border of the fibula.
Nerve: The superficial peroneal nerve.
Blood Vessels: The branches of the anterior tibial artery and vein.
Techniques: Side kick, roundhouse kick.
Effects: Excruciating pain on the ankle, loss of balance and mobility.

APPLICATIONS

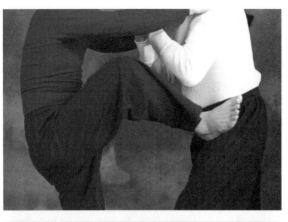

Stomp Kick on the Squatting Bone-Orifice

The Squatting Bone-Orifice is located in the lateral crease of the hip. If you are a good kicker, lift your leg and stomp the bottom of the heel into the point to cause excruciating pain that can paralyze the leg. Other options are an elbow strike, thumb press, hammer fist or knifehand strike.

Kick the Ring of Jumping

The Ring of Jumping is located slightly below the lateral center of the hip. Kicking this spot causes severe pain in the hip and incapacitates the leg. It is great spot to hit when the opponent does a back kick (or other spinning technique). As soon as he turns his body, throw a front pushing kick at the Ring of Jumping. He'll not only lose his balance, but also suffer sustained pain throughout the fight. Additional effective techniques are roundhouse kick and knee kick.

Knee Kick to the Wind Market

The Wind Market is located in the midline of the lateral thigh. Kicking this spot causes spasm of the outer thigh muscles. This is a good spot to strike with a knee in close fighting or with a roundhouse kick at a distance. Lift your knee and throw it in a circular motion to hit the target at a perpendicular angle.

Knee Kick to the Central River

The Central River is on the lateral thigh above the knee. This is a popular spot to strike to slow down a fast moving opponent. At long or medium distance, throw quick roundhouse kicks. If your opponent changes stance to avoid your kick, use the same kick on his inner thigh. If he clinches, throw repetitive knee kicks to the Central River. This technique will slow the opponent and make it easier for you to attack at will.

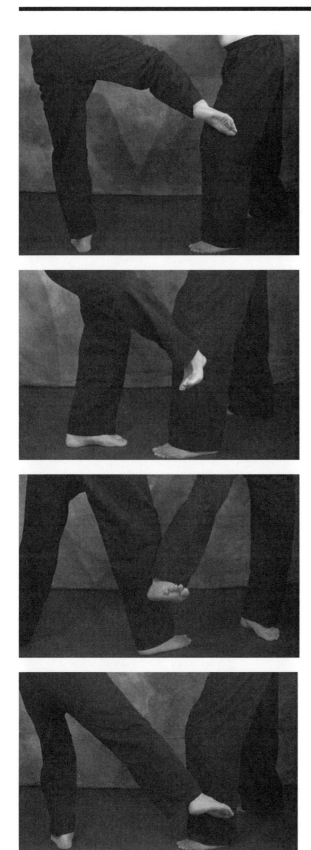

Roundhouse Kick to the Knee Yang Joint

The Knee Yang Joint is located lateral to the knee joint. In a standing fight, this is a good spot to attack with a roundhouse kick, side kick or knee kick. In ground combat, repeated elbow strikes to the Knee Yang Joint can damage the knee.

Heel Kick to the Yang Mound Spring

The Yang Mound Spring is in the depression on the upper lateral shin. Striking this spot with a heel kick, side kick, roundhouse kick, elbow or hammer fist causes acute pain in the leg and disables the leg. This is a useful target in close quarter fighting.

Heel Kick to the Outer Hill

The Outer Hill is above the ankle. This is a good target to attack on a heavier opponent who has overpowered you. As soon as he closes in, throw a roundhouse kick or heel kick to the target (depending on whether you are facing toward or away from him). Kicking the Outer Hill causes sharp pain in the shin and possibly fracture of the fibula.

Roundhouse Kick to the Yang Assistance

The Yang Assistance is above and anterior to the ankle. This is a good tactical spot to distract the opponent. For example, kick this spot with a rear leg roundhouse kick and when the opponent stumbles, attack his face with combination punches or strikes.

VITAL POINTS ON THE FOOT

ANTERIOR FOOT

Divided Ravine (ST41)

Location: At the junction of the dorsal foot and leg.
Nerves: The superficial and deep peroneal nerves.
Blood Vessels: The anterior tibial artery and vein.
Techniques: Side kick, stomp kick, forearm press.
Effects: Sharp pain on the ankle joint and foot, structural damage to the joint.

Hill Ruins (GB40)

Location: Anterior, inferior to the external malleolus.
Nerve: The branch of the superficial peroneal nerve.
Blood Vessel: The branch of the anterolateral malleolar artery.
Techniques: Thumb press, stomp kick.
Effects: Unbearable pain on the foot, loss of mobility.

Central Mound (LV04)

Location: 1 cun anterior to the medial malleolus, in the depression on the medial side of the tendon of the anterior tibial muscle.
Nerves: The branch of the medial dorsal cutaneous nerve, the saphenous nerve.
Blood Vessel: The anterior medial malleolar artery.
Techniques: Stomp kick.
Effects: Acute pain in the foot.

Surging Yang (ST42)

Location: In the depression between the 2nd and 3rd metatarsal bones and the cuneiform bone.
Nerves: The branches of the superficial and deep peroneal nerves.

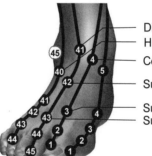

Divided ravine (ST41)
Hill ruins (GB40)
Central mound (LV04)
Surging yang (ST42)
Supreme surge (LV03)
Sunken valley (ST43)

Blood Vessels: The dorsal artery and vein of the foot.
Techniques: Stomp kick.
Effects: Severe pain on the instep.

Supreme Surge (LV03)

Location: In the depression of the junction of the 1st and 2nd metatarsal bones.
Nerve: The branch of the deep peroneal nerve.
Blood Vessel: The 1st dorsal metatarsal artery.
Techniques: Thumb press, knuckle press, stomp kick.
Effects: Unbearable pain in the foot, loss of mobility.

Sunken Valley (ST43)

Location: In the depression of the junction of the 2nd and 3rd metatarsal bones.
Nerve: The medial dorsal cutaneous nerve of the foot.
Blood Vessels: The dorsal venous network of the foot.
Techniques: Stomp kick, thumb press, knuckle press.
Effects: Acute pain in the foot.

APPLICATIONS

Stomp Kick to the Divided Ravine

The Divided Ravine is at the junction of the top of the foot and the leg. The peroneal nerves and tibial artery and vein branch out to the toes in this region. A stomp kick on this spot can not only cause unbearable pain but also damage the structure of the joint. This is a good technique to soften up an opponent who is clinching or grabbing you.

Strike the Hill Ruins

The Hill Ruins is located below the ankle on the instep. This spot is rich with small veins and nerves. A thumb press, knuckle punch or knifehand strike can cause excruciating pain in the foot and impair the opponent's mobility. A side stomp kick can disable the function of the ankle momentarily.

Stomp the Central Mound

The Central Mound is located on top of the instep. This is the junction of the leg and ankle where nerves and arteries branch out to the toes. A side stomp kick can damage the joint and blood vessels in this region, resulting in the opponent's inability to put weight on his foot. After the kick, push the opponent backward while your foot is still stomping on his foot for added impact, however be aware that this can result in permanent damage to the tendons and ligaments of the foot.

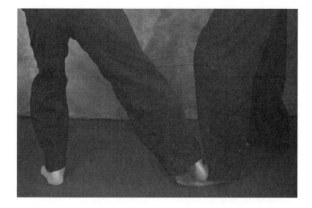

Stomp Kick to the Surging Yang

The Surging Yang is in the depression near the top of the instep. A stomp kick to this spot can disable the function of the foot. If done properly, the opponent may react by bending his body forward, allowing you to throw a knee kick to his face or go for a side headlock and take him to the ground.

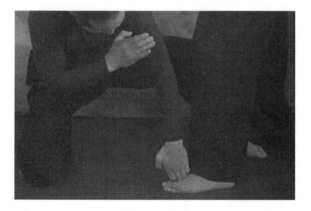

Knuckle Punch to the Supreme Surge

The Supreme Surge is located in the depression of the bones of the foot. Pressing this spot causes excruciating pain and sustained pressure can numb the entire leg. This technique is useful when you are caught by a front headlock. While inserting one hand into the lock to try to loosen the opponent's grip, strike or press this spot to distract him.

Stomp on the Sunken Valley

The Sunken Valley is in the middle of the instep. Stomping this spot causes acute pain in the foot that spreads up to the hip through the peroneal nerve. A stomp kick with the bottom of the heel can fracture or dislocate the metatarsal bones, making it impossible for the opponent to stand comfortably or place his weight on the foot.

INTERIOR FOOT

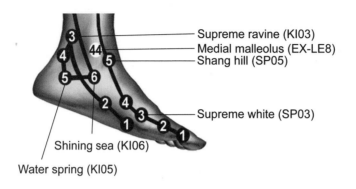

Supreme ravine (KI03)
Medial malleolus (EX-LE8)
Shang hill (SP05)
Supreme white (SP03)
Shining sea (KI06)
Water spring (KI05)

Supreme Ravine (KI03)

Location: In the depression posterior to the Medial Malleolus (EX-LE8).
Nerve: The tibial nerve.
Blood Vessels: The posterior tibial artery and vein.
Techniques: Thumb press, sweeping kick.
Effects: Electrifying pain in the ankle.

Medial Malleolus (EX-LE8)

Location: On the pyramid-shaped process of the tibia that projects at the ankle.
Nerves: The branches of peroneal nerve.
Blood Vessels: The branches of the peroneal artery.
Techniques: Roundhouse kick, sweep kick.
Effects: Acute pain in the ankle, loss of mobility.

Shang Hill (SP05)

Location: In the depression distal and inferior to the medial malleolus.
Nerves: The medial crural cutaneous nerve, the branch of the superficial peroneal nerve.
Blood Vessels: The medial tarsal artery, the great saphenous vein.
Techniques: Stomp kick, side kick, thumb press.
Effects: Acute pain in the ankle, loss of mobility.

Supreme White (SP03)

Location: Proximal and inferior to the head of the 1st metatarsal bone.
Nerves: The branches of the saphenous and superficial peroneal nerves.
Blood Vessels: The branches of the medial tarsal and plantar arteries.
Techniques: Thumb press.
Effects: Sharp pain in the foot.

Shining Sea (KI06)

Location: 1 cun below the medial malleolus.
Nerve: The medial crural cutaneous nerve.
Blood Vessels: The posterior tibial artery and vein.
Techniques: Sweeping kick, thumb press.
Effects: Sharp pain in the interior ankle.

Water Spring (KI05)

Location: 1 cun below the Supreme Ravine (KI03).
Nerve: The medial crural cutaenous nerve.
Blood Vessels: The branch of the posterior tibial artery and vein.
Techniques: Thumb press, sweeping kick.
Effects: Sharp and sustaining pain in the foot.

APPLICATIONS

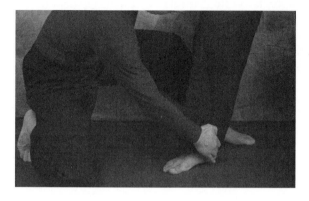

Thumb Press on the Supreme Ravine

The Supreme Ravine is located in the depression behind the ankle. Due to the presence of the tibial nerve, the impact on this spot is directly transmitted to the upper leg. Press the spot with your thumb or strike it with the middle fingertip. In a stand up fight, an inside sweeping kick also causes electrifying pain in the ankle.

Kick the Medial Malleolus

The Medial Malleolus is the protruding bone at the bottom of the tibia, on the inner ankle. Kicking this spot can cause pain and permanent damage to the ankle. The precise target you need to aim for is the bottom of the protruding bone where the medial ligament of ankle begins. Striking this spot causes tormenting pain in the ankle due to damage to the ligament and loss of mobility.

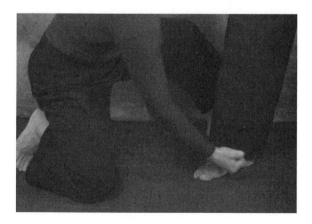

Strike the Shang Hill

The Shang Hill is located in the depression in front of and below the inner ankle. A hammer fist strike, knifehand strike or thumb press causes sharp pain that spreads to the shin and instep. Strike at an angle to penetrate deeply into the crease between the ankle and leg and increase the pain of the strike.

Squeeze the Supreme White

The Supreme White is located on the instep next to the head of the 1st metatarsal bone. Squeeze the Supreme White with the proximal phalange of your thumb while grabbing the outer foot with your fingers to increase the force of your squeezing.

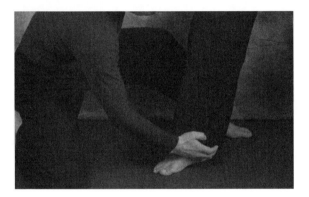

Knifehand Strike to the Shining Sea

The Shining Star is located below the medial malleolus. A thumb press, knuckle punch, or knife-hand strike generates excruciating pain in the leg. This is a good target to attack when you are grabbed and desperate.

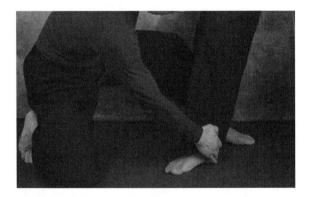

Strike the Water Spring

The Water Spring is on the posterior inner ankle. This is an excellent target to strike or press from the rear to generate electrifying pain along the rear ankle. When you are caught in a headlock from the side or front, use this technique to ease the grab.

EXTERIOR FOOT

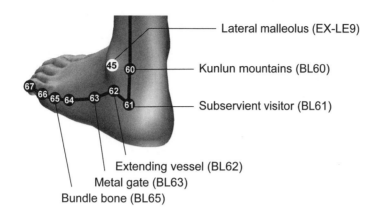

Lateral malleolus (EX-LE9)

Kunlun mountains (BL60)

Subservient visitor (BL61)

Extending vessel (BL62)

Metal gate (BL63)

Bundle bone (BL65)

Lateral Malleolus (EX-LE9)

Location: At the tip of the pyramid-shaped process of the fibula that projects at the ankle.
Nerves: The superficial peroneal nerves.
Blood Vessel: The lateral malleolus artery.
Techniques: Side kick, front kick, sweep kick.
Effects: Sharp pain on the outer ankle.

Kunlun Mountains (BL60)

Location: In the depression between the external malleolus and Achilles tendon.
Nerve: The sural nerve.
Blood Vessels: The small saphenous vein, the postero-external malleolar artery and vein.
Techniques: Thumb press, knuckle press.
Effects: Sharp pain in the lower leg.

Subservient Visitor (BL61)

Location: In the posterior depression below the external malleolus.
Nerve: The branch of the sural nerve.
Blood Vessels: The branches of the peroneal artery and vein.
Techniques: Sweeping kick, thumb press, knuckle press, knuckle punch.
Effects: Tormenting pain below the posterior ankle.

Extending Vessel (BL62)

Location: In the depression below the external malleolus.
Nerve: The sural nerve.
Blood Vessel: The external malleolar artery.
Techniques: Sweeping kick, thumb press, knuckle press.
Effects: Acute pain on the foot.

Metal Gate (BL63)

Location: In the depression lateral to the cuboid bone.
Nerve: The lateral dorsal cutaneous nerve of the foot.
Blood Vessels: The lateral plantar artery and vein.
Techniques: Stomp kick, thumb press, knuckle press.
Effects: Acute pain on the foot.

Bundle Bone (BL65)

Location: On the lateral side of the foot, posterior and inferior to the head of the 5th metatarsal bone.
Nerve: The lateral dorsal cutaneous nerve.
Blood Vessels: The plantar digital artery and vein.
Techniques: Stomp kick, thumb press, squeezing.
Effects: Sharp pain on the foot.

APPLICATIONS

Kick the Lateral Malleolus

The Lateral Malleolus is at the bottom of the fibula which is connected to the ankle joint by the calcaneofibular ligament. Kicking this spot causes unbearable pain in the ankle. When you are wearing shoes, kick with the heel. A simultaneous attack to the Lateral Malleolus and the calcaneofibular ligament can make the opponent crippled momentarily and potentially cause permanent damage to the ankle.

Roundhouse Kick to the Kunlun Mountains

The Kunlun Mountains is located in the depression behind the ankle on the outside of the foot. In a street fight, deliver a roundhouse kick from the side or rear to ensure precise contact with the target. This is a good way to take down a larger opponent by chopping at his base and then pulling him down to the ground.

Thumb Press on the Subservient Visitor

The Subservient Visitor is located in the depression below and behind the ankle on the outside of the foot and is the spot where the peroneus brevis tendon travels downward to connect to the 5th metatarsal bone. Pressing this spot with the tip of your thumb causes excruciating pain in the rear ankle.

Knifehand to the Extending Vessel

The Extending Vessel is located in the depression below the ankle on the outside of the foot. If your hand is well-hardened by training, strike this point with your knifehand at a slightly upward angle. A thumb press is also effective for generating sharp pain. Kicking with the tip of a pointed shoe produces intense pain that can cripple an opponent.

Punch the Metal Gate

The Metal Gate is located in the depression lateral to the cuboid bone. Striking this spot with the middle knuckle causes stabbing pain in the outer foot. Other effective techniques are the stomp kick, thumb press, knuckle press, and knuckle punch.

Stomp the Bundle Bone

The Bundle Bone is located on the lateral side of the foot, next to the head of the 5th metatarsal bone. Stomping with the bottom of the foot can fracture the bones of the foot causing intense pain. If you are on the ground with few options, drop your elbow on the Bundle Bone. Your opponent may jump like a startled rabbit. Additional effective techniques are a thumb press and squeezing the point.

VITAL POINT
APPLICATIONS

CHAPTER 10

VITAL POINT
STRIKING DRILLS

*Vital Point Striking Drills are designed to help you con-
dition your body to the mental image of the techniques.
By practicing the drills, you can enhance the precision,
speed and naturalness of your performance. Begin with
a single technique. Once you're comfortable with it, add
another one, and continue to add more as you progress.
Ultimately, you'll be able to execute 3 to 5 techniques in
one second or less. Keep in mind though that a thousand
mile journey begins with the first step. Start slowly and
practice steadily. Speed and power come as result of
diligent and honest effort. These sample drills are just
the beginning. Once you understand how to practice the
drills, create your own combinations to suit your needs.*

EXERCISE #1

Standing Fight Striking Drill 1

General Guide: Drilling is a process of conditioning the body to a mental image of the technique. Through repetition, you can eliminate things that hinder your performance and techniques become automatic. Begin the drill slowly so that you can teach your muscles each step properly. Speed comes naturally as you progress.

Practice Guide:

Single Technique Practice: Practice 10 repetitions of Technique #1 and then practice 10 repetitions of Technique #2 on the right side. Repeat the set from the left side.

Technique Description:

#1: Lead hand punch to the White Bone-Orifice (GV25)
#2: Lead foot front kick to the Medial Eyes of the Knee (EX-LE4)

EXERCISE #2

STANDING FIGHT STRIKING DRILL 2

General Guide: Practice Techniques #1 and 2 as a combination. Focus on your rhythm. Pay more attention to your precision than speed.

Practice Guide:

> Progressive Group Practice: Practice 4 repetitions of Techniques #1 and 2 as a combination on the right side. Repeat the set from the left side.

Technique Description:

> #1: Lead hand punch to the White Bone-Orifice (GV25)
> #2: Lead foot front kick to the Medial Eyes of the Knee (EX-LE4)

EXERCISE #3

STANDING FIGHT STRIKING DRILL 3

General Guide: In this drill practice how to shift your weight efficiently. Discover your optimal stance width for quick smooth transitions between front hand striking and rear hand striking.

Practice Guide:

    1) Stage One: Practice #1 and 2 as a combination, then #3 as an independent technique.
       Practice 10 repetitions on each side.
    2) Stage Two: Progressive Group Practice
       Practice #1-3 as a combination 5 times on the right side. Repeat the entire set from the left side.

Technique Description:

    #1: Lead hand punch to the White Bone-Orifice (GV25)
    #2: Lead foot front kick to the Medial Eyes of the Knee (EX-LE4)
    #3: Rear hand palm strike to the Dorsal Center (AD-UE5)

EXERCISE #4

STANDING FIGHT STRIKING DRILL 4

General Guide: In this drill practice how to commit yourself to overcoming the inertia of consecutive techniques without losing the center of your bodily force.

Practice Guide:
1) Stage One: Single Technique Practice
Practice Technique #4 10 times on each side.
2) Stage Two: Progressive Group Practice
Practice #1-4 as a combination 5 times on the right side. Repeat the set from the left side.

Technique Description:
#1: Lead hand punch to the White Bone-Orifice (GV25)
#2: Lead foot front kick to the Medial Eyes of the Knee (EX-LE4)
#3: Rear hand palm strike to the Dorsal Center (AD-UE5)
#4: Rear foot roundhouse kick to the Recover Flow (KI07)

EXERCISE #5

STANDING FIGHT STRIKING DRILL 5

General Guide: In this drill practice how to magnify the attacking force by coiling and uncoiling your muscles. Particularly after technique #4, drop your left foot in front of you and rotate your upper body to throw a right punch to the chin for a knockout.

Practice Guide:
1) Stage One: Single Technique Practice
   Practice Technique #5 10 times on each side.
2) Stage Two: Progressive Group Practice
   Practice #1-5 as a combination 5 times on the right side. Repeat the set from the left side.

Technique Description:
   #1: Lead hand punch to the White Bone-Orifice (GV25)
   #2: Lead foot front kick to the Medial Eyes of the Knee (EX-LE4)
   #3: Rear hand palm strike to the Dorsal Center (AD-UE5)
   #4: Rear foot roundhouse kick to the Recover Flow (KI07)
   #5: Lead hand punch to the Sauce Receptacle (CV24)

EXERCISE #6

STANDING FIGHT STRIKING DRILL 6

General Guide: In this drill, practice how to penetrate into the center of the opponent's power.

Practice Guide:
1) Stage One: Single Technique Practice
   Practice Technique #6 10 times on each side.
2) Stage Two: Progressive Group Practice
   Practice #1-6 as a combination 5 times on the right side. Repeat the set from the left side.

Technique Description:
#1: Lead hand punch to the White Bone-Orifice (GV25)
#2: Lead foot front kick to the Medial Eyes of the Knee (EX-LE4)
#3: Rear hand palm strike to the Dorsal Center (AD-UE5)
#4: Rear foot roundhouse kick to the Recover Flow (KI07)
#5: Lead hand punch to the Sauce Receptacle (CV24)
#6: Rear knee kick to the Groin (AD-T1)

EXERCISE #7

STANDING FIGHT STRIKING DRILL 7

General Guide: In this drill practice how to anticipate your opponent's reaction and respond appropriately. For instance, when you do a left knee kick to the groin he may bend forward in pain, then throw your right uppercut to his Solar Plexus (Turtledove Tail) or the under his chin (Ridge Spring).

Practice Guide:
1) Stage One: Single Technique Practice
   Practice Technique #7 10 times on each side.
2) Stage Two: Progressive Group Practice
   Practice #1-4 as Combination 1 and #5-7 as Combination 2. Repeat Combinations 1 and 2 in sequence 5 times on the right side. Repeat the entire set from the left side.

Technique Description:
#1: Lead hand punch to the White Bone-Orifice (GV25)
#2: Lead foot front kick to the Medial Eyes of the Knee (EX-LE4)
#3: Rear hand palm strike to the Dorsal Center (AD-UE5)
#4: Rear foot roundhouse kick to the Recover Flow (KI07)
#5: Lead hand punch to the Sauce Receptacle (CV24)
#6: Rear knee kick to the Groin (AD-T1)
#7: Lead hand uppercut to the Turtledove Tail (CV15)

EXERCISE #8

STANDING FIGHT STRIKING DRILL 8

General Guide: In this drill, practice how to commit your body to full attack and retreat, then attack with the second wave of a left roundhouse kick to the rear of the knee.

Practice Guide:
  1) Stage One: Single Technique Practice
     Practice Technique #8 10 times on each side. (Move your left foot forward, retreat, then left roundhouse kick and drop your left foot in front. Reverse when you change stance.)
  2) Stage Two: Progressive Group Practice
     Practice #1-5 as Combination 1 and #6-8 as Combination 2. Repeat Combinations 1 and 2 in sequence 5 times on the right side. Repeat the entire set from the left side.

Technique Description:
  #1: Lead hand punch to the nose
  #2: Lead foot front kick to the kneecap
  #3: Rear hand palm tap to the opponent's rear hand
  #4: Rear foot roundhouse kick to the inner lead ankle
  #5: Lead hand punch to the chin
  #6: Rear knee kick to the groin
  #7: Lead punch to the Solar Plexus
  #8: Step back and rear foot roundhouse kick to the Knee Joint (LV07)

EXERCISE #9

STANDING FIGHT STRIKING DRILL 9

General Guide: In this drill practice how to launch a surprise third wave attack. After Technique #8 (roundhouse kick to the rear knee), withdraw the kicking foot to the rear, then boldly shoot a rear roundhouse kick to the carotid artery on the neck. This is a powerful combination for a knockout: a good target, a powerful technique, and the element of surprise.

Practice Guide:

> Practice #1-5 as Combination 1, then #6-8 as Combination 2, and finally practice Technique #9 with full concentration as a single technique. Repeat the sequence 5 times on each side.

Technique Description:

> #1: Lead hand punch to the nose
> #2: Lead foot front kick to the kneecap
> #3: Rear hand palm tap to the opponent's rear hand
> #4: Rear foot roundhouse kick to the inner lead ankle
> #5: Lead hand punch to the chin
> #6: Rear knee kick to the groin
> #7: Lead punch to the Solar Plexus
> #8: Step back and rear foot roundhouse kick to the Knee Joint (LV07)
> #9: Step back and rear foot roundhouse kick to the Protuberance Assistance (LI18)

EXERCISE #10

GROUND FIGHT DRILL 1

General Guide: From the guard position, practice pre-emptive striking before he punches you. If he punches you, cover your face, and respond with counter strikes, or trap his hands and strike back.

Practice Guide:
  Practice Techniques #1-4 as single techniques 5 times. When you are confident, practice #1 and 2 as a combination. Then practice #1-2-3 as a sequence. Finally combine #1-2-3-4 as a sequence.

Technique Description:
  #1: Left punch to the White Bone-Orifice (GV25)
  #2: Right punch to the Great Bone-Orifice (ST03)
  #3: Left palm block and right punch to the Four Whites (ST02)
  #4: Left hand trapping and right palm heel strike to the Ridge Spring (CV23)

271

EXERCISE #11

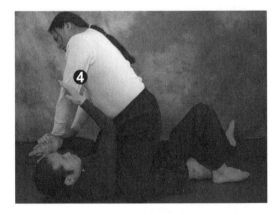

GROUND FIGHT DRILL 2

General Guide: From the guard position, practice pre-emptive striking before he punches you. When he begins to punch you, control his arm and topple him off.

Practice Guide:

Practice Techniques #1-2 as a combination. Practice #3 and #4 independently and then combine them into a combination of #1-2-3-4.

Technique Description:

#1: Left punch to the White Bone-Orifice (GV25)
#2: Right punch to the Great Bone-Orifice (ST03)
#3: Left hand wrist control and right fingertip thrust or punch to the Great Horizontal (SP15)
#4: Left hand wrist control and right knifehand strike to the Small Sea (SI08)

CAUTION

In the following chapters, Book 3 introduces sample-training scenarios. The techniques in this book can be very dangerous. You should practice these drills with utmost caution and should not strike vital points on another person in practice. Furthermore, when using any technique in self-defense, your actions should always be justified and in compliance with the laws of your place of residence.

Alternatives are presented for your personal expansion of your training repertoire. You may incorporate these techniques in any sequences that are appropriate: before or after presented techniques, as substitutes for presented techniques, as a solo application, or in combination with other techniques that you find workable.

CHAPTER 11

STANDING FIGHT APPLICATIONS

*Success in a standing fight is often determined by your ability
to control the distance and angles and throw overpowering
techniques.*

*Being overpowering means your fitness must be at an optimal
level. A technique without physical power is like a paper tiger.
Distance control comes from experience and confidence about
your actions in relation to the techniques your opponent tries
to execute. Angle control comes from your capacity to spot an
opening immediately and precisely strike the target by maneuvering your bodily weapon according to the target presented.*

*With this knowledge of distance, angle and technique in
mind, your goal is to discover what you can do in potentially
dangerous situations through practice and adaptation of the
sample scenarios in the following pages.*

AGAINST REAR SHOULDER GRAB

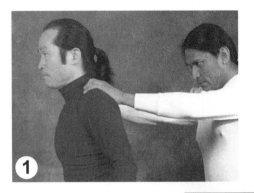

1. Recognize the situation: try to see or feel the position of the opponent's arms to prepare the best counterattack.

Focus: Find the weakest spot.

2. Strike the Groin (AD-T1) with a hammer fist or backfist.
3. Immediately punch to the Seal Hall (EX-HN3). You may do both techniques simultaneously, as shown in step 3.

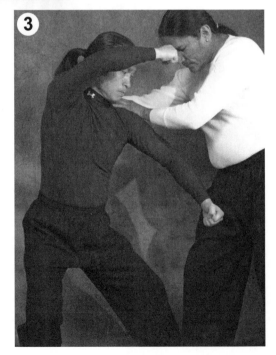

ALTERNATIVE TECHNIQUES

Palm strike to the Great Bone-Orifice (ST03)

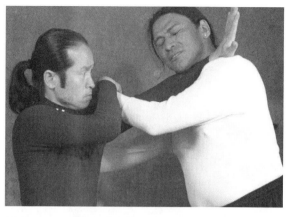

Forearm push to the Protuberance Assistance (LI18) while controlling his wrist

Forearm push to the Adam's Apple (AD-N1) while twisting the wrist downward (focusing your power on his wrist)

Forearm push to the Protuberance Assistance (LI18) while twisting his wrist downward (focusing your power on his neck)

Breaking his wrist downward by pressing the Lumbar Pain Point (EX-UE7) with your right thumb while barricading the Protuberance Assistance (LI18) with your forearm

277

AGAINST REAR BEAR HUG

1. Strike the Groin (AD-T1) with a hammer fist.
2. Rear headbutt to the Temporal Hairline (GB07).
3. Grab the wrists and press them down and inward.
4. Unlock his grip.
5. Twist one wrist outward while pivoting your body counterclockwise.
6. Press the Exterior Pericardium (EX-UE8) for more control.

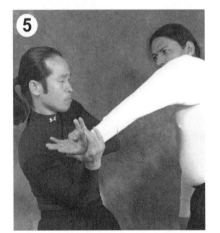

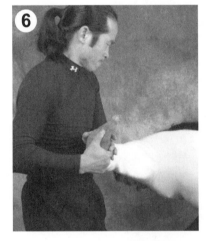

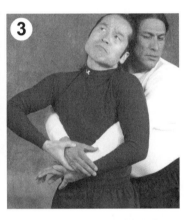

7. Pull him toward you and elbow strike to the upper elbow.
8. Pull the wrist inward and elbow strike the Spirit Tower (GV10).
9. Choke his neck with your left inner forearm.
10. Lower his wrist and transfer his wrist to your other hand.
11. Hook punch to the Capital Gate (GB25).
12. Elbow strike on the Spirit Hall (BL44).

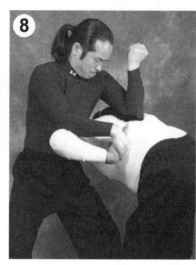

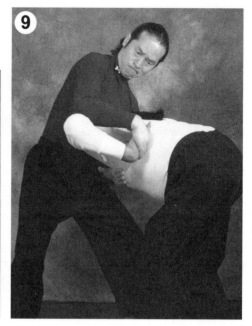

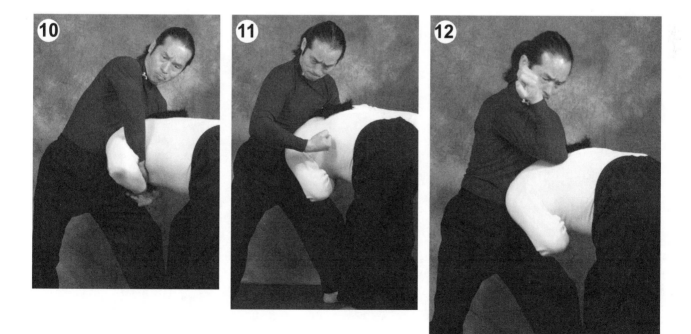

AGAINST REAR BEAR HUG 2

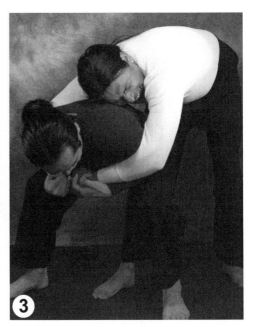

1. Breathe in deeply.
2. Breathe out and lower your center of the gravity.
3. Bend your body forward.
4. Strike the Groin (AD-T1) with a hammer fist.
5. Stomp kick to the Surging Yang (ST42).
6. Put your foot behind his.
7. Elbow strike to the Sea of Blood (SP10).
8. Push your chest forward and execute a rear headbutt to his face.

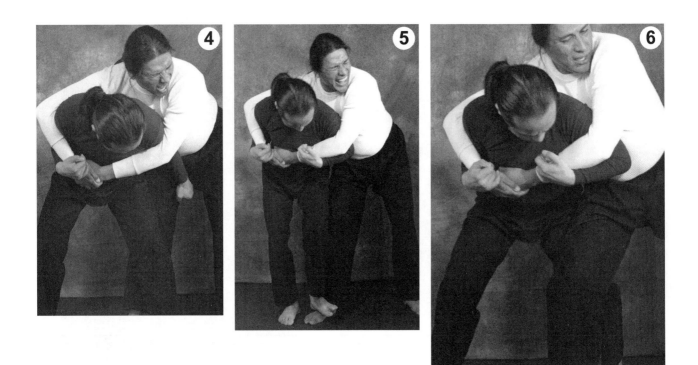

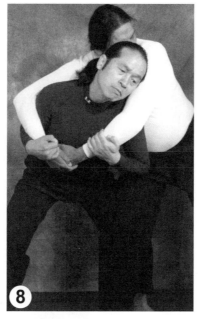

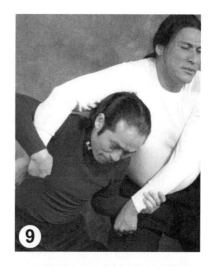

9. Unlock his grip and move your body backward.
10. Grab his wrist and press the Dispersing Riverbed (TW12).
11. Press him forward.
12. Execute an armbar using your shoulder.
13. Knifehand strike to the Celestial Well (TW10).

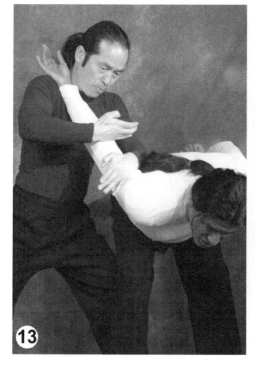

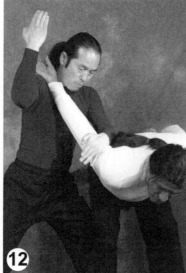

ALTERNATIVE TECHNIQUES

Hooking hand press

Elbow strike to the Will Chamber (BL52)

Punch to the Lesser Sea (HT03)

Hammer fist to the Stomach Transport (BL21)

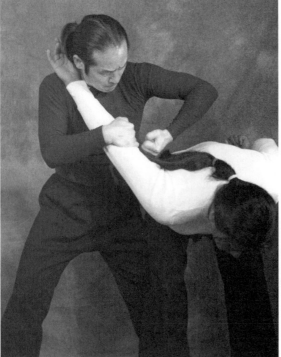

Elbow strike to the Kidney Transport (BL23)

Elbow strike to the Stomach Transport (BL21)

Hammer fist to the Shoulder Well (GB21)

Backfist to the Auricle (AD-H2)

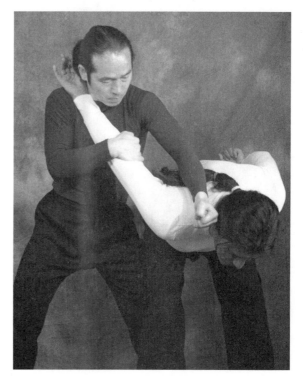

AGAINST FRONT WRIST GRAB

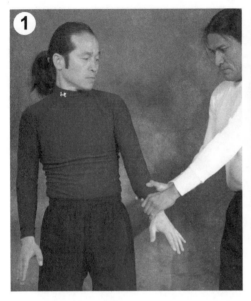

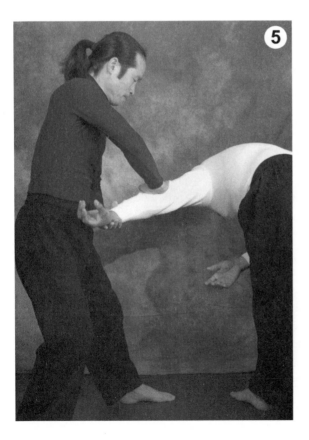

1. Open your fingers for strength.
2. Twist your left wrist inward and right fingertip thrust to the Ridge Spring (CV23).
3. Rotate your left wrist upward and grab his wrist with your right hand.
4. Rotate your left wrist further to break his grip and push the Clear Cold Abyss (TW11) with your right palm.
5. Pull his wrist and press his elbow downward to the ground.

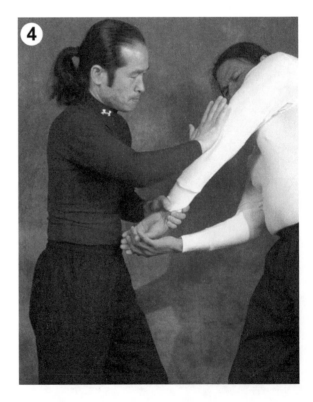

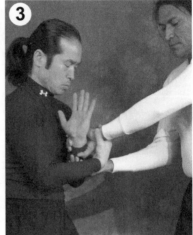

ALTERNATIVE TECHNIQUES

Vertical punch to the Eyeball (AD-H1)

Vertical punch to the Great Bone-Orifice (ST03)

Vertical punch to the Florid Canopy (CV20)

Fingertip thrust to the Energy Abode (ST11)

Fingertip thrust to the Empty Basin (ST12)

Palm heel strike to the White Bone-Orifice (GV25)

Knifehand strike to the Shoulder Well (GB21)

Thumb press to the Cubit Marsh (LU05)

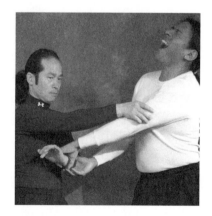

Thumb press to the Lower Biceps (AD-UE1)

285

ALTERNATIVE TECHNIQUES (CONTINUED)

Palm heel strike to the Celestial Well (TW10)

Fingertip thrust to the Abdominal Lament (SP16)

Fingertip thrust to the Outer Mound (ST26)

Fingertip thrust to the Waterway (ST28)

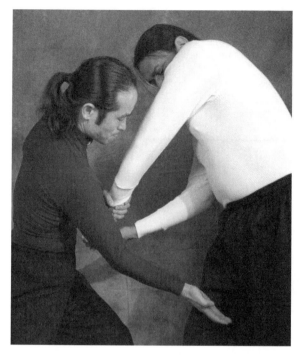

Palm heel strike to the Groin (AD-T1)

Elbow strike to the Blue Spirit (HT02)

Elbow strike to the Spirit Hall (BL44)

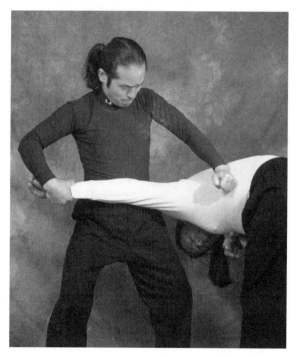

Hammer fist to the Camphorwood Gate (LV13)

AGAINST FRONT WRIST GRAB (BOTH HANDS)

1. Move the left wrist up while twisting outward and the right wrist down, twisting downward.

2. Grab the opponent's Lumbar Pain Point (EX-UE7) with your right hand.

3. Free your left wrist by continuing to twist and pull.

4. Elbow strike to the closest target on his head.

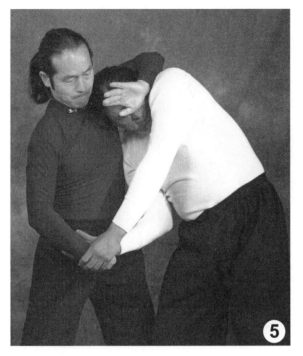

5. Pull his wrist and simultaneously press his head toward you with your left arm.

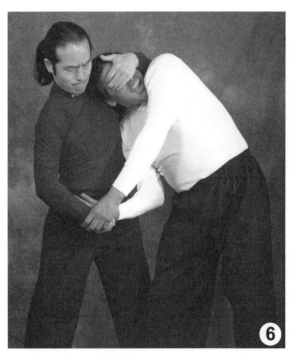

6. Slap his Eyeballs (AD-H1) with your palm and compress them.

7. Twist his wrist forcefully inward to bring his head toward you.

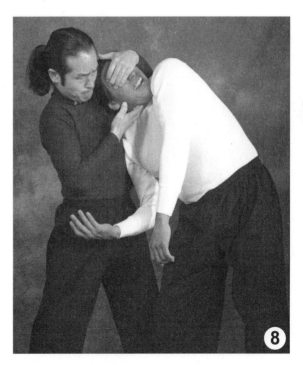

8. Fingertip thrust or knuckle punch to the Protuberance Assistance (LI18).

ALTERNATIVE TECHNIQUES

Elbow strike to the Celestial Spring (PC02)

Elbow strike to the Great Bone-Orifice (ST03)

Elbow strike to the Celestial Storehouse (LU03)

Elbow strike to the Leading Valley (GB08)

Punch to the Protuberance Assistance (LI18)

Thumb press to the Lower Biceps (AD-UE1)

Knee kick to the Wind Market (GB31)

Stomp kick to the Divided Ravine (ST41)

Against Rear Wrist Grab

1. Open your fingers for strength and control.
2. Drop your center of the gravity tilting your torso slightly forward, and simultaneously bend your elbows and spread your arms.
3. Bring your right arm over your head, with your palm facing forward and rotate the opponent's right wrist upside down.
4. Control the opponent's right wrist by pressing the Union Valley (LI04).

5. After gaining control of the wrist, punch the
   Lively Center (KI26).
6. Knee kick to the Gate of Abundance (BL37).
7. Rear choke on the Adam's Apple (AD-N1).
8. Palm strike to the Eyeballs (AD-H1).

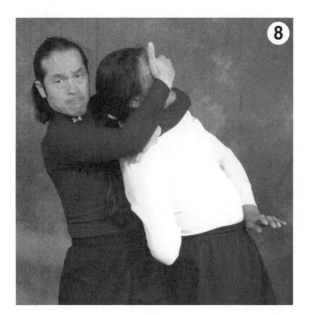

ALTERNATIVE TECHNIQUES

Hip snap to the Curved Bone (CV02)

Back kick to the Groin (AD-T1)

Thumb press to the Small Sea (SI08)

Knifehand strike to the Celestial Well (TW10)

Elbow strike to the Clear Cold Abyss (TW11)

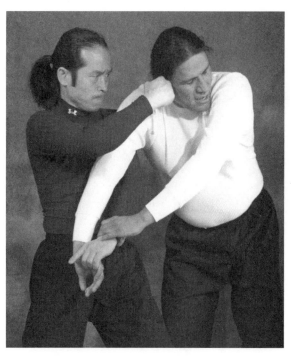

Punch to the Temple (EX-HN5)

Palm heel strike to the White Bone-Orifice
(GV25)

Palm heel strike to the Auditory Convergence
(GB02)

ALTERNATIVE TECHNIQUES (CONTINUED)

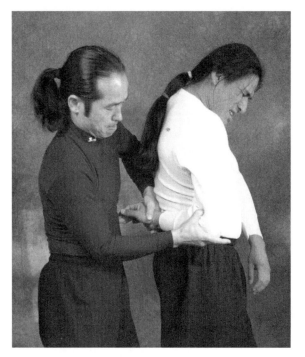

Thumb press to the Pool at the Bend (LI11)

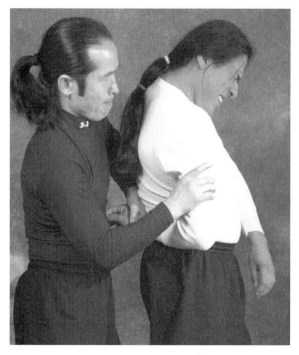

Thumb press to the Blue Spirit (HT02)

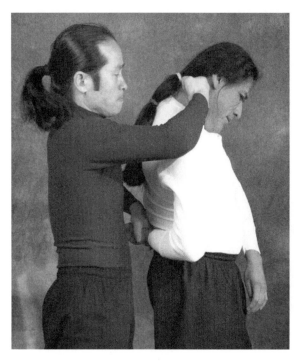

Punch to the Wind Pool (GB20)

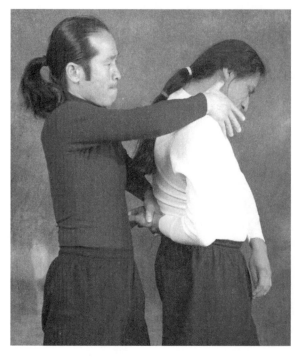

Thumb press to the Wind Screen (TW17)

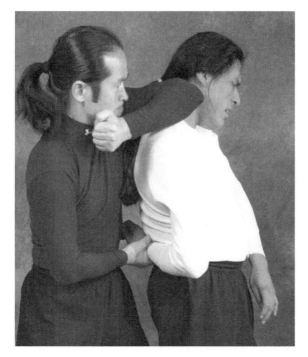

Elbow strike to the Wind Screen (TW17)

Fingertip thrust or knuckle punch to the Wind Pool (GB20)

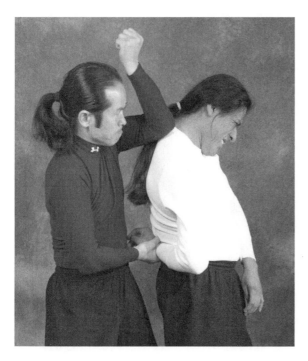

Elbow strike to the Great Hammer (GV14)

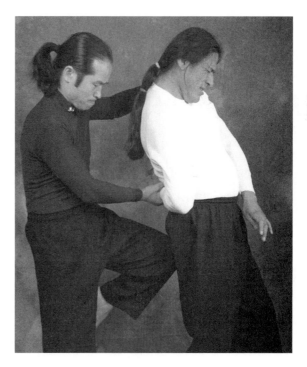

Knee kick to the Lumbar Transport (GV02)

AGAINST REAR CHOKE

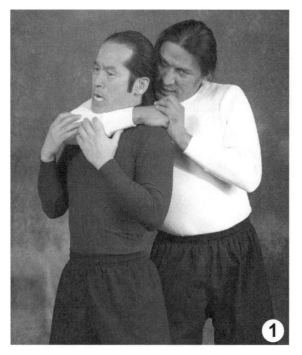

1. Stick your chin down into the opponent's forearm for breathing space.

2. Bring the chin down deeper and raise your elbow.

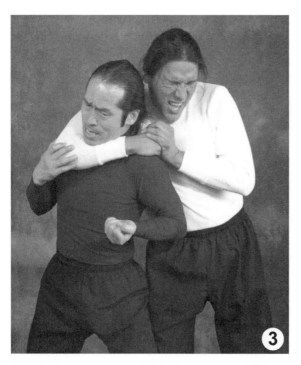

3. Elbow strike to the Spirit Gate Tower (CV08), aka the umbilicus.

4. Immediately hammer fist to the Groin (AD-T1).

298

5. As he reacts, bend forward and throw another elbow strike to the Waterway (ST28).

6. Immediately press the Third Space (LI03) with your left middle finger and press the Elbow Bone-Orifice (LI12) with your right fingers.

7. Move your whole body backward under his armpit keeping his arm against your body.

8. Pull his wrist upward behind him to secure an armlock.

AGAINST REAR CHOKE AND ARM LOCK

1. Tuck in your chin to gain breathing space and align your neck for strength.
2. Pivot your body outward on your right foot.
3. While rotating your body, right elbow strike to the Capital Gate (GB25).
4. Bend your body forward to disrupt his balance.

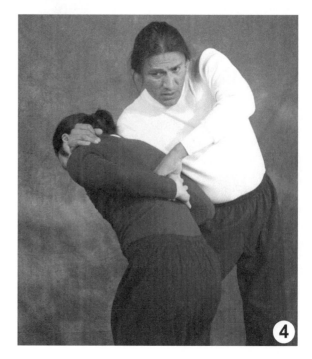

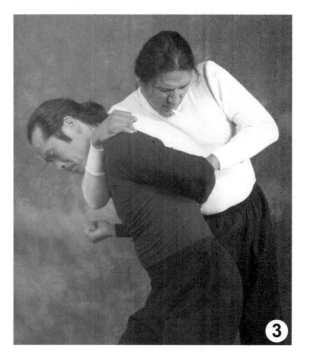

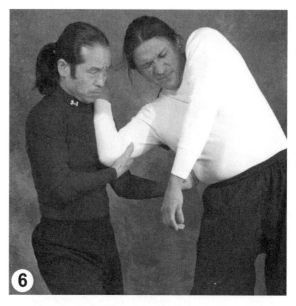

5. Pivot further into his body and press the Blue Spirit (HT02) with your right thumb.
6. Left punch to the Capital Gate (GB25).
7. Left elbow strike to the Celestial Pillar (BL10).
8. Apply an L-shape outward arm lock with a thumb press to the Lesser Sea (HT03).

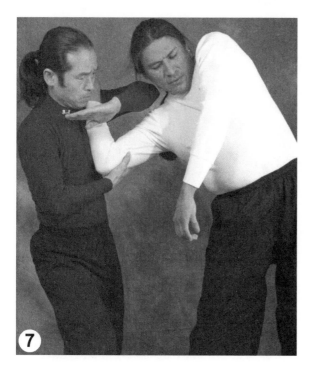

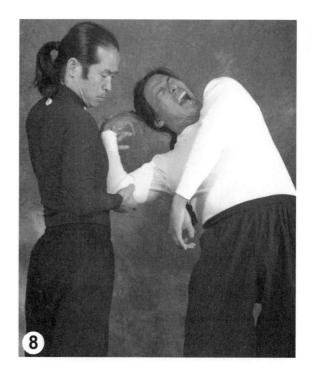

ALTERNATIVE TECHNIQUES

Thumb press to the Lesser Sea (HT03) and forearm strike to the Jaw Chariot (ST06)

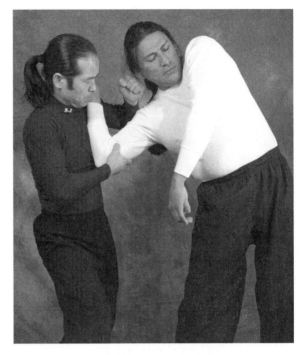

Thumb press to the Lesser Sea (HT03) and backfist to the Auditory Palace (SI19)

Wrist lock and knuckle punch to the Eyeball (AD-H1)

Wrist lock and knifehand strike to the White Bone-Orifice (GV25)

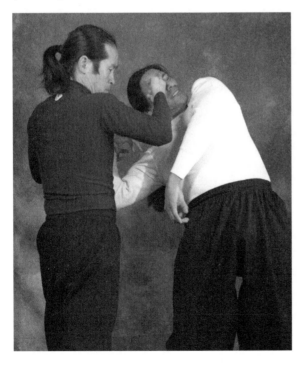

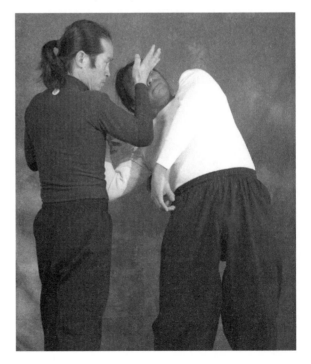

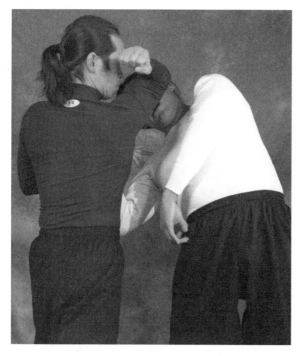

Wrist lock and elbow strike to the Great Bone-Orifice (ST03)

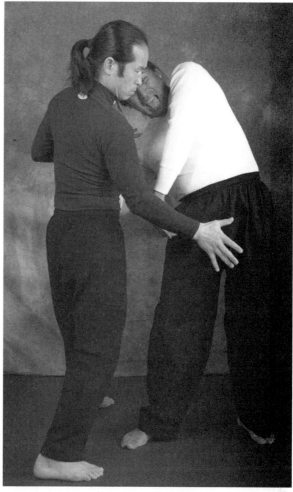

Wrist lock and palm strike to the Groin (AD-T1)

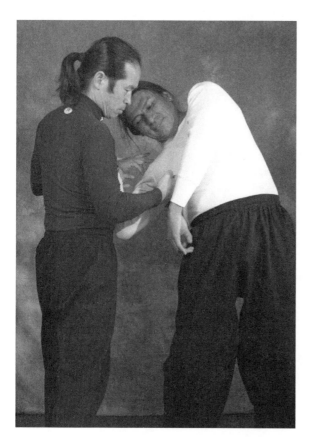

Wrist lock and thumb tip thrust to the Highest Spring (HT01)

AGAINST REAR CHOKE AND ARM LOCK 2

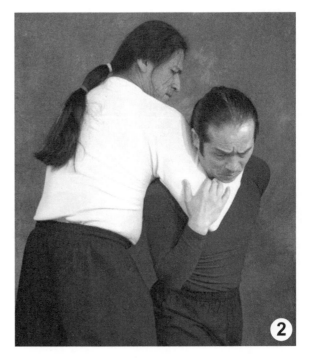

1. Tuck your chin downward for breathing space and strength.
2. Pivot your body outward and press the Arm Five Li (LI13) with your fingers.
3. Rotate your body toward him.
4. Pull your chin down and disrupt his balance.

5. Grab his wrist with your left hand.
6. Apply a wrist lock with a thumb press to the Lesser Sea (HT03).
7. Palm strike to the Jaw Chariot (ST06).
8. Grab his shoulder and kick downward to the Knee Yang Joint (GB33).

ALTERNATIVE TECHNIQUES

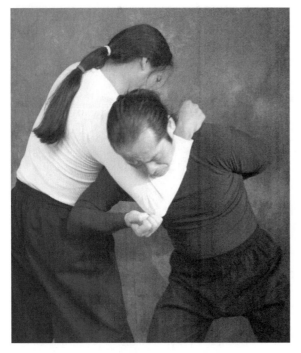

Elbow strike to the Ring of Jumping (GB30)

Wrist lock by pressing the Lumbar Pain Point (EX-UE7) with your left thumb

Elbow strike to the Philtrum (GV26)

Elbow strike to the Florid Canopy (CV20)

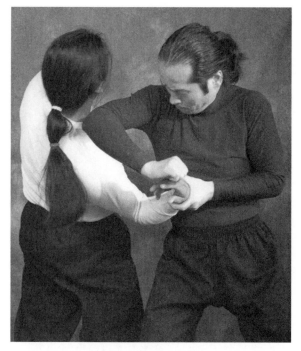

Elbow strike to the Energy Door (ST13)

Palm heel strike to the Great Bone-Orifice (ST03)

Leg sweep takedown

Heel Kick to the Supporting Sinews (BL56)

AGAINST FRONT TACKLE

1. Spread your feet and lean forward for balance.
2. Squat to lower your center of gravity and control his body.
3. Quickly elbow strike to the Great Hammer (GV14).
4. Another elbow snap to the Spirit Door (BL42).
5. Slide back and press his body to the ground.
6. Elbow strike to the Spirit Hall (BL44).

Focus: Balance by sliding back, leaning forward, loading your weight on the opponent's body, and going with the flow of the fight. Keep riding him while attacking the back and side of the body, and trying to apply a choke.

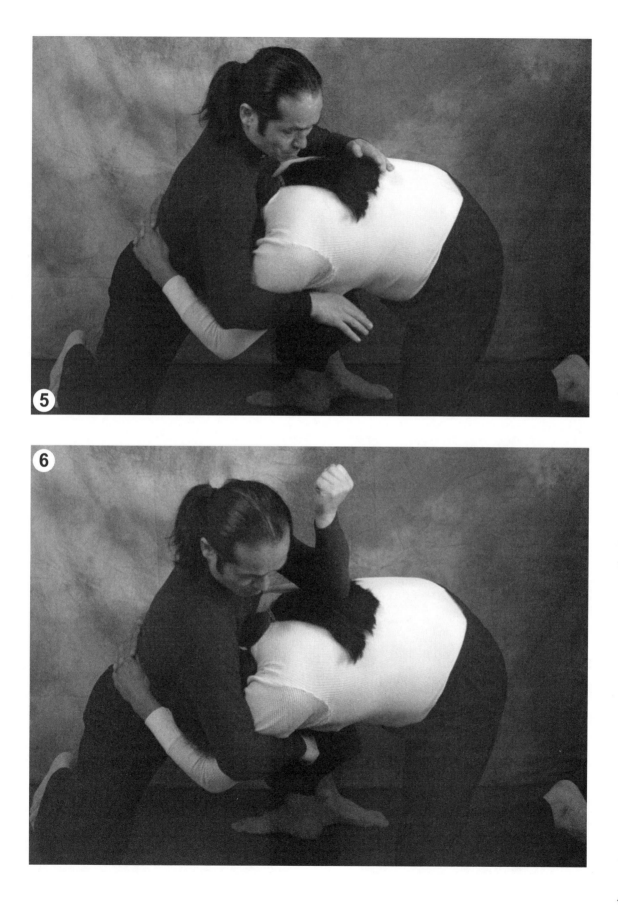

ALTERNATIVE TECHNIQUES

Elbow strike to the Unyielding Space (GV18)

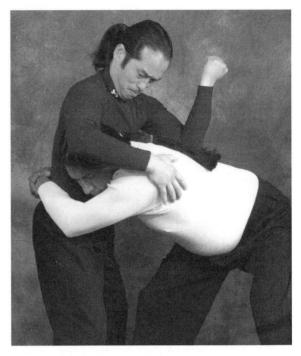

Elbow strike to the Stomach Transport (BL21)

Punch to the Celestial Pillar (BL10)

Knuckle punch to the Capital Gate (GB25)

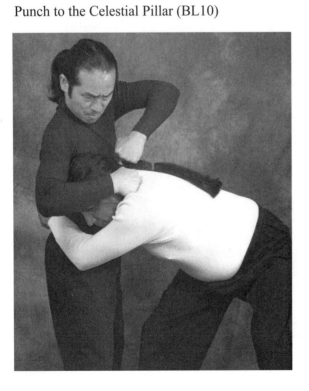

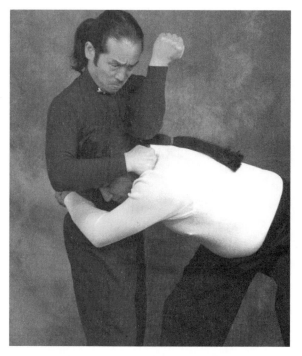

Elbow strike to the Crooked Wall (SI13)

Punch to the Will Chamber (BL52)

Palm heel strike to the Abdominal Lament (SP16)

AGAINST REAR TACKLE

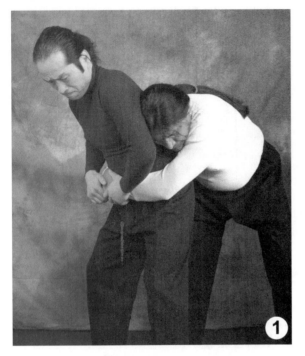

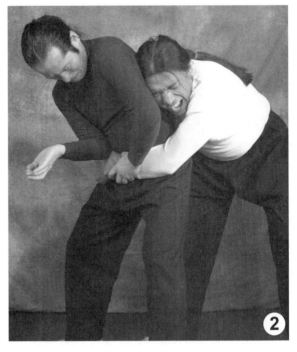

1. Lower your center of gravity and secure his forearm by pressing it firmly against your body.
2. Elbow strike to the Dorsal Center (AD-UE5).
3. Lower your body and drop your hip backward onto his thigh.
4. Grab his ankle or pants leg and pull.

5. Sit down on his knee as he falls.
6. Pull his ankle toward you and check his kick with your foot.
7. Press the Instep Yang (BL59) with your left inner forearm and press the Supreme White (SP03) with your right outer forearm.

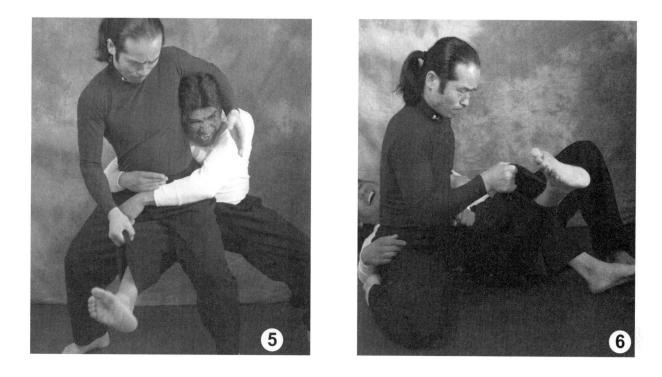

ALTERNATIVE TECHNIQUES

Headlock while pressing the Auricle (AD-H2) with your inner forearm

Palm heel strike to the Spirit Court (GV24)

Punch to the Temple (EX-HN5)

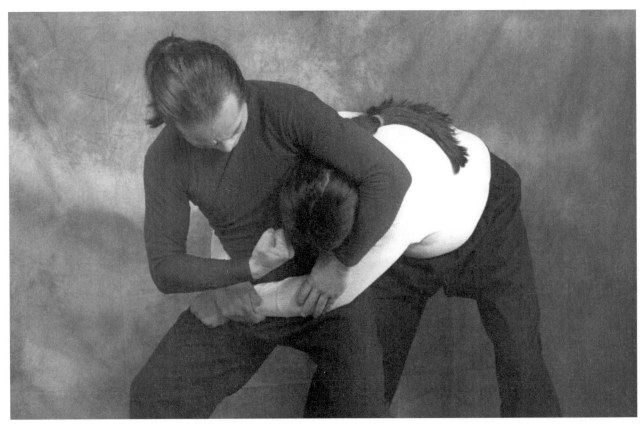

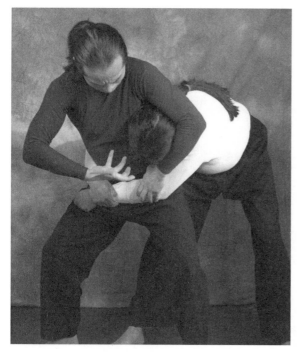

Gouge the Eyeball (AD-H1)

Finger pull on the White Bone-Orifice (GV25)

Press the Taking Flight (BL58) with your left inner wrist and knifehand strike to the Inner Calf (AD-LE6)

AGAINST SIDE HEAD LOCK

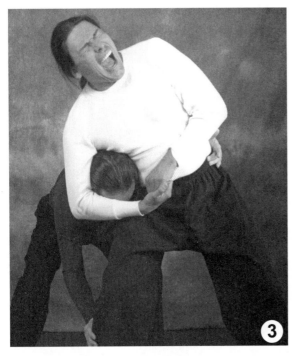

1. Move your left foot slightly backward and press the Linking Path (GB28) with your left fingertips.

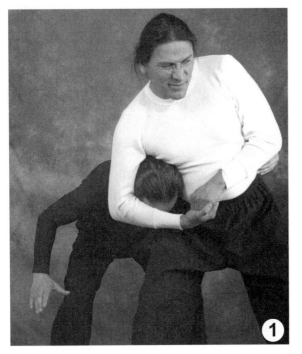

2. Press the Supporting Sinews (BL56) with your right thumb tip.

3. Move your right foot slightly forward to add more power to your thumb press while simultaneously breaking his balance.

4. Pull his left hip downward in a circular path to the ground.

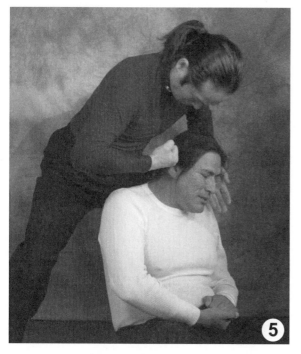

5. Immediately strike his left Eardrum (AD-H3) with your left palm and punch to the Leading Valley (GB08) with your right fist.

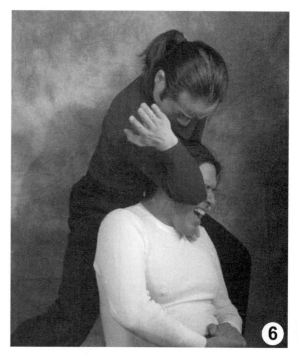

6. Elbow strike to the Auditory Palace (SI19).

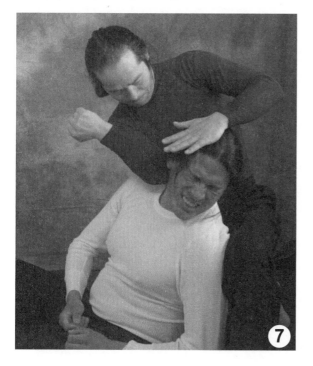

7. Immediately palm heel strike to the Forehead Fullness (GB04) and elbow strike to the Empty Basin (ST12).

Focus: Wisely select what strike to use at what time. The timing and order of the strikes vary according to his reactions and your readiness.

ALTERNATIVE TECHNIQUES

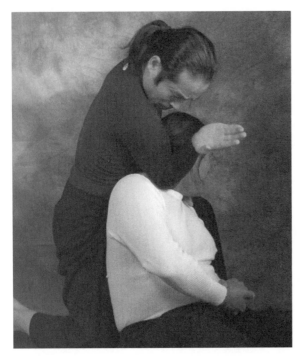

Elbow strike to the Energy Abode (ST11)

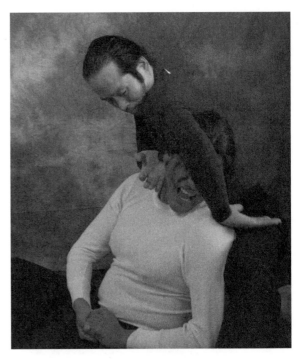

Forearm press to the White Bone-Orifice
(GV25) and knifehand strike to the
Protuberance Assistance (LI18)

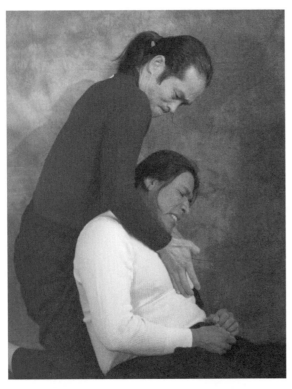

Knifehand strike to the Lively Center (KI26)

Palm heel strike to the Eyeball (AD-H1)

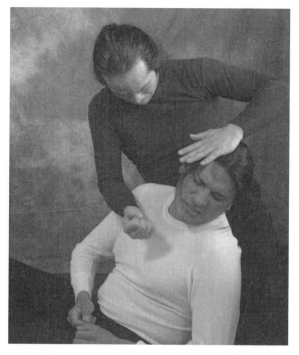

Palm heel strike to the Forehead Fullness (GB04) and hammer fist to the Lively Center (KI26)

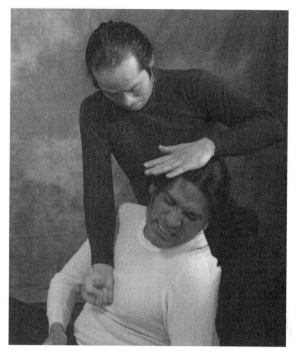

Palm heel strike to the Forehead Fullness (GB04) and hammer fist to the Breast Center (ST17)

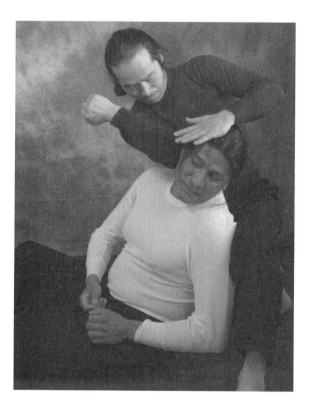

Palm heel strike to the Forehead Fullness (GB04) and elbow strike to the Celestial Pillar (BL10)

Focus: Whatever technique you apply, be prepared to maintain control of the neck and head. If you lose control of them, grab his shoulder and then go for the neck to regain control.

319

CHAPTER 12

GROUND FIGHT APPLICATIONS

Success in groundfighting is determined by leverage, strength, technique, and tactical flexibility. There is no room to experiment with many things on the ground. Stick with your best basic weapons until you succeed in exploiting the opponent's weak points. Once you find a technique that works, focus on finishing it. When you've got a solid lock on his neck or arm, stick to it. Don't let it go, no matter what position you end up in, until you tap him out or choke him out. Watch for ambush attacks. If your opponent suddenly begins to pin you down and relentlessly hit you, which often occurs quickly and unexpectedly, cover your face, focus on striking the most vulnerable spots you can reach to inflict maximum pain, and then transition to a position that gives you better control. Always strive to secure your breathing space and leverage on the ground.

FROM GUARD POSITION

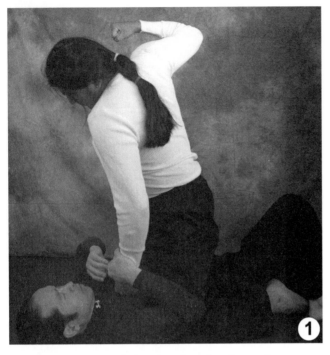

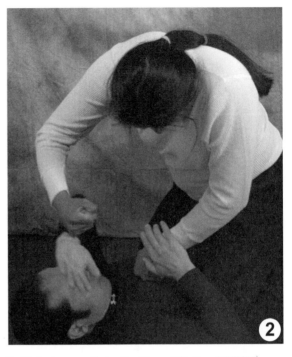

1. Prepare to control the situation: bend your knees, cover your face, and grab whatever body part is presented to you by your opponent.
2. Protect yourself and look for a chance to counter.

3. Counterpunch to the Four Whites (ST02).
4. Grab his wrist and pull downward, then palm heel strike to the Sauce Receptacle (CV24).

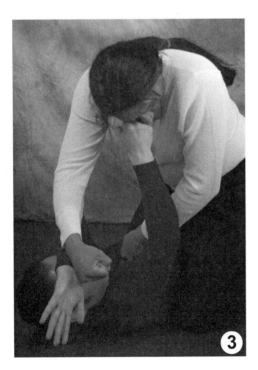

ALTERNATIVE TECHNIQUES

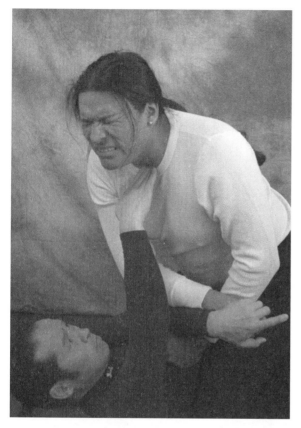

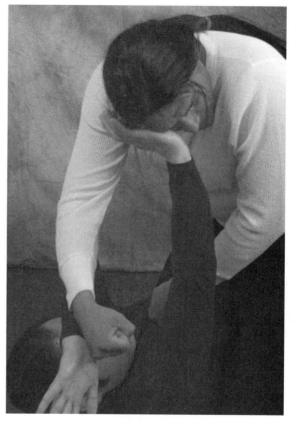

Fingertip thrust to the Celestial Chimney (CV22)

Palm heel strike to the Eyeball (AD-H1)

Punch to the Great Bone-Orifice (ST03)

Arc hand strike to the Adam's Apple (AD-N1)

Palm heel strike to the Ridge Spring (CV23)

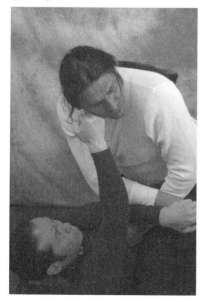

AGAINST CHOKING IN GUARD POSITION

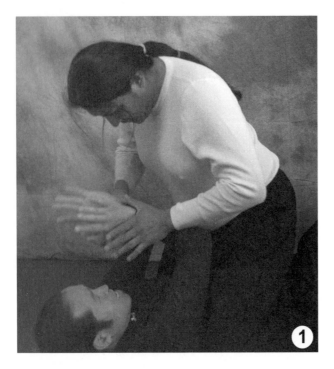

1. Fight to push his hands off your neck. Keep your knees bent and your feet flat on the ground at all times.
2. Cross your forearms and grab one of his wrists.
3. Twist his wrist to the side while pivoting and lifting your hip toward his weak spot.
4. Knifehand strike to the Small Sea (SI08).

Focus 1: Make his position as unstable as possible by: 1) moving your hip constantly to unbalance him; 2) throwing knee kicks to the Lumbar Transport (GV02) for distraction; 3) causing pain by elbow striking the Winnower Gate (SP11) on the front of his thigh.

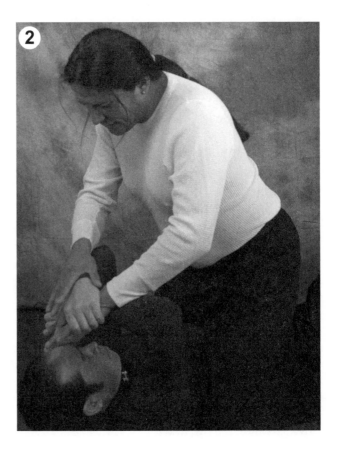

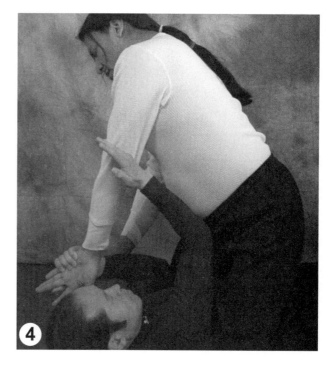

Focus 2: Until you reach the tipping point, do everything possible to help topple him off of you: 1) push his elbow joint; 2) push his knee toward your foot to destabilize his balance; 3) shrimp your body to expand your leverage and reduce his.

Focus 3: Leave every door open for maneuvering: 1) throw him to the side; 2) throw him over your head; 3) roll out from under him if the situation permits; 4) immobilize his arm; 5) beat him into submission.

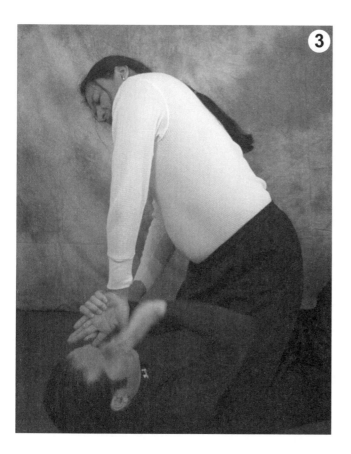

Alternative Techniques

Wrist lock and punch the Sun and Moon (GB24)

Wrist lock and fingertip thrust to the Great Horizontal (SP15)

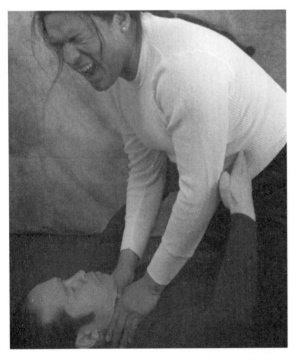

Fingertip thrust to the Abdominal Lament (SP16)

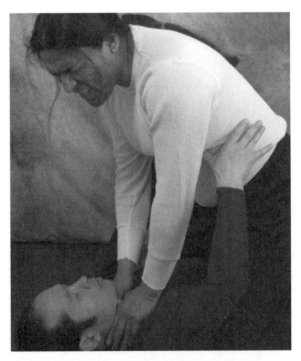

Thumb press to the Not Contained (ST19)

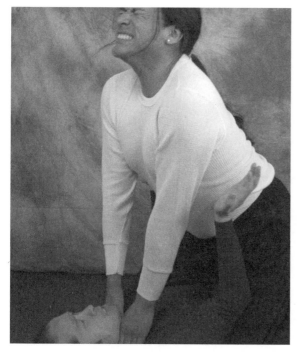

Knifehand strike the Camphorwood Gate (LV13)

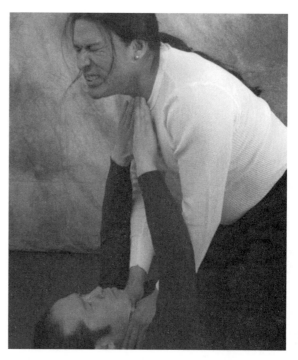

Double fingertip press the Energy Abode (ST11)

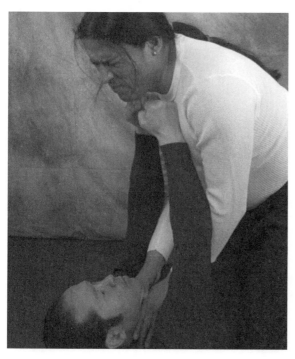

Double hammer fists to the Lively Center (KI26)

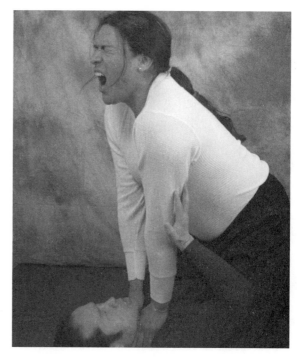

Double palm heel strikes to the Celestial Well (TW10)

ALTERNATIVE TECHNIQUES (CONTINUED)

Block his sight by slapping the White Bone-Orifice (GV25)

Pull his arm and strike the Adam's Apple (AD-N1)

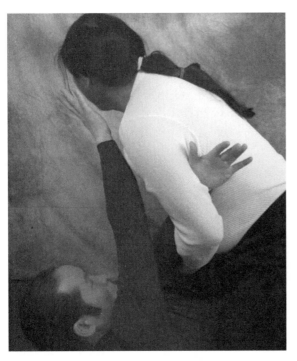

Pull his arm and slap his Eardrum (AD-H3)

Pull his arm and fingertip thrust to the Ridge Spring (CV23)

Pull his arm and backfist strike to the Temple (EX-HN5)

Pull his arm and slap the Sauce Receptacle (CV24)

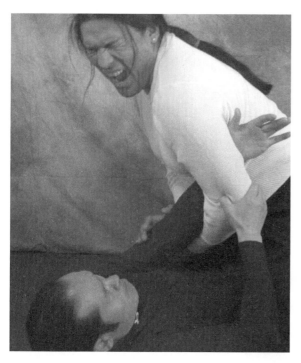

Pull his arm and thumb press to the Arm Five Li (LI13)

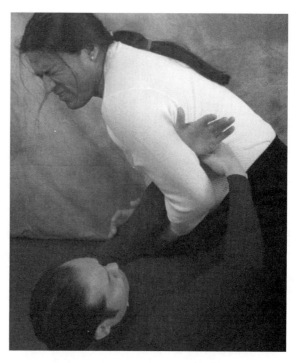

Pull his arm and punch to the Camphorwood Gate (LV13)

AGAINST ARM PIN

1. Center yourself as much as possible: keep your knees and elbows bent at all times, your feet flat on the floor and your chin tucked in.

2. Knee kick to the Lumbar Transport (GV02). If one kick does not work, keep kicking. As you're kicking, bring your arms as close to your body as possible, and slide your body toward your opponent's hips little by little.

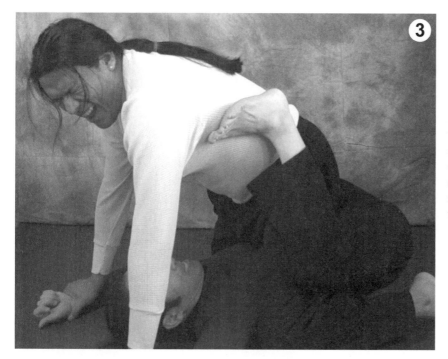

3. When you are able to maneuver relatively freely, breathe in and raise your feet high on your opponent's sides. With a forceful exhalation, kick, with both inner ankle bones, inwardly to the Capital Gate (GB25).

4. Then, stick the toes of your feet into the Highest Spring (HT01) under the armpit, and topple him off you upward, downward, or sideways.

AGAINST ARM PIN 2

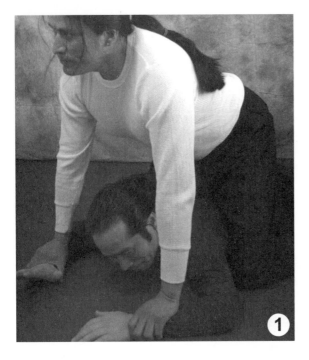

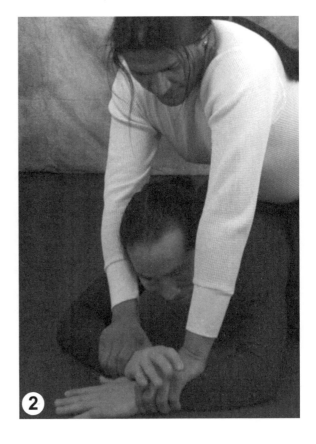

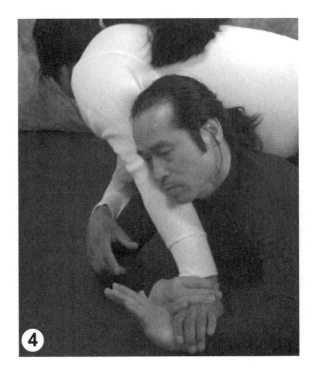

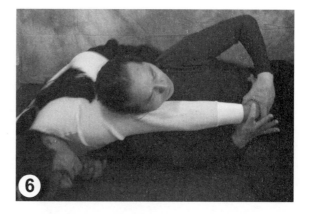

1. Keep one knee and your elbows bent for leverage.
2. Shrimp your body. When your opponent tries to adjust his balance bring your right hand, grab his left wrist.
3. Move your head around behind his left arm and press the right side of your face against the Celestial Well (TW10).
4. Hold your grip firmly and lean your head toward his elbow.
5. Crawl upward and press his elbow harder to the ground while twisting his wrist.
6. As his head hits the ground crawl up further and raise your hip while pressing his elbow with your whole body weight downward diagonally.
7. Press his elbow with your head and raise your body.
8. Press the Dispersing Riverbed (TW12) with your right palm. Progressively raise your body to maintain control.

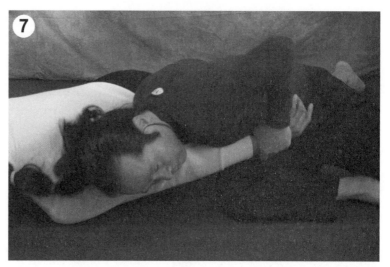

Focus: Don't be in a hurry. If you are, you'll lose him or fall prey to a counter. Establish your leverage inch-by-inch but solidly. Take your time because the key here is your absolute control.

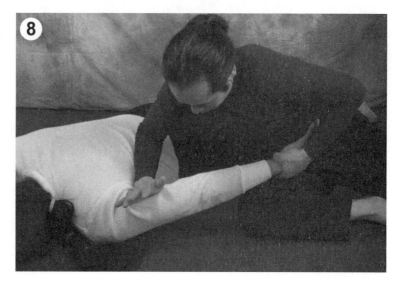

333

ALTERNATIVE TECHNIQUES

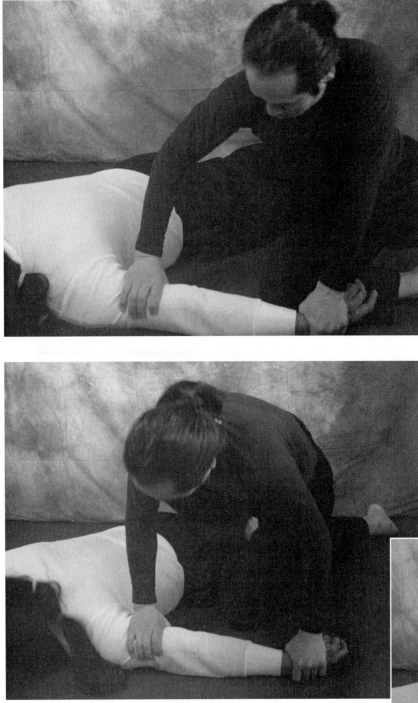

Pin the arm through wrist control and a thumb press to the Blue Spirit (HT02)

Press his upper arm by loading your body weight through your right arm. If he tries to pull his arm out, strike the Lesser Sea (HT03) with your right knee.

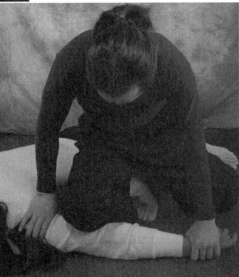

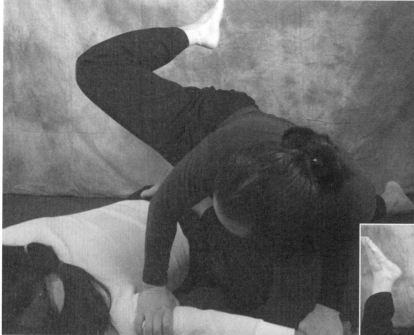

Knee strike to the Mute's Gate (GV15)

Caution: Striking the occipital ridge in the rear of the head is extremely dangerous and can cause death or brain damage. Never practice this technique on another person. A heavy bag or practice dummy is a good alternative for practice.

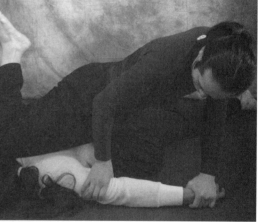

Knee kick to the Stomach Transport (BL21)

Focus: The Stomach Transport (BL21) is located between the 12th thoracic vertebra and the 1st lumbar vertebra. It is on the rear inner upper part of the kidney. Kicking this spot can cause severe pain in the body and possible death. Do not practice this technique on a partner.

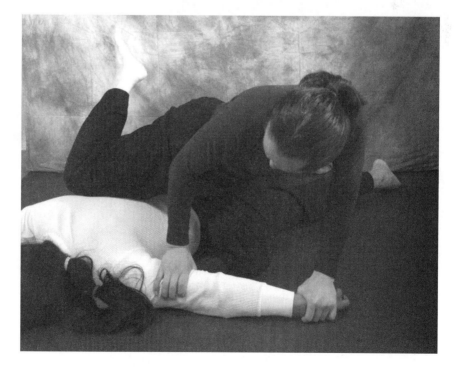

ALTERNATIVE TECHNIQUES (CONTINUED)

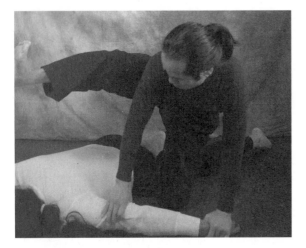

Arm pin and heel drop kick to the Central Shoulder Transport (SI15)

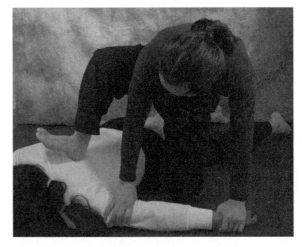

Arm pin and heel drop kick to the Spirit Hall (BL44)

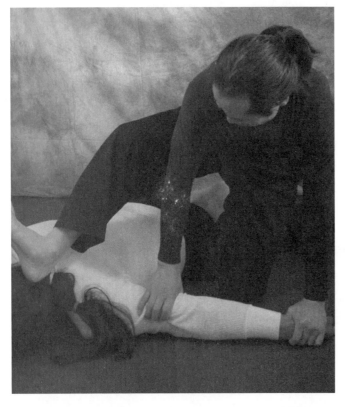

Arm pin and heel drop kick to the Wind Pool (GB20)

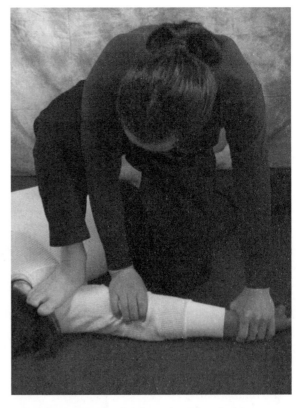

Arm pin and stomp kick to the Blue Spirit (HT02)

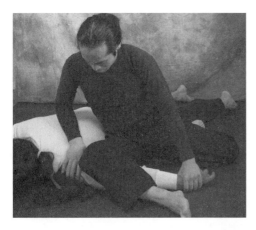

Arm pin and leg press to the
Clear Cold Abyss (TW11)

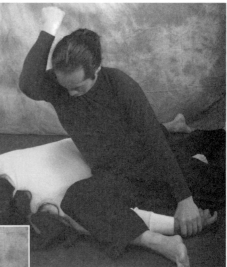

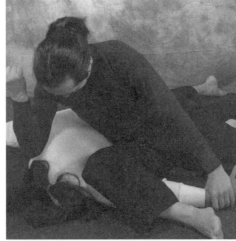

Leg arm pin and elbow strike
to the Crooked Wall (SI13)

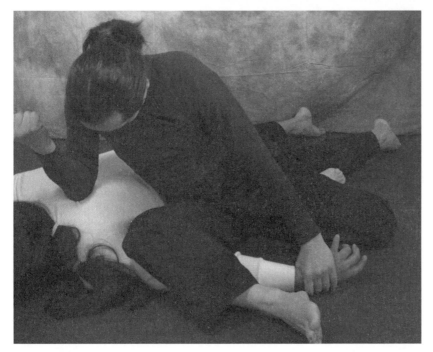

Leg arm pin and elbow strike
to the Spirit Path (GV11)

CHAPTER 13

KNIFE DEFENSE APPLICATIONS

To survive a knife attack, you need to control Four Elements of Knife-defense: 1) distance, 2) defense, 3) weapon, 4) target. Try to maintain a safe distance. Keep track of the blade: what section of your body is being attacked and what angle of attack you need to respond to. Determine what bodily weapon to use and what targets are available to attack. For defense, use your lead hand and arm. For offense use both hands and arms, and feet and legs. Mentally segment your defense into high, middle, and low sections and the angles of attack into inward, outward, upward, downward, or diagonal. The targets of your defensive techniques will be the closest or the most easily accessible ones such as the groin, eyes, vital points on the arm and others that the opponent may present in response to your actions or reactions.

AGAINST FRONTAL MID-SECTION THRUST 1

1. Prepare the Four Control Elements of Knife-defense: 1) distance, 2) defense, 3) weapon, 4) target. In this case, you are too close to step back so prepare for the risk of getting cut.
2. V-block against his forearm with your forearm as you move out of the attacking line.
3. As he extends his arm to reach you, move your body to keep the knife away from you. Snap his wrist with your wrist in an upward circular motion.
4. Guide his wrist clockwise.
5. As his wrist goes downward, palm heel strike to the Great Bone-Orifice (ST03).
6. Immediately control his left arm with your left hand (or left knifehand strike to the Collection Orifice (LU06) to snap away the knife), and right palm heel strike to the Auditory Convergence (GB02).
7. Apply a right arm rear choke while wrapping up his left arm.
8. Complete the choke.

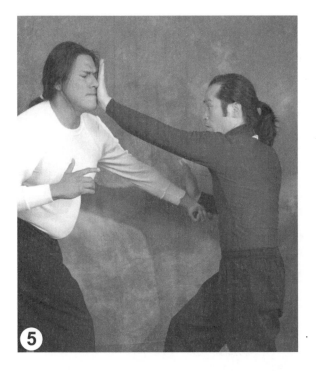

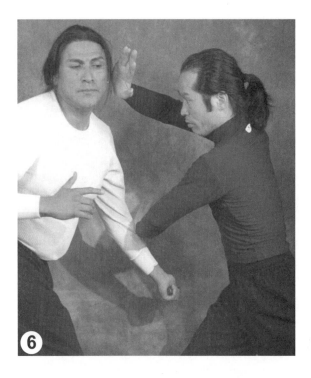

ALTERNATIVE TECHNIQUES

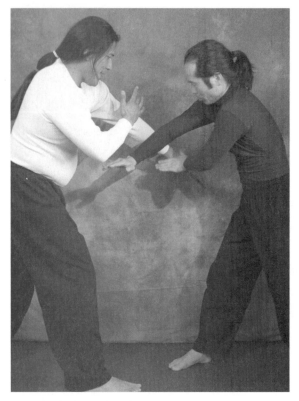

Double forearm block

Palm and arm block

Palm block and palm heel strike to the Sauce
Receptacle (CV24)

Cut-in and elbow strike to the Wind Pool (GB20)

CAUTION 1

ERROR #1: Wrist cut

ERROR #2: Neck thrust

ERROR #3: Forearm slash

Caution: A miscalculation of the angle and path of the knife is common in knife fighting. The result is getting cut on hand, wrist, forearm, face, neck or torso as shown here.

To avoid getting cut, keep your distance and find practical weapons that are longer than the knife or that can shield you. Examples are clothing like a shirt or jacket (snap at his eyes or roll around your forearm), belt, umbrella, bag or chair.

To minimize the risk of getting cut, move your arms in circular motions protecting your vital targets.

CAUTION 2

Random thrusts   *Sudden change of course*

Caution: Expect the unexpected. If not, you'll be frustrated, scared, defeated, or killed. Cuts may result from accidental or unexpected maneuvers by the opponent, so try to stay cool, keep a safe distance from the opponent and figure out what your options are. Sometimes, you are no match for an opponent. If that's the case, run.

Deep thrust

344

AGAINST FRONTAL MID-SECTION THRUST 2

1. At a safe distance, keep track of the blade.
2. When your opponent thrusts, respond instinctively to deflect the blade at this close distance. Use your forearm to guide the blade off the centerline.

3. Strike the Sauce Receptacle (CV24) with your palm heel.
4. Wrap your arm around his neck, palm heel strike to the Jaw Chariot (ST06) to disorient him and finish with a rear choke.

345

ALTERNATIVE TECHNIQUES

Wrist grab and thumb press to the Outer Pass (TW05), and backfist to the Jaw Chariot (ST06)

Under arm backfist strike to the Great Reception (ST05)

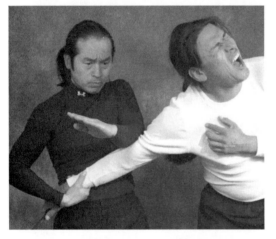

Forearm press to the Celestial Well (TW10)

Punch to the Temple (EX-HN5)

Wrist grab and elbow strike to the Sun and Moon (GB24)

Wrist grab and elbow strike to the Temple (EX-HN5)

ALTERNATIVE TECHNIQUES (CONTINUED)

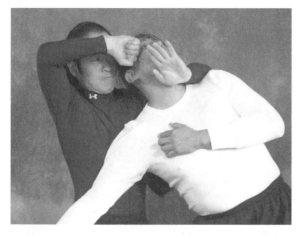

Rear choke and punch to the Temple (EX-HN5)

Rear choke and knifehand to the Protuberance Assistance (LI18)

Rear choke and elbow strike to the Great Bone-Orifice (ST03)

Rear choke and fingertip thrust to the Protuberance Assistance (LI18)

Wrist control and head control by pressing the Adam's Apple (AD-N1) with your radial wrist crease

347

AGAINST FRONTAL MID-SECTION THRUST 3

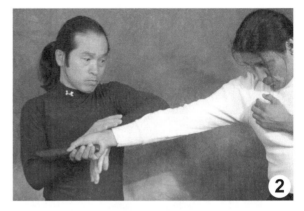

1. Assess the situation and mentally prepare.
2. Deflect the blade with your hands and move your body out of the attacking line.
3. Move closer to the opponent's body, while simultaneously throwing a right palm heel to the White Bone-Orifice (GV25), and left palm heel strike to the Spirit Path (GV11).

4. Apply a choke by going under the opponent's arm and pressing the Protuberance Assistance (LI18) with your inner forearm.

ALTERNATIVE TECHNIQUES

Wrist grab and backfist to the Temple (EX-HN5)

Arm control, knee press to the Bend Center (BL40)

Wrist grab, forearm press on the neck, and knee kick to the Supporting Sinews (BL56)

Wrist grab and knee kick to the Great Horizontal (SP15)

349

ALTERNATIVE TECHNIQUES (CONTINUED)

Wrist grab and thumb press to the Lumbar Pain Point (EX-UE7) and the Dorsal Center (AD-UE5)

Wrist grab and hammer fist to the Groin (AD-T1)

Wrist grab, thumb press to the Exterior Pericardium (EX-UE8) and forearm press to the Protuberance Assistance (LI18)

350

AGAINST FRONTAL MID-SECTION THRUST 4

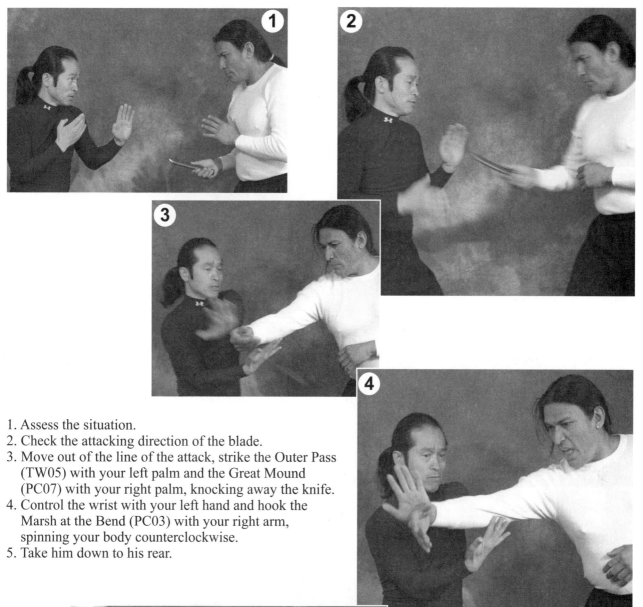

1. Assess the situation.
2. Check the attacking direction of the blade.
3. Move out of the line of the attack, strike the Outer Pass (TW05) with your left palm and the Great Mound (PC07) with your right palm, knocking away the knife.
4. Control the wrist with your left hand and hook the Marsh at the Bend (PC03) with your right arm, spinning your body counterclockwise.
5. Take him down to his rear.

AGAINST FRONTAL MID-SECTION THRUST 5

1. Prepare yourself mentally and physically.
2. When your opponent thrusts, deflect the blade with your hands and move your body out of the attacking line.
3. Simultaneously grab and pull his right wrist, trap his arm with your left arm in V-shape, press his Lower Biceps (AD-UE1) with your upper arm and push your chest against his elbow.
4. Lower your torso, displace his shoulder and add more pressure to his elbow.

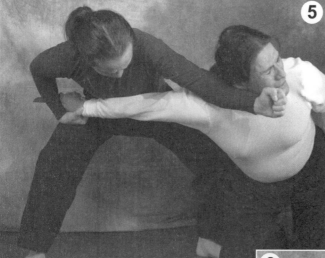

5. Backfist to the Great Bone-Orifice (ST03) when he tries to reach for you.
6. Upper arm press to the Upper Arm (LI14).
7. Drop your torso against his elbow and control his arm and shoulder on the ground.

AGAINST SLASHING 1

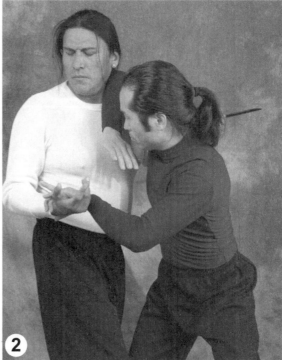

1. Check the distance. In this case, you should either step back or strike first.
2. Before he lowers his weapon, step diagonally into his centerline and strike the Protuberance Assistance (LI18) with your right elbow. Do it quickly and powerfully.
3. Immediately, throw an upward left elbow strike to the Not Contained (ST19).
4. Grab his wrist with your right arm and control his neck with your arm.

5. Choke his neck from the rear and control his wrist.
6. Move backward and bring his head to the ground.
7. Control the wrist firmly and elbow strike to the Wind Pool (GB20).

Focus: A pre-emptive strike is also called a cut-in, which means cutting through the space between the line of the attack and his defense. Two critical elements for a cut-in in are timing and angle: the timing for attacking his weakest point and the safest angle for your entry.

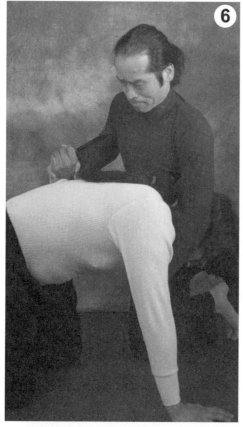

AGAINST SLASHING 2

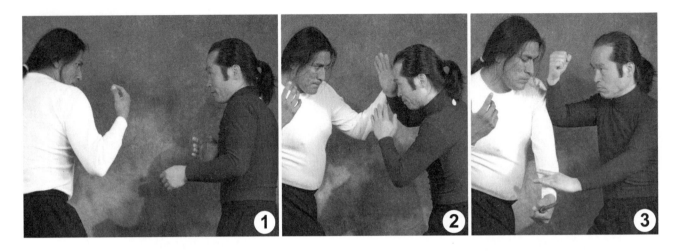

1. Assess the opponent's intentions.
2. Block his attack with your forearm. Deflect the force by moving his left forearm in a clockwise circular path.
3. After the circular deflection, control his left wrist with your left hand, and strike with your right backfist to the Eyeball (AD-H1).

4. Immediately, pull his left arm toward you and press the Dispersing Riverbed (TW12) with your forearm.
5. Move your right foot into his center, take him to a kneeling position by loading your body weight onto his upper arm.

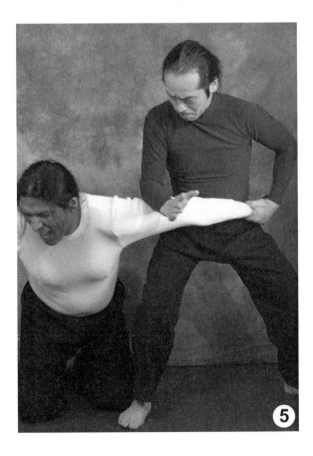

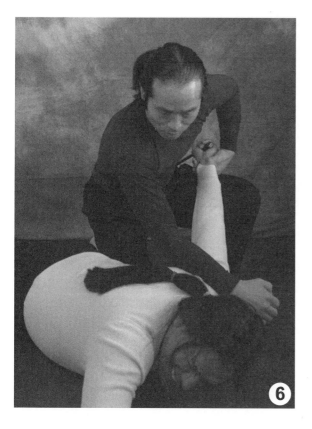

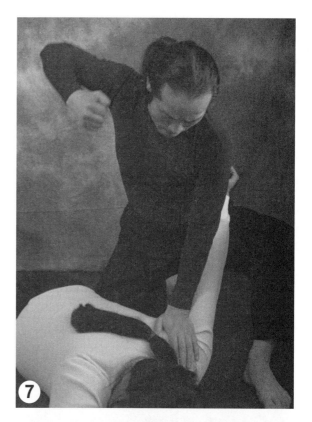

6. Pressing the Celestial Spring (PC02) with your forearm, follow the dropping path of his body, and position yourself right next to his torso while controlling his wrist and shoulder.
7. Secure his arm by placing his wrist on your thigh (with his palm facing upward) and pressing his scapula region.
8. Punch to the Mute's Gate (GV15).

Focus: You should constantly adjust your foot position and body angle when he exerts his force or resists in order to take advantage of what happens during the course of the confrontation. Based on solid technique, be adaptive.

ALTERNATIVE TECHNIQUES

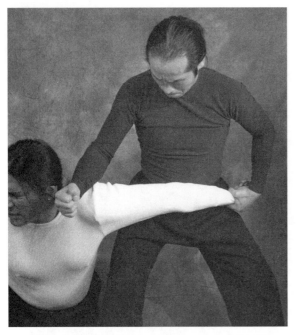

Backfist to the Auditory Convergence (GB02)

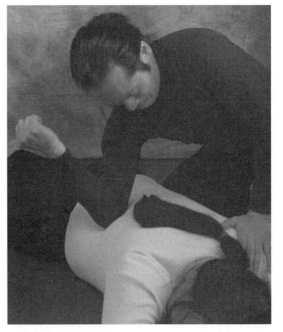

Elbow strike to the Will Chamber (BL52)

Palm heel strike to the Jade Pillow (BL09)

Knifehand strike to the Wind Pool (GB20)

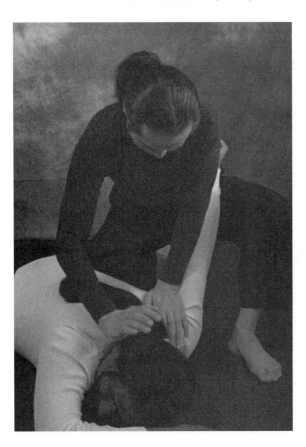

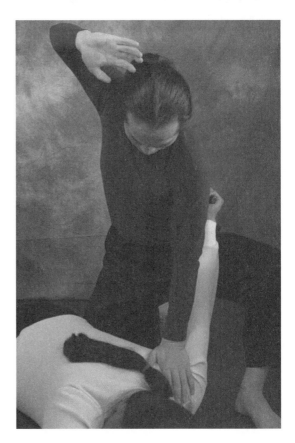

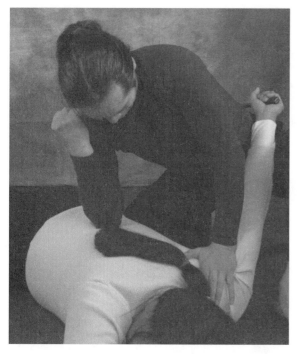

Elbow strike to the Kidney Transport (BL23)

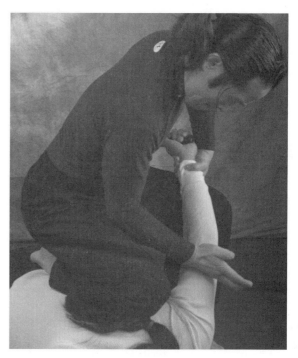

Knifehand strike to the Blue Spirit (HT02)

Knee kick to the Small
Intestine Transport
(BL27)

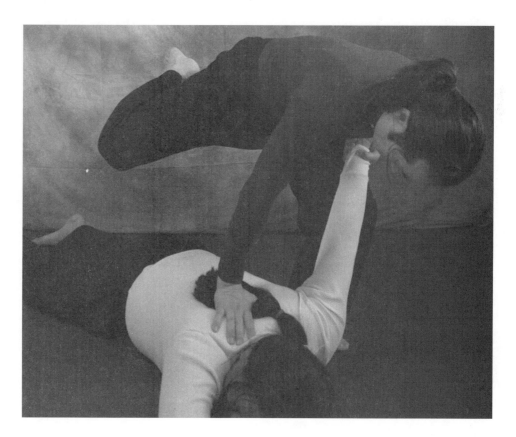

AGAINST ICE-PICK GRIP 1

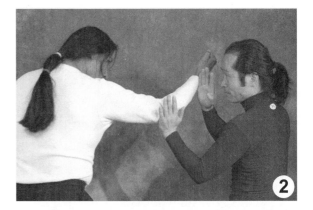

1. Keep your eyes on the blade.
2. As he lowers his weapon, move your body out of the attacking line, deflect his forearm with your hands, grab and twist his wrist, and guide it around your body.
3. Press the Small Sea (SI08) on his rear elbow with your left palm.
4a. Bring his wrist backward and then upward for an arm lock.
4b. (alternative) If his resistance is too great to manipulate for a rear arm lock, pull his wrist around your right waist and press his elbow toward the ground. You should follow his body while loading your weight onto his elbow.

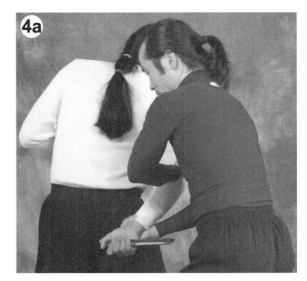

AGAINST ICE-PICK GRIP 2

1. Keep your eyes on the blade and raise your guard.
2. As he lowers his weapon, move out of the line of attack and deflect his elbow with your left palm.
3. While controlling his elbow, hook his forearm with your right arm and press his arm to bend against your torso.
4. Grab his wrist with your left hand and walk him backward to take him down.

Caution: You should move out of the line of the attack to avoid getting stabbed on your shoulder or back. To establish control, press his Lower Biceps (AD-UE1) (#3) and grab his wrist (#4) simultaneously and forcefully.

AGAINST ICE-PICK GRIP 3

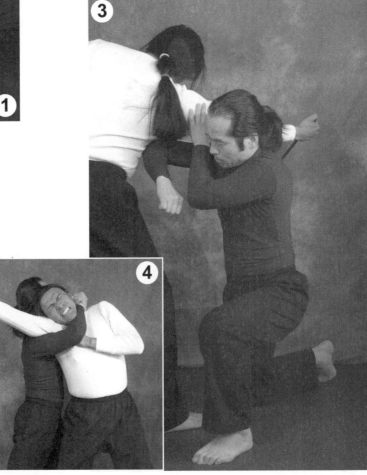

1. Prepare yourself mentally and physically.
2. As he lowers his weapon, deflect his forearm with your left hand.
3. Kneel on your left knee and strike the Abdominal Lament (SP16) with your right elbow.
4. Immediately, hook his neck with your right arm, grab your right wrist with your left and constrict the Protuberance Assistance (LI18).

AGAINST ICE-PICK GRIP 4

1. Raise your guard and watch the blade.
2. As he lowers his weapon, block his forearm with your right outer forearm.
3. In a circular motion grab his wrist with your right hand, and press his elbow with your left palm.
4. Left roundhouse kick to the Posterior Lower Thigh (AD-LE2).
5. As he falls backward, calculate the proper distance and drop his elbow on your thigh. The vital target on his arm is Dispersing Riverbed (TW12).

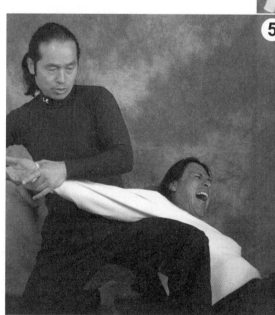

363

AGAINST ICE-PICK GRIP 5

1. Prepare yourself for the attack.
2. As he lowers his weapon, deflect his forearm with your palms.
3. Control his right shoulder with your left palm and his arm with your right hand.
4. Control his torso by pressing the Will Chamber (BL52) with your palm, and hook his neck with your right arm, pressing the Protuberance Assistance (LI18).

5. Pull his neck counterclockwise toward the center of your body while pressing the Suspended Pivot (GV05) with your hand to arch his back.
6. Constrict his neck tighter by planting the top edge of your radius into the Protuberance Assistance (LI18).
7. Grab your right wrist with your left hand to complete the choke. Pivot your body counterclockwise to intensify the force.

Caution: Choking the carotid artery can be fatal. In a few seconds, the subject can lose consciousness and continued constriction can lead to death. You should learn this type of technique from a professional instructor. Do not try this technique unsupervised.

AGAINST REVERSE GRIP ATTACK

1. Watch the blade. In this case, the opponent is trying to conceal it under his arm.
2. Evade or grab the attacking wrist with your right hand.
3. While controlling the attacking wrist with your right hand, punch to the Great Reception (ST05).

4. Immediately, shoot a roundhouse kick to the Bend Center (BL40).

5. Drop your left foot right behind him, grab his shoulders, and throw a knee kick to the Gate of Abundance (BL37).

6. Pull him down clockwise to the ground. As he lands, elbow strike to the Great Bone-Orifice (ST03) against the force of his falling.

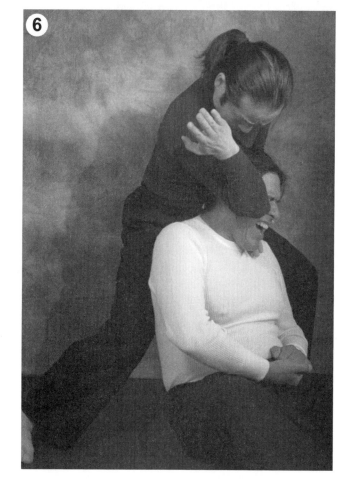

AGAINST REAR SHOULDER GRAB

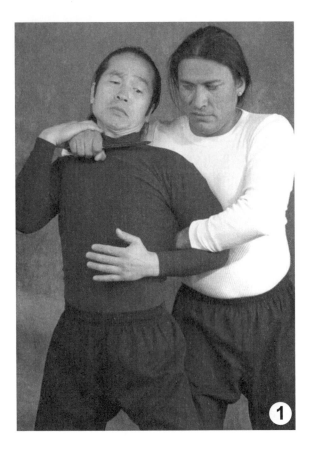

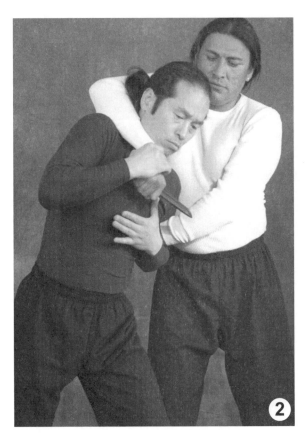

1. Press the Great Mound (PC07) on the opponent's inner wrist with your right thumb. Secure more breathing space by pulling down on his wrist. Open your left hand and press it firmly on your stomach for leverage.
2. Lower and rotate your body counter-clockwise toward the opponent while pressing his right wrist against your body firmly.
3. Grab his wrist with both hands.

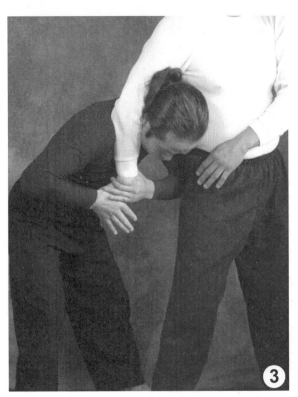

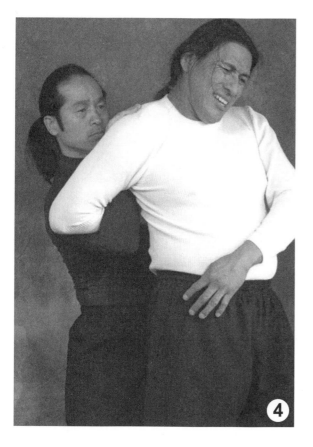

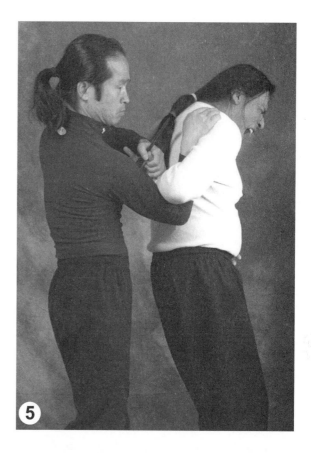

4. Push his wrist upward behind him.
5. Insert your right forearm under his arm and rest your hand on his right scapula. Your left hand should hold his right wrist firmly.
6. Take the knife from him with your left hand.

CHAPTER 14

GUN DEFENSE
APPLICATIONS

Defending against a gun is impossible unless it is within your reach and you are skillful and confident enough to take action. One error means death. It is the holder of the gun who dictates the situation by his action, your reaction, and his counter-reaction. Your goal is to finish the situation with your initial reaction or for your reaction to lessen the imminent danger of the conflict. If you can de-escalate the situation verbally, use every possible means to resolve it without physical endangerment. If not, your final option is to attempt to disarm the opponent. The process of disarming may lead to death, either accidental or intentional on the part of either you or your assailant.

The bottom line is you need to control everything: the psyche and body of the opponent, the weapon, and your own mind and actions. You should check the intent and action of the assailant, then respond. The optimal result is positioning yourself at a distance where you can grab the weapon. Once in grabbing range, it's essential to control the assailant's arm. Grab and pull his wrist, grab the barrel of the gun, hook and snatch the gun out of his hand.

AGAINST GUN FROM THE FRONT 1

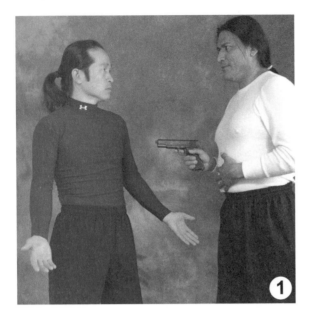

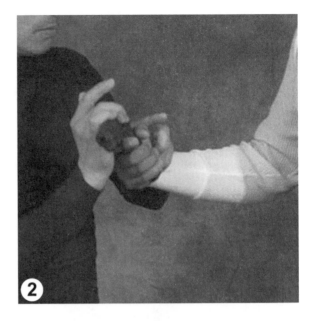

1. Stay cool and control yourself. Position yourself at a distance where you can grab the weapon.
2. Grab and press the opponent's wrist, pressing your thumb on the Dorsal Center (AD-UE5) and grab the barrel of the gun, as you move your body out of the firing line.
3. Hyperflex his wrist and twist his wrist counterclockwise.
4. Snatch the gun out of his hand.
5. Aim the gun at him and command him to back off.

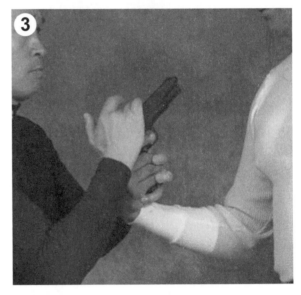

AGAINST GUN FROM THE FRONT 2

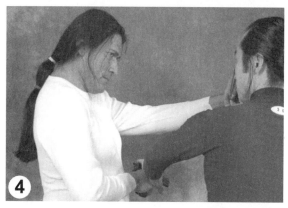

1. Stay cool and identify what the assailant wants from you.
2. Give him what he wants.
3. Distract his attention with the object in your right hand.
4. Move out of the firing line, grab the gun with your left hand and push it slightly away from you.
5. Grab his right hand with both hands while pressing your right thumb on the Dorsal Center (AD-UE5) and rotate his arm counterclockwise.
6. Snatch the gun, aim it at him, and command him to back off.

AGAINST GUN FROM THE FRONT 3

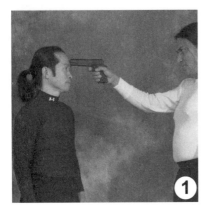

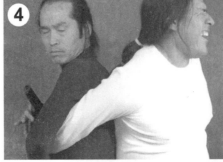

1. Stay cool. If you sense imminent death, be prepared to act.
2. Move your head out of the firing line (outward toward him) and palm strike to the Celestial Well (TW10) with your left palm, while securing his wrist with your right hand.
3. Move your body toward his elbow and push him forward.
4. Wrap his arm with yours and pivot your body to increase the pain in his arm and keep the gun away from him.
5. Control his arm with your left arm, and take the gun out of his hand.

AGAINST GUN FROM THE REAR 1

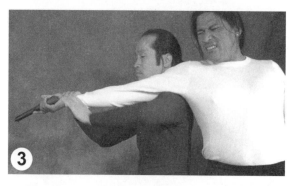

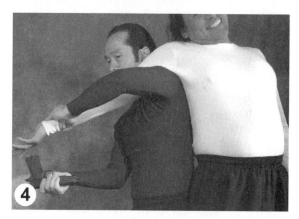

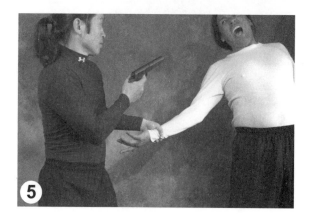

1. Per his command, raise your hands and try to figure out which side is the outside of his arm.
2. Calmly but quickly pivot your body clockwise on your right foot, moving your head out of the firing line, and raise your right forearm to cover your head.
3. Continue to pivot, while hooking the Inner Passage (PC06) downward with your hands and pulling the Dispersing Riverbed (TW12) against your shoulder, and grabbing his wrist with your left hand.
4. Control his wrist with your left hand and disarm him.
5. Continue to pivot under his armpit while controlling his wrist with your left hand, and aiming the gun at him.

AGAINST GUN FROM THE REAR 2

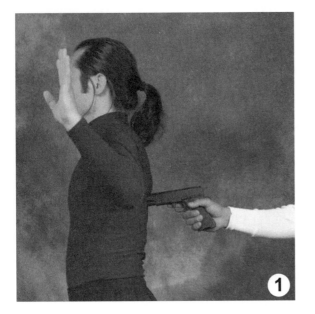

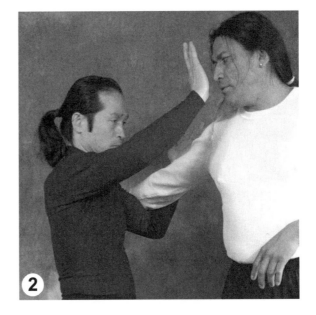

1. Stay cool. Per his command, raise your hands and try to figure out which side is the inside of his arm.
2. Calmly but quickly pivot your body counterclockwise on your left foot, moving your body out of the firing line, while hooking his elbow in V-shape with your left arm, and palm heel striking to the Philtrum (GV26).
3. Press the Dispersing Riverbed (TW12) with your left palm heel and right palm, and move back to take him down.
4. Kneel down with great force causing unbearable pain in his right shoulder.
5. Using the momentum from step #4, take him down to the ground and press his arm with his wrist locked on your left shoulder.
6. Take his gun with your right hand.
7. Control his arm with your left hand and shoulder, and prepare to aim the gun at the assailant to end the conflict.

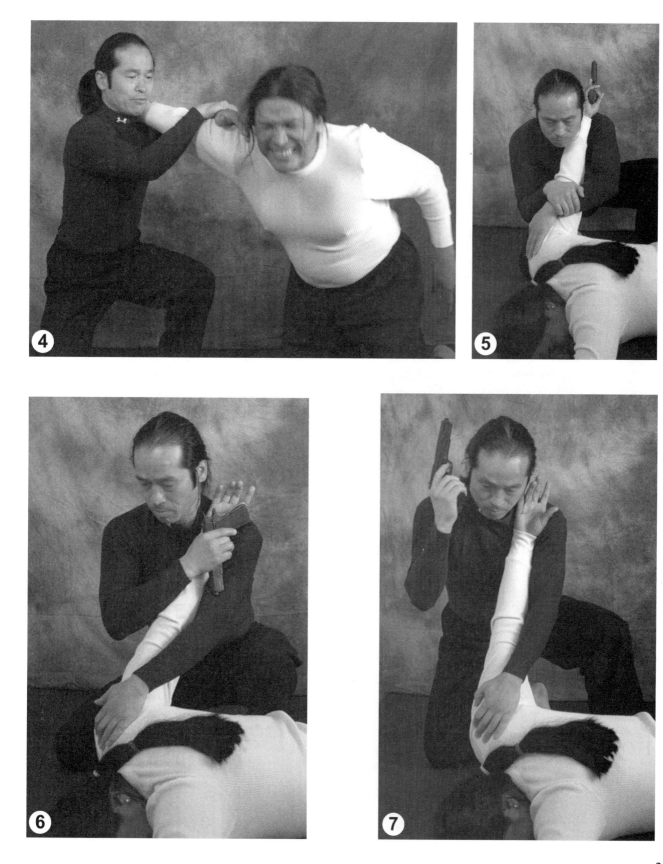

AGAINST GUN FROM THE REAR 3

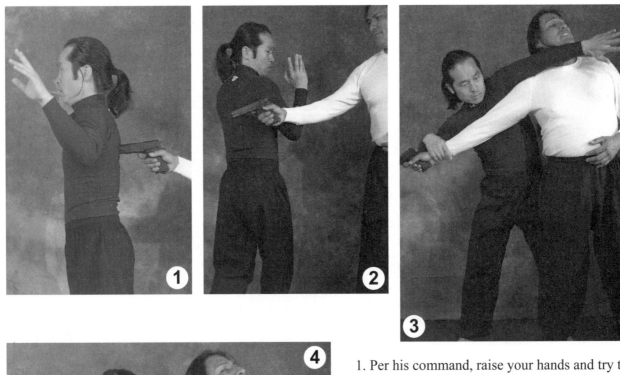

1. Per his command, raise your hands and try to figure out which side is the outside of his arm.
2. Calmly but quickly pivot your body clockwise on your right foot, moving your body out of the firing line, cover your body with V-shaped forearm.
3. Continue to pivot, while grabbing his wrist with your right hand, and press the Protuberance Assistance (LI18) with your elbow away from you.
4. Lower your center of the gravity and press the Union of Yang (BL55) with your left knee.
5. As he falls backward, bring your knee right under his right arm and drop his elbow on your thigh. Press the Canopy (ST15) on his chest with your left palm heel to prevent him from standing up.
6. Press his wrist downward with your left hand and take his gun with your right hand.
7. Erect your body and prepare to pivot.
8. Pivot your body counterclockwise on your left heel, without standing up, and hold his wrist firmly with your left hand, twisting it counterclockwise as you pivot. Sit on him as you finish the pivot, using your body weight to magnify the pain in his wrist. Aim the gun at him and finish the conflict.

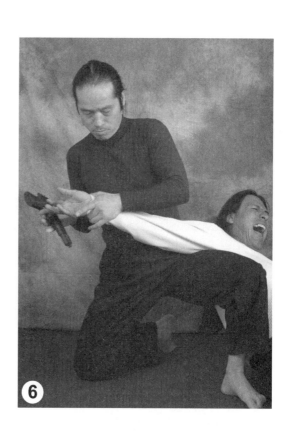

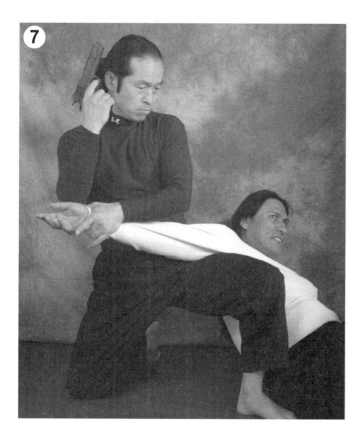

AGAINST GUN POINTED ON THE HEAD FROM THE REAR

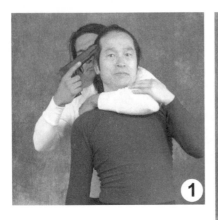

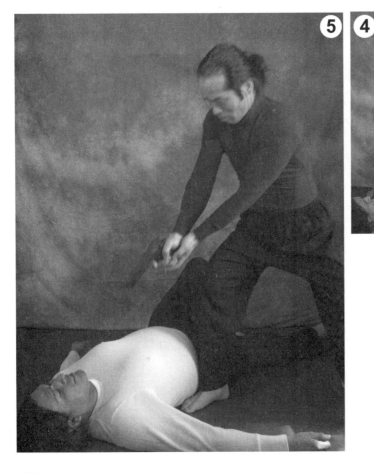

1. Stay cool. Secure leverage on his elbow crease with your left hand.
2. Grab the gun barrel with your right hand.
3. Pull the gun downward while pressing the Pool at the Bend (LI11) on his left arm with your left hand. Twist your body by moving your hip backward. Using momentum, throw him around your body clockwise and take the gun.
4. Aim the gun at the opponent and finish the conflict.

APPENDIX

MERIDIAN CHARTS & TERMS

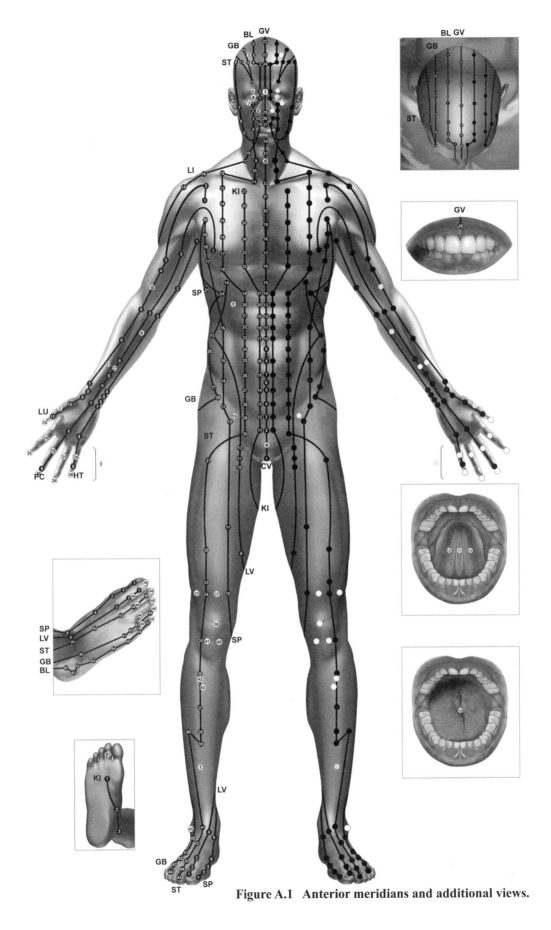

Figure A.1 Anterior meridians and additional views.

Meridian Abbreviations

LU: Lung Meridian
LI: Large Intestine Meridian
ST: Stomach Meridian
SP: Spleen Meridian
HT: Heart Meridian
SI: Small Intestine Meridian
BL: Bladder Meridian
KI: Kidney Meridian
PC: Pericardium Meridian
TW: Triple Warmer Meridian
GB: Gallbladder Meridian
LV: Liver Meridian
GV: Governing Vessel Meridian
CV: Conception Vessel Meridian

THE 48 EXTRA POINTS (WHITE DOTS)

#1-15: The Head and Neck Points (EX-HN1-15)
#16: The Chest and Abdomen Points (EX-CA1)
#17-25: The Back Points (EX-B1-9)
#26-36: The Upper Extremities Points (EX-UE1-11)
#37-48: The Lower Extremities Points (EX-LE1-12)

The 16 ADDITIONAL POINTS
(GRAY DOTS)

a-c: The Head Points (AD-H1-3)
d: The Neck Point (AD-N1)
e-f: The Trunk (AD-T1-2)
g-k: The Arm (AD-UE1-5)
l-q: The Leg (AD-LE1-6)

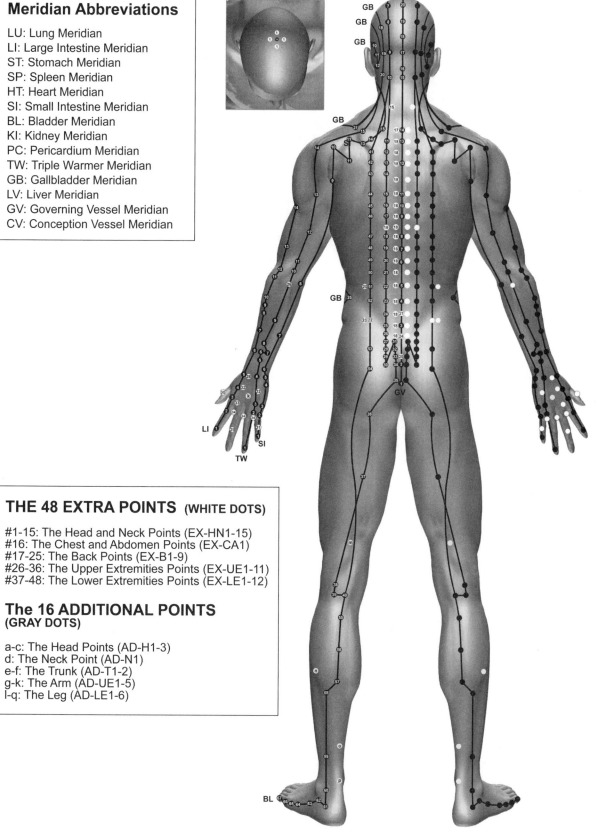

Figure A.2   Posterior meridians and additional view.

383

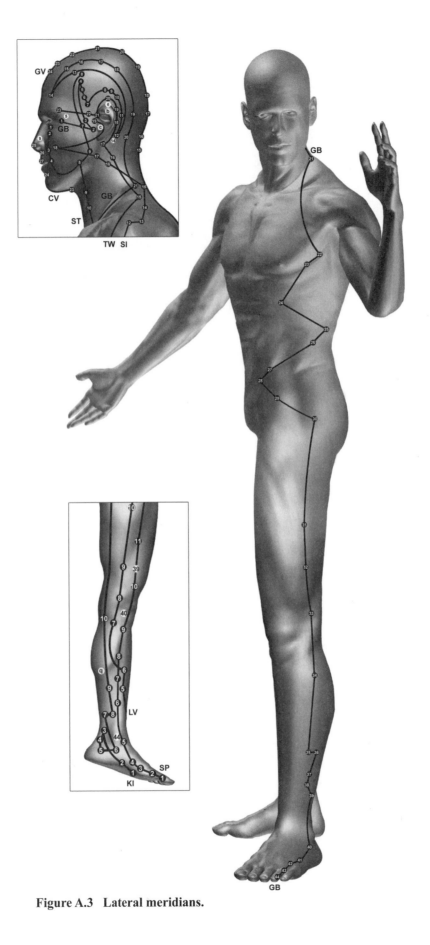

Figure A.3 Lateral meridians.

Table A.1 Meridian Terms

THE LUNG MERIDIAN OF THE HAND

Code	Pinyin	Chinese	Korean	English
LU01	Zhōngfǔ	中府	중부	Central Treasury
LU02	Yúnmén	雲門	운문	Cloud Gate
LU03	Tianfǔ	天府	천부	Celestial Storehouse
LU04	Xiábái	俠白	협백	Guarding White
LU05	Chizé	尺澤	척택	Cubit Marsh
LU06	Kǒngzuì	孔最	공최	Collection Orifice
LU07	Lìequē	列缺	열결	Broken Sequence
LU08	Jīngqú	經渠	경거	Channel Ditch
LU09	Tàiyuān	太淵	태연	Supreme Abyss
LU10	Yújì	魚際	어제	Fish Border
LU11	Shàoshāng	少商	소상	Lesser Shang

THE LARGE INTESTINE MERIDIAN OF THE HAND

Code	Pinyin	Chinese	Korean	English
LI01	Shángyáng	商陽	상양	Shang Yang
LI02	Erjián	二間	이간	Second Space
LI03	Sānjiān	三間	삼간	Third Space
LI04	Hégǔ	合穀	합곡	Union Valley
LI05	Yángxī	陽溪	양계	Yang Ravine
LI06	Piānlì	偏曆	편역	Veering Passageway
LI07	Wēnliū	溫溜	온류	Warm Dwelling
LI08	Xiàlián	下廉	하염	Lower Ridge
LI09	Shànglián	上廉	상염	Upper Ridge
LI10	Shǒusānlǐ	手三里	수삼리	Arm Three Li
LI11	Qūchí	曲池	곡지	Pool at the Bend
LI12	Zhǒuliáo	肘髎	주료	Elbow Bone-Orifice
LI13	Shōuwǔlǐ	手五里	수오리	Arm Five Li
LI14	Bìnào	臂臑	비뇨	Upper Arm
LI15	Jiānyú	肩髃	견우	Shoulder Bone
LI16	Jùgǔ	巨骨	거골	Great Bone
LI17	Tiāndǐng	天鼎	천정	Celestial Tripod
LI18	Fútū	扶突	부돌	Protuberance Assistant
LI19	Kǒuhéliáo	口禾髎	구화료	Grain Bone-Orifice
LI20	Yíngxiāng	迎香	영향	Welcoming Fragrance

THE STOMACH MERIDIAN OF THE FOOT

Code	Pinyin	Chinese	Korean	English
ST01	Chéngqì	承泣	승읍	Tear Container
ST02	Sìbái	四白	사백	Four Whites
ST03	Jùliáo	巨髎	거료	Great Bone-Orifice
ST04	Dìcāng	地倉	지창	Earth Granary
ST05	Dàyíng	大迎	대영	Great Reception
ST06	Jiáchē	頰車	협차	Jaw Chariot
ST07	Xiàguān	下關	하관	Below the Joint
ST08	Tóuwéi	頭維	두유	Head Corner
ST09	Rényíng	人迎	인영	Man's Prognosis
ST10	Shuǐtū	水突	수돌	Water Prominence
ST11	Qìshě	氣舍	기사	Energy Abode
ST12	Quēpén	缺盆	결분	Empty Basin
ST13	Qìhù	氣戶	기호	Energy Door
ST14	Kùfáng	庫房	고방	Storeroom
ST15	Wūyì	屋翳	옥예	Canopy
ST16	Yìngchuāng	膺窗	흉창	Breast Window
ST17	Rǔzhōng	乳中	유중	Breast Center
ST18	Rǔgēn	乳根	유근	Breast Root
ST19	Bùróng	不容	불용	Not Contained
ST20	Chéngmǎn	承滿	승만	Bearing Fullness
ST21	Liángmén	梁門	양문	Beam Gate
ST22	Guānmén	關門	관문	Gate of Passage
ST23	Tàiyǐ	太乙	태을	Supreme Unity
ST24	Huáròumén	滑肉門	활육문	Slippery Flesh Gate
ST25	Tiānshū	天樞	천추	Celestial Pivot
ST26	Wàilíng	外陵	외능	Outer Mound
ST27	Dàjù	大巨	대거	Great Gigantic
ST28	Shuǐdào	水道	수도	Waterway
ST29	Guīlái	歸來	귀래	Return & Arrive
ST30	Qìchōng	氣沖	기충	Surging Energy
ST31	Bìguān	髀關	비관	Thigh Joint
ST32	Fútù	伏兔	복토	Crouching Rabbit
ST33	Yīnshì	陰市	음시	Yin Market
ST34	Liángqiū	梁丘	양구	Beam Hill
ST35	Dúbí	犢鼻	독비	Calf's Nose
ST36	Zúsānlǐ	足三里	족삼리	Leg Three Li

ST37	Shàngjùxū	上巨虛	상거허	Upper Great Hollow
ST38	Tiáokǒu	條口	조구	Ribbon Opening
ST39	Xiàjùxū	下巨虛	하거허	Lower Great Hollow
ST40	Fēnglóng	豐隆	풍륭	Bountiful Bulge
ST41	Jiěxī	解溪	해계	Divided Ravine
ST42	Chōngyáng	沖陽	충양	Surging Yang
ST43	Xiàngǔ	陷穀	함곡	Sunken Valley
ST44	Nèitíng	內庭	내정	Inner Court
ST45	Lìduì	厲兌	예태	Severe Mouth

THE SPLEEN MERIDIAN OF THE FOOT

Code	Pinyin	Chinese	Korean	English
SP01	Yǐnbái	隱白	은백	Hidden White
SP02	Dàdū	大都	대도	Great Metropolis
SP03	Tàibái	太白	태백	Supreme White
SP04	Gōngsūn	公孫	공손	Yellow Emperor
SP05	Shāngqiū	商丘	상구	Shang Hill
SP06	Sānyīnjiāo	三陰交	삼음교	Three Yin Intersection
SP07	Lòugǔ	漏穀	루곡	Leaking Valley
SP08	Dìjī	地機	지기	Earth's Crux
SP09	Yīnlíngquán	陰陵泉	음능천	Yin Mound Spring
SP10	Xuèhǎi	血海	혈해	Sea of Blood
SP11	Jìmén	箕門	기문	Winnower Gate
SP12	Chōngmén	沖門	충문	Surging Gate
SP13	Fùshě	府舍	부사	Bowel Abode
SP14	Fùjié	腹結	복결	Abdominal Bind
SP15	Dàhéng	大橫	대횡	Great Horizontal
SP16	Fùāi	腹哀	복애	Abdominal Lament
SP17	Shídòu	食竇	식두	Food Orifice
SP18	Tiānxī	天溪	천계	Celestial Ravine
SP19	Xiōngxiāng	胸鄉	흉향	Chest Village
SP20	Zhōuróng	周榮	주영	Supreme Glory
SP21	Dàbāo	大包	대포	Great Embrace

THE HEART MERIDIAN OF THE HAND

Code	Pinyin	Chinese	Korean	English
HT01	Jíquán	極泉	극천	Highest Spring
HT02	Qīnglíng	青靈	청영	Blue Spirit
HT03	Shàohǎi	少海	소해	Lesser Sea
HT04	Língdào	靈道	영도	Spirit Pathway
HT05	Tōnglǐ	通里	통리	Connecting Li
HT06	Yīnxì	陰隙	음극	Yin Cleft
HT07	Shénmén	神門	신문	Spirit Gate
HT08	Shàofǔ	少府	소부	Lesser Mansion
HT09	Shàochōng	少沖	소충	Lesser Surge

THE SMALL INTESTINE MERIDIAN OF THE HAND

Code	Pinyin	Chinese	Korean	English
SI01	Shàozé	少澤	소택	Lesser Marsh
SI02	Qiángǔ	前谷	전곡	Front Valley
SI03	Hòuxī	後溪	후계	Back Ravine
SI04	Wàngǔ	腕骨	완골	Wrist Bone
SI05	Yánggǔ	陽谷	양곡	Yang Valley
SI06	Yǎnglǎo	養老	양노	Nursing the Aged
SI07	Zhīzhèng	支正	지정	Branch Right
SI08	Xiǎohǎi	小海	소해	Small Sea
SI09	Jiānzhēn	肩貞	견정	True Shoulder
SI10	Nàoshū	臑俞	뇌유	Upper Arm Transport
SI11	Tiānzōng	天宗	천종	Celestial Gathering
SI12	Bǐngfēng	秉風	병풍	Grasping the Wind
SI13	Qūyuán	曲垣	곡원	Crooked Wall
SI14	Jiānwàishū	肩外俞	견외유	Outer Shoulder Transport
SI15	Jiānzhōngshū	肩中俞	견중유	Central Shoulder Transport
SI16	Tiānchuāng	天窗	천창	Celestial Window
SI17	Tiānróng	天容	천용	Celestial Countenance
SI18	Quánliáo	顴膠	관료	Cheek Bone-Orifice
SI19	Tīnggōng	聽宮	청궁	Auditory Palace

THE BLADDER MERIDIAN OF THE FOOT

Code	Pinyin	Chinese	Korean	English
BL01	Jīngmíng	睛明	청명	Eyes Bright
BL02	Zánzhú	攢竹	찬죽	Bamboo Gathering
BL03	Méichōng	眉沖	미충	Eyebrow Ascension
BL04	Qǔchā	曲差	곡차	Deviating Turn
BL05	Wǔchù	五處	오처	Fifth Place
BL06	Chéngguāng	承光	승광	Light Guard
BL07	Tōngtiān	通天	통천	Celestial Connection
BL08	Luòquè	絡卻	락각	Declining Meridian
BL09	Yùzhěn	玉枕	옥침	Jade Pillow
BL10	Tiānzhù	天柱	천주	Celestial Pillar
BL11	Dàzhù	大杼	대저	Great Shuttle
BL12	Fēngmén	風門	풍문	Wind Gate
BL13	Fèishū	肺俞	폐유	Lung Transport
BL14	Juéyīnshū	厥陰俞	궐음유	Reverting Yin Transport
BL15	Xīnshū	心俞	심유	Heart Transport
BL16	Dūshū	督俞	독유	Governing Transport
BL17	Géshū	膈俞	격유	Diaphragm Transport
BL18	Gānshū	肝俞	간유	Liver Transport
BL19	Dǎnshū	膽俞	담유	Gallbladder Transport
BL20	Pǐshū	脾俞	비유	Spleen Transport
BL21	Wèishū	胃俞	위유	Stomach Transport
BL22	Sānjiāoshū	三焦俞	삼초유	Triple Warmer Transport
BL23	Shènshū	腎俞	신유	Kidney Transport
BL24	Qìhǎishū	氣海俞	기해유	Sea-of-Energy Transport
BL25	Dàchángshū	大腸俞	대장유	Large Intestine Transport
BL26	Guānyuánshū	關元俞	관원유	Origin Pass Transport
BL27	Xiǎochángshū	小腸俞	소장유	Small Intestine Transport
BL28	Pángguāngshū	膀胱俞	방광유	Bladder Transport
BL29	Zhōnglǔshū	中膂俞	중여유	Central Backbone Transport
BL30	Báihuánshū	白環俞	백환유	White Ring Transport
BL31	Shàngliáo	上髎	상료	Upper Bone-Orifice
BL32	Cìliáo	次髎	차료	Second Bone-Orifice
BL33	Zhōngliáo	中髎	중료	Central Bone-Orifice
BL34	Xiàliáo	下髎	하료	Lower Bone-Orifice
BL35	Huìyáng	會陽	회양	Meeting of Yang
BL36	Chéngfú	承扶	승부	Support & Assist

BL37	Yīnmén	殷門	은문	Gate of Abundance
BL38	Fúxì	浮郄	부극	Superficial Cleft
BL39	Wěiyáng	委陽	위양	Bend Yang
BL40	Wěizhōng	委中	위중	Bend Center
BL41	Fùfēn	附分	부분	Attached Branch
BL42	Pòhù	魄戶	백호	Spirit Door
BL43	Gāohuāng	膏肓	고황	Diaphragm Vital Transport
BL44	Shéntáng	神堂	신당	Spirit Hall
BL45	Yìxǐ	譩譆	의희	Sighing Giggling
BL46	Géguān	膈關	격관	Diaphragm Pass
BL47	Húnmén	魂門	혼문	Spirit Gate
BL48	Yánggāng	陽綱	양강	Yang Headrope
BL49	Yìshě	意舍	의사	Reflection Abode
BL50	Wèicāng	胃倉	위창	Stomach Granary
BL51	Huāngmén	肓門	황문	Diaphragm Vital Gate
BL52	Zhìshì	志室	지실	Will Chamber
BL53	Bāohuāng	胞肓	포황	Bladder Membrane
BL54	Zhìbiān	秩邊	질변	Sequential Border
BL55	Héyáng	合陽	합양	Union of Yang
BL56	Chéngjīn	承筋	승근	Supporting Sinews
BL57	Chéngshān	承山	승산	Supporting Mountain
BL58	Fēiyáng	飛揚	비양	Taking Flight
BL59	Fùyáng	跗陽	부양	Instep Yang
BL60	Kūnlún	昆侖	곤윤	Kunlun Mountains
BL61	Púcān	僕參	복삼	Subservient Visitor
BL62	Shēnmài	申脈	신맥	Extending Vessel
BL63	Jīnmén	金門	금문	Metal Gate
BL64	Jīnggǔ	京骨	경골	Capital Bone
BL65	Shùgǔ	束骨	속골	Bundle Bone
BL66	Zútōnggǔ	足通穀	족통곡	Foot Connecting Passage
BL67	Zhìyīn	至陰	지음	Extremity of Yin

THE KIDNEY MERIDIAN OF THE FOOT

Code	Pinyin	Chinese	Korean	English
KI01	Yǒngquán	湧泉	용천	Bubbling Spring
KI02	Rángǔ	然榖	연곡	Blazing Valley
KI03	Tàixī	太溪	태계	Supreme Ravine
KI04	Dàzhōng	大鐘	대종	Great Goblet
KI05	Shuǐquán	水泉	수천	Water Spring
KI06	Zhàohǎi	照海	조해	Shining Sea
KI07	Fùliū	複溜	복류	Recover Flow
KI08	Jiāoxìn	交信	교신	Intersection Reach
KI09	Zhùbīn	築賓	축빈	Guest House
KI10	Yīngǔ	陰榖	음곡	Yin Valley
KI11	Hénggǔ	橫骨	횡골	Pubic Bone
KI12	Dàhè	大赫	대혁	Great Manifestation
KI13	Qìxué	氣穴	기혈	Energy Orifice
KI14	Sìmǎn	四滿	사만	Fourfold Fullness
KI15	Zhōngzhù	中注	중주	Central Flow
KI16	Huāngshū	肓俞	황유	Huang Transport
KI17	Shāngqū	商曲	상곡	Shang Bend
KI18	Shíguān	石關	석관	Stone Pass
KI19	Yīndū	陰都	음도	Yin Metropolis
KI20	Tōnggǔ	通谷	통곡	Connecting Valley
KI21	Yōumén	幽門	유문	Dark Gate
KI22	Bùláng	步廊	보랑	Corridor Walk
KI23	Shénfēng	神封	신봉	Spirit Seal
KI24	Língxū	靈墟	영허	Spirit Ruins
KI25	Shéncáng	神藏	신장	Spirit Storehouse
KI26	Yùzhōng	彧中	욱중	Lively Center
KI27	Shūfǔ	俞府	유부	Transport Mansion

THE PERICARDIUM MERIDIAN OF THE HAND

Code	Pinyin	Chinese	Korean	English
PC01	Tiānchí	天池	천지	Celestial Pool
PC02	Tiānquán	天泉	천천	Celestial Spring
PC03	Qūzé	曲澤	곡택	Marsh at the Bend
PC04	Xìmén	隙門	극문	Cleft Gate
PC05	Jiānshǐ	間使	간사	Intermediary Courier
PC06	Nèiguān	內關	내관	Inner Passage
PC07	Dàlíng	大陵	대능	Great Mound
PC08	Láogōng	勞宮	노궁	Work Palace
PC09	Zhōngchōng	中沖	중충	Central Hub

THE TRIPLE WARMER MERIDIAN OF THE HAND

Code	Pinyin	Chinese	Korean	English
TW01	Guānchōng	關沖	관충	Passage Hub
TW02	Yèmén	液門	액문	Humor Gate
TW03	Zhōngzhǔ	中渚	중저	Central Islet
TW04	Yángchí	陽池	양지	Yang Pond
TW05	Wàiguān	外關	외관	Outer Pass
TW06	Zhīgōu	支溝	지구	Branch Ditch
TW07	Huìzōng	會宗	회종	Convergence and Gathering
TW08	Sānyángluò	三陽絡	삼양락	Three Yang Connection
TW09	Sìdú	四瀆	사독	Four Rivers
TW10	Tiānjǐng	天井	천정	Celestial Well
TW11	Qīnglěngyuān	清冷淵	청냉연	Clear Cold Abyss
TW12	Xiāoluò	消濼	소락	Dispersing Riverbed
TW13	Nàohuì	臑會	뇌회	Upper Arm Convergence
TW14	Jiānliáo	肩髎	견료	Shoulder Bone-Orifice
TW15	Tiānliáo	天髎	천료	Celestial Bone-Orifice
TW16	Tiānyǒu	天牖	천용	Celestial Window
TW17	Yìfēng	翳風	예풍	Wind Screen
TW18	Chìmài	瘈脈	계맥	Spasm Vessel
TW19	Lúxī	顱息	로식	Skull Rest
TW20	Jiǎosūn	角孫	각손	Angle Vertex
TW21	Ermén	耳門	이문	Ear Gate
TW22	Erhéliáo	耳和髎	이화료	Harmony Bone-Orifice
TW23	Sīzúkōng	絲竹空	시죽공	Silk Bamboo Orifice

THE GALLBLADDER MERIDIAN OF THE FOOT

Code	Pinyin	Chinese	Korean	English
GB01	Tóngzǐliáo	瞳子髎	동자료	Pupil Bone Orifice
GB02	Tīnghuì	聽會	청회	Auditory Convergence
GB03	Shàngguān	上關	상관	Upper Gate
GB04	Hànyàn	頜厭	함염	Forehead Fullness
GB05	Xuánlú	懸顱	현로	Suspended Skull
GB06	Xuánlí	懸厘	현리	Suspended Tuft
GB07	Qūbìn	曲鬢	곡빈	Temporal Hairline Curve
GB08	Shuāigǔ	率谷	솔곡	Leading Valley
GB09	Tiānchōng	天沖	천충	Celestial Hub
GB10	Fúbái	浮白	부백	Floating White
GB11	Tóuqiàoyīn	頭竅陰	두규음	Head Portal Yin
GB12	Wángǔ	完骨	완골	Completion Bone
GB13	Běnshén	本神	본신	Root Spirit
GB14	Yángbái	陽白	양백	Yang White
GB15	Tóulínqì	頭臨泣	두임읍	Head Overlooking Tears
GB16	Mùchuāng	目窗	목창	Eye Window
GB17	Zhèngyíng	正營	정영	Upright Construction
GB18	Chénglíng	承靈	승영	Spirit Support
GB19	Nǎokōng	腦空	뇌공	Brain Hollow
GB20	Fēngchí	風池	풍지	Wind Pool
GB21	Jiānjǐng	肩井	견정	Shoulder Well
GB22	Yuānye	淵腋	연액	Armpit Abyss
GB23	Zhéjīn	輒筋	첩근	Sinew Seat
GB24	Rìyuè	日月	일월	Sun and Moon
GB25	Jīngmén	京門	경문	Capital Gate
GB26	Dàimài	帶脈	대맥	Girdling Vessel
GB27	Wǔshū	五樞	오추	Fifth Pivot
GB28	Wéidào	維道	유도	Linking Path
GB29	Jūliáo	居髎	거료	Squatting Bone-Orifice
GB30	Huántiào	環跳	환도	Ring of Jumping
GB31	Fēngshì	風市	풍시	Wind Market
GB32	Zhōngdú	中瀆	중독	Central River
GB33	Xīyángguān	膝陽關	슬양관	Knee Yang Joint
GB34	Yánglíngquán	陽陵泉	양능천	Yang Mound Spring
GB35	Yángjiāo	陽交	양교	Yang Intersection
GB36	Wàiqiū	外丘	외구	Outer Hill

GB37	Guāngmíng	光明	광명	Light Bright
GB38	Yángfǔ	陽輔	양보	Yang Assistance
GB39	Xuánzhōng	懸鐘	현종	Suspended Bell
GB40	Qiūxū	丘墟	구허	Hill Ruins
GB41	Zúlínqì	足臨泣	족임읍	Foot Overlooking Tears
GB42	Dìwǔhuì	地五會	지오회	Earth Fivefold Convergence
GB43	Xiáxī	俠溪	협계	Pinched Ravine
GB44	Zúqiàoyīn	足竅陰	족규음	Foot Portal Yin

THE LIVER MERIDIAN OF THE FOOT

Code	Pinyin	Chinese	Korean	English
LV01	Dàdūn	大敦	대돈	Great Pile
LV02	Xíngjiān	行間	행간	Moving Between
LV03	Tàichōng	太沖	태충	Supreme Surge
LV04	Zhōngfēng	中封	중봉	Central Mound
LV05	Lígōu	蠡溝	루곡	Woodworm Canal
LV06	Zhōngdū	中都	중도	Central Metropolis
LV07	Xīguān	膝關	슬관	Knee Joint
LV08	Qūquán	曲泉	곡천	Spring at the Bend
LV09	Yīnbāo	陰包	음포	Yin Bladder
LV10	Zúwǔlǐ	足五里	족오리	Foot Five Li
LV11	Yīnlián	陰廉	음염	Yin Corner
LV12	Jímài	急脈	급맥	Urgent Pulse
LV13	Zhāngmén	章門	장문	Camphorwood Gate
LV14	Qīmén	期門	기문	Cycle Gate

THE GOVERNING VESSEL MERIDIAN

Code	Pinyin	Chinese	Korean	English
GV01	Chángqiáng	長強	장강	Lasting Strong
GV02	Yāoshū	腰俞	요유	Lumbar Transport
GV03	Yāoyángguān	腰陽關	요양관	Lumbar Yang Joint
GV04	Mìngmén	命門	명문	Life Gate
GV05	Xuánshū	懸樞	현추	Suspended Pivot
GV06	Jǐzhōng	脊中	척중	Spinal Center
GV07	Zhōngshū	中樞	중추	Central Pivot
GV08	Jīnsuō	筋縮	근축	Sinew Contraction
GV09	Zhìyáng	至陽	지양	Extremity of Yang
GV10	Língtái	靈台	영태	Spirit Tower
GV11	Shéndào	神道	신도	Spirit Path
GV12	Shēnzhù	身柱	신추	Body Pillar
GV13	Táodào	陶道	도도	Kiln Path
GV14	Dàzhuī	大椎	대추	Great Hammer
GV15	Yǎmén	啞門	아문	Mute's Gate
GV16	Fēngfǔ	風府	풍부	Wind Mansion
GV17	Nǎohù	腦戶	뇌호	Brain Door
GV18	Qiángjiān	強間	강간	Unyielding Space
GV19	Hòudǐng	後頂	후정	Behind the Vertex
GV20	Bǎihuì	百會	백회	Hundred Convergences
GV21	Qiándǐng	前頂	전정	Before the Vertex
GV22	Xìnhuì	囟會	신회	Fontanel Meeting
GV23	Shàngxīng	上星	상성	Upper Star
GV24	Shéntíng	神庭	신정	Spirit Court
GV25	Sùliáo	素髎	소료	White Bone-Orifice
GV26	Rénzhōng	人中	인중	Philtrum
GV27	Duìduān	兌端	태단	Extremity of the Mouth
GV28	Yínjiāo	齦交	온교	Gum Intersection

THE CONCEPTION VESSEL MERIDIAN

Code	Pinyin	Chinese	Korean	English
CV01	Huìyīn	會陰	회음	Meeting of Yin
CV02	Qūgǔ	曲骨	곡골	Curved Bone
CV03	Zhōngjí	中極	중극	Central Pole
CV04	Guānyuán	關元	관원	Passage of Origin
CV05	Shímén	石門	석문	Stone Gate
CV06	Qìhǎi	氣海	기해	Sea of Energy
CV07	Yīnjiāo	陰交	음교	Yin Intersection
CV08	Shénquè	神闕	신궐	Spirit Gate Tower
CV09	Shuǐfēn	水分	수분	Water Divide
CV10	Xiàwǎn	下脘	하완	Lower Venter
CV11	Jiànlǐ	建裏	건리	Interior Strengthening
CV12	Zhōngwǎn	中脘	중완	Central Venter
CV13	Shàngwǎn	上脘	상완	Upper Venter
CV14	Jùquè	巨闕	거궐	Great Tower Gate
CV15	Jiūwěi	鳩尾	구미	Turtledove Tail
CV16	Zhōngtíng	中庭	중정	Center Palace
CV17	Dànzhōng	膻中	단중	Chest Center
CV18	Yùtáng	玉堂	옥당	Jade Hall
CV19	Zǐgōng	紫宮	자궁	Purple Palace
CV20	Huágài	華蓋	화개	Florid Canopy
CV21	Xuánjī	璿璣	선기	Jade Pearl
CV22	Tiāntū	天突	천돌	Celestial Chimney
CV23	Liánquán	廉泉	염천	Ridge Spring
CV24	Chéngjiāng	承漿	승장	Sauce Receptacle

REFERENCES

Barmeier, J. 1996. *The Brain*. San Diego, CA: Lucent Books.

Christensen, L. W. 2008. *Defensive Tactics: Modern Arrest & Control Techniques for Today's Police Warrior*. Santa Fe, NM: Turtle Press.

Clemente, C. 1985. *Gray's Anatomy of the Human Body*. Philadelphia, PA: Lippincott Williams & Wilkins.

Edelson, E. 1991. *The Nervous System*. New York: Chelsea House.

Greenfield, S. A. 1996. *The Human Mind Explained*. New York: Henry Holt.

Grounds, T. B. 2006. *The Bare Essentials Guide for Martial Arts Injury Care & Prevention*. Santa Fe, NM: Turtle Press.

Hanho. 1992. *Combat Strategy: Junsado The Way of the Warrior*. Hartford, CT: Turtle Press.

Hay, J.G., and Reid, J.G. 1982. *The Anatomical and Mechanical Bases of Human Motion*. Englewood Cliffs, NJ: Prentice-Hall, Inc.

Ji, Z. 1991. *Physiological Basis of Modernized TCM* (in Chinese). Beijing, China: Xueyuan Press.

Kim, S. H. 2000. *Martial Arts After 40*. Hartford, CT: Turtle Press.

Kim, S. H. 1993. *Ultimate Fitness Through Martial Arts*. Hartford, CT: Turtle Press.

Kim, S. H. 2004. *Ultimate Flexibility: A Complete Guide to Stretching for Martial Arts*. Santa Fe, NM: Turtle Press.

Knapp, S. N. 2007. *A Los Angeles Bouncer's Guide to Practical Fighting*. Santa Fe, NM: Turtle Press.

Merskey, H., Loeser, D. J., and Dubner, R. 1975. *The Paths of Pain*. International Association for the Study of Pain.

Onello, R. M. 2007. *Boxing: Advanced Tactics & Strategies*. Santa Fe, NM: Turtle Press.

Parker, S. 1997. *The Brain and Nervous System*. Austin, TX: Raintree/Steck-Vaughn.

Sage, G.H. 1984. *Motor Learning and Control: A Neuropsychological Approach*. Dubuque, IA: Wm. C. Brown Publishers.

Shen, Z. 1995. *Traditional Chinese Medicine* (in Chinese). Shanghai, China: Shanghai Science and Technology Press.

Simon, S. 1997. *The Brain: Our Nervous System*. New York: Morrow.

Turkington, C. 1996. *The Brain Encyclopedia*. New York: Facts on File.

Wade, N., ed. 1998. *The Science Times Book of the Brain*. New York: Lyons Press.

Wall, M., Huh, J., and Mattox K. 2005. Thoracic Vascular Trauma. *Vascular Surgery*.

Xie, Z., Lou, Z., and Huang, X. 1994. *Classified Dictionary of Traditional Chinese Medicine*, Beijing, China: New World Press.

GLOSSARY

Acromial: Of or relating to the outer end of the spine of the scapula.

Anterior: Situated toward the front of the body.

Apex: A narrowed or pointed end of an anatomical structure, for example the ear.

Arteriole: A small branch of an artery leading to a capillary.

Articular: Of or relating to a joint.

Auricular: Of or relating to the ear.

Autonomic: Of or pertaining to the autonomic nervous system.

Axilla: The cavity beneath the junction of the arm and shoulder; commonly called the armpit.

Axon: A long fiber of a nerve cell that carries outgoing messages.

Biceps: The large flexor muscle of the front of the upper arm.

Brachial: Of or relating to the arm.

Cardiac: Of, relating to, situated near or acting on the heart.

Carotid Artery: Either of the two main arteries that supply blood to the head.

Carpal: Of or relating to the group of bones supporting the wrist.

Celiac: Of or relating to the abdominal cavity.

Cephalic: Of or relating to the head.

Cervical: Of or relating to the neck.

Circumflex: Bending around.

Clavicle: The narrow elongated S-shaped bone on either side of the neck; commonly called the collarbone.

Coccygeal: Of or relating to the coccyx.

Coccyx: A small bone that consists of four fused vertebrae which form the terminus of the spinal column; commonly called the tailbone.

Condyle: The prominence of a bone, normally appearing in pairs that look like knuckles at one end of the bone.

Cranial: Of or relating to the skull.

Crest: A ridge on a bone.

Cun: A traditional Chinese unit of length relative to an individual's body which is used to located acupoints. The traditional measure is the width of a person's thumb at the knuckle. However, a cun varies depending on the point being located. For example, the distance between the nipples is 8 cun and this 8 cun measurement can be used to find other points on the chest, and there are always 3 cun from the eyebrow to the hairline, however this distance may vary depending on the size of the individual's head. The distance across all four fingers when held together is also 3 cun.

Cutaneous: Of or relating to the skin.

Dermis: A layer of skin beneath the epidermis consisting of connective tissue which cushions the body.

Diaphragm: The partition of muscle and connective tissue separating the chest and abdominal cavities.

Digital: Of or relating to the fingers or toes.

Distal: Situated away from the point of attachment or origin or a central point.

Dorsal: Located near, on, or toward the back.

Dorsum: The back.

Epicondyle: A prominence on the distal part of a long bone that is the site of the attachment of muscles and ligaments.

Epigastric: Situated upon or over the stomach.

External: Able to be perceived outwardly.

Femoral: Of or relating to the femur or thigh.

Femur: The bone of the leg that extends from the hip to the knee, it is the longest and largest bone in the human body.

Fibula: The outer and smaller of the two bones of the leg below the knee, the slenderest bone of the human body in proportion to its length.

Fossa: An anatomical pit, groove, or depression.

Ganglion: A mass of nerve tissue containing neurons that is located outside the central nervous system.

Gastrocnemius: The largest and most superficial muscle of the calf.

Gluteal: Of or relating to the buttocks.

Great Trochanter: A rough prominence on the upper part of the femur.

Hiatus: A passage through an anatomical part or organ.

Humerus: The longest bone of the upper arm.

Hyoid Bone: A U-shaped bone or complex of bones that is situated between the base of the tongue and the larynx.

Hypochondrium: The abdominal regions on either side of the epigastric region, above the lumbar regions; the flank regions of the trunk.

Hypogastric: Of or relating to the lower abdominal cavity.

Iliac: Of or relating to the lowest abdominal regions.

Inferior: Situated below and closer to the feet than another part of an upright body.

Inguinal: Of, relating to or situated in the region of the groin.

Intercostal: Situated between the ribs.

Interneuron: A neuron that exclusively signals another neuron.

Jugular: Of or relating to the throat or neck.

Lateral: Of or relating to the side.

Lumbar: Of or relating to the trunk or the vertebrae between the thoracic vertebrae and sacrum.

Malleolus: A strong pyramid-shaped process of the tibia or filbula that projects at the ankle; commonly called the ankle bone.

Mandible: The lower jaw.

Mastoid Process: The process of the temporal bone behind the ear.

Median: Situated in the middle; lying on the plane that divides the body into left and right halves.

Metacarpal: Of or relating to the bones of the hand.

Metatarsal: Of or relating to the bones of the foot.

Midsagittal: In the median region of the suture between the parietal bones of the skull.

Neuron: A nerve cell that sends and receives electrical signals over long distances.

Nociceptor: A sensory receptor that sends signals that cause the perception of pain in response to potentially damaging stimulus.

Occipital: Of or relating to the compound bone that forms the posterior part of the skull.

Olecranon: The large process of the ulna that projects behind the elbow and forms the bony prominence of the elbow.

Ophthalmic: Of, relating to or near the eye.

Orbital: The bony cavity that encloses and protects the eye; commonly called the eye socket.

Palmar: Of or relating to the palm of the hand.

Parasympathetic: Pertaining to that part of the autonomic nervous system consisting of nerves and ganglia that arise from the cranial and sacral regions and function in opposition to the sympathetic system.

Patella: A thick flat triangular movable bone that forms the anterior point of the knee and protects the front of the knee joint.

Pelvic: Of, relating to, or located in or near the pelvis.

Plexus: A network of nerves or blood vessels.

Pons: A band of nerve fibers in the brain that connect the midbrain, medulla, and cerebrum.

Popliteal: Of or relating to the back of the leg behind the knee joint.

Posterior: Situated behind.

Protuberance: Something that is bulging beyond the surrounding or adjacent surface.

Pubic Symphysis: The rigid articulation of the two pubic bones in the lower abdomen; commonly called the pubic bone.

Pulmonary: Relating to or carried on by the lungs.

Quadriceps: Large extensor muscle of the front thigh.

Radial: Of, relating to, or situated near the thumb side of the hand or forearm.

Ramus: A projecting part or branch (pl. rami).

Sacral: Of, relating to or near the sacrum.

Sacrum: The part of the spinal column that consists of five fused vertebrae diminishing in size to the apex at the lower end which bears the coccyx.

Sartorius: A muscle that arises from the iliac spine, crosses the front of the thigh to insert on the upper part of the tibia, it is the longest muscle in the human body.

Scapula: Either of a pair of large flat triangular bones of the upper back; commonly called shoulder blade.

Sternocleidomastoid: A thick superficial muscle on each side of the neck that arises from the sternum and the clavicle.

Sternum: A compound bone that lies in the median central part of the body, about seven inches (18 centimeters) long; commonly called the breastbone.

Subcostal: Situated below a rib.

Superficial: Of, relating to or located near the surface.

Superior: Situated toward the head and further away from the feet than another part of an upright body.

Supraorbital: Situated above the eye.

Sympathetic: Pertaining to the part of the autonomic nervous system consisting of nerves arising from the thoracic and lumbar regions of the spinal cord, and functioning in opposition to the parasympathetic system.

Tarsal: Of or relating to the bones of the foot.

Temporal: Of or relating to the temple or the sides of the skull.

Thenar Muscle: Any of the muscles that comprise the musculature of the thumb.

Thoracic: Of, relating to, located within, or involving the thorax.

Thorax: The part of the body between the neck and the abdomen.

Tibia: The inner and larger of the two bones of the leg between the knee and ankle.

Tibial: Of, relating to, or located near a tibia.

Trachea: The main trunk of the system of tubes by which air passes to and from the lungs; commonly called the windpipe.

Transverse: At a right angle to the long axis of the body.

Transverse Cubital Crease: The line across the inside of the arm at the elbow.

Trapezius: A large flat triangular muscle of each side of the upper back.

Triceps: The large extensor muscle situated along the back of the upper arm.

Ulnar: Located on the same side of the forearm as the ulna bone.

Umbilicus: A depression in the middle of the abdomen that is the point of former attachment of the umbilical cord; commonly called the navel or belly button.

Vascular: Of or relating to the blood vessels.

Venule: A small vein.

Vertebra: Any of the bony or cartilaginous segments that make up the spinal column. (pl. vertebrae)

Vesical: Of or relating to the bladder.

Vestibular: Of or relating to the vestibule of the inner ear.

Viscera: The organs in the cavities of the body, especially those in the abdominal cavity.

Xiphoid Process: The smallest and lowest portion of the human sternum.

INDEX

Index

ABOUT THE AUTHOR

Sang H. Kim is an internationally respected author of 12 martial arts books, including the best sellers *Ultimate Flexibility, Ultimate Fitness through Martial Arts, Combat Strategy* and *Teaching: the Way of the Master*, and star of over 100 martial arts instructional DVDs and video downloads programs including *Ultimate Fitness, Self-defense Encyclopedia, Knife-defense, Power Breathing*, Junsado Training Series, and Complete Taekwondo Series.

He won the 1976 Korean National Championship and was named Instructor of the Year by the Korean government in 1983. As a special agent during his military service, he developed tactical combat methods for hand-to-hand and hand-to-weapon combat for covert operatives.

To advance his education, he studied abroad in US in 1985 and has since traveled to Europe, North and South America and Asia to present seminars on martial arts and motivational skills. He earned a BS degree in English Literature, an MS degree in Sports Science and a Ph.D. in Sports Media Studies.

He taught Taekwondo at Trinity College from 1987 to 1998 and was a technical advisor for Wesleyan University and the University of Connecticut. He has spoken on Sports Philosophy, Fighting Strategy and Motivation at Yale University, Gordonstoun School in Scotland, Brunell University in London, and private and public organizations in Bermuda, Ireland, Korea, Spain, Germany, Austria and the United Kingdom.

He has been featured in magazines and newspapers including Black Belt, Taekwondo times, Taekwondo People, WTF Magazine, Combat, Fighter's Magazine-UK, Cumbernauld Gazette-Scotland, Delta Sky, Vitality, Bottom Line Business, Korea Herald, Donga Newspaper-Seoul, Chosun Daily-Seoul, and Choongang Central Daily-New York. His books and films have been reviewed in the Dallas Observer, Hartford Current, Worcester Telegram, El Nacional (Oklahoma), the Herald News, Inner-self Magazine, Memphis Business Journal, The Observer, San Francisco Sun Reporter, The New York Times, The Star Gazette, The Times, and 90 more publications.

His books include *Ultimate Flexibility, Ultimate Fitness Through Martial Arts, Teaching: the Way of The Master, Taekwondo Kyorugi, Instructor's Desk Reference, Martial Arts After 40, the Art of Harmony, Combat Strategy, Muye Dobo Tongji*, and *1,001 Ways To Motivate Yourself and Others* (translated in 22 languages). His DVDs include *Ultimate Fitness, Self-defense Encyclopedia, Power Breathing, Beginner's Taekwondo, Martial Arts of Korea*, Complete Taekwondo Series and Junsado Combat Training Series.

He developed Law Enforcement Safety & Survival programs for local, state and federal law enforcement agencies, and VIP Security programs for international agencies in the US, UK, and Canada.

He has also produced over a dozen documentaries on the international subjects including *The Real Royal Trip, Ki: the Science of Energy, Zen for Martial Arts, 100 Years of Tradition* for Connecticut State Police, and *Admiral Yi Sun-shin and the Turtle Boat, Dong Ahn Geo: Zen Buddhism* (English Edition).

He wrote, produced and directed Zen Man-his first martial arts feature film in 2006 and is currently producing and directing his second feature film in Santa Fe, New Mexico.

MORE TITLES FROM TURTLE PRESS

Drills for Grapplers
Groundfighting Pins and Breakdowns
Defensive Tactics
Secrets of Unarmed Gun Defenses
Point Blank Gun Defenses
Security Operations
Vital Leglocks
Boxing: Advanced Tactics and Strategies
Grappler's Guide to Strangles and Chokes
Fighter's Fact Book 2
The Armlock Encyclopedia
Championship Sambo
Complete Taekwondo Poomse
Martial Arts Injury Care and Prevention
Timing for Martial Arts
Strength and Power Training
Complete Kickboxing
Ultimate Flexibility
Boxing: A 12 Week Course
The Fighter's Body: An Owner's Manual
The Science of Takedowns, Throws and Grappling for Self-defense
Fighting Science
Martial Arts Instructor's Desk Reference
Solo Training
Solo Training 2
Fighter's Fact Book
Conceptual Self-defense
Martial Arts After 40
Warrior Speed
The Martial Arts Training Diary for Kids
Teaching Martial Arts
Combat Strategy
The Art of Harmony
Total MindBody Training
1,001 Ways to Motivate Yourself and Others
Ultimate Fitness through Martial Arts
Taekwondo Kyorugi: Olympic Style Sparring

For more information:
Turtle Press
1-800-77-TURTL
e-mail: orders@turtlepress.com

http://www.turtlepress.com